EXPERIMENTS IN GROWTH

EXPERIMENTS IN

(*Spiritual* growth, that is)

by BETSY CAPRIO

Ave Maria Press • Notre Dame, Indiana 46556

To Jane Blair Whitworth
my dear mother
who likes my family, my dog
and my books.

Design and layout: *Charles E. Jones*
Robert L. Mutchler
Tom Hojnacki

International Standard Book Number: 0-87793-114-3
Library of Congress Catalog Card Number: 76-22268

Printed in the United States of America.

CONTENTS

THE GROWTH EXPERIMENTS

CREATION AND RE-CREATION, and fun and games:

PRAYER:

STORIES AND SYMBOLS:

INTRODUCTION

I hope very much that you like this book, and I thought that (even though it's a serious book about a serious subject) it might be fun to give you a picture of how it was written.

The roots of many of the ideas which you'll find in *Experiments in Growth* are so exciting, so stimulating (see Chapter One), that working with them can lead to a bad case of mental indigestion. This began to happen to me, and as an antidote—sort of an Alka-Seltzer for the mind—I found myself alternating my writing time for this book with TV-watching time. It became a habit for me to break up my day with the noontime, four-hanky soap opera, *Search for Tomorrow,* which provided a complete change of pace from the heavy worlds of religion, education and psychology. This went on for a couple of years; while this book was being written the cast of that long-lived drama and I sloshed through

    4 deaths
    4 adulterous affairs
    4 weddings
    3 divorces
    2 May-December romances
    2 murder trials
    1 establishment of paternity
    1 case each of hysterical blindness, heart attack, attempted suicide (wrist-
        slashing)
    1 mercy-killing (pulled plug on oxygen tank)
    1 attempted murder (locked victim in prison freezer)
    1 teenaged drugs-plus-I-hate-my-mother routine
    1 perforated liver

and endless buckets of tears. At this point, of course, I'm wondering if snatches of all this melodrama have slipped out into this collection of ideas for spiritual growth. Maybe that's not a bad thing—you'll have to decide.

Now, more in the vein of our important topic, I'd like to tell you that the book you're holding is a couple of things:

— First, it's a companion volume to an earlier book for religion teachers (*Experiments in Prayer,* Ave Maria Press, 1973) and a sequel to a more theoretical cassette tape (*Prayer Ideas for Religion Teachers,* Ave Maria Press, 1974). Both urge religious educators (and others who help people pray) to experiment with enabling students to *experience* God as well as learn information about Him. In these two works, I tried to emphasize the need for effective prayer—the most familiar path to religious experience—as an integral part of every religion class, so that kids could learn to "taste the Lord." *Experiments in Growth* is a recipe book, like its predecessor, but it's a broader book which includes meaningful praying as just one of many ways of spiritual growth.

As in *Experiments in Prayer,* the exercises in this book are written up as if they are to be used in religion classrooms. You can see that it would be easy for facilitators/enablers (what word are you using this year?) to adapt them to other settings: homes, retreat houses, growth centers, churches and temples and synagogues, or wherever people grow. I especially hope that adults—teachers, in particular—will find *Experiments in Growth* a sort of spiritual workbook that helps them work alone, on their own.

Although I'm writing from the Christian perspective, I would also hope that these ideas could be easily translated into the repertories of people of all faiths—or even people with no religious commitment. Just so you don't have to guess, perhaps I should add that my own religious commitment for the past 19 years has been to the Roman Catholic Church, but that my work is colored, surely, by childhood training as an Anglican and childhood memories of black evangelical worship in the South. My mentors, religiously speaking, are people like Thomas Merton (of course) and Elizabeth Seton, and—going back—Dominic the friar, as well as C. S. Lewis and Sigrid Undset and a whole clutch of artists and musicians—past and present, popular and academic, famous and folk. On psychological fronts, the substructure for the ideas I share with you is drawn largely from the work of Carl Jung and Abraham Maslow, religious (with a small "r") men in the best sense of that word. I've spent 25 years exploring spiritual growth skills, primarily, I guess, because I've been very much in need of them.

My training has been in education, not theology, and so you'll see books of many persuasions referred to in *Experiments in Growth;* from each I have drawn what fits my Church's framework. . . . I would hope readers would adjust the ideas here to fit the shadings of their own beliefs. Educationally, this book would be classified as humanistic (but that's not the same as Humanistic). Theologically, it's intended to be in harmony with the declarations of the Second Vatican Council of the early 1960's. The two fit together just fine, as evidenced in the United States by the present ongoing work for the *National Catechetical Directory.*

— Second, this book is a very tentative and small step in a continuing joyful work: the hooking-up of research in humanistic psychology and humanistic education to the older field of religious education. Chapter One, for those who like theory, goes

into this synthesizing more deeply, so here I'll just note that there are, indeed, problems in the hooking-up. The literature of humanistic psychology and education is sprawling and very large; much of it is experimental and tentative, "on the path" and evolving daily. Even the language and vocabulary of these approaches are an area of shifting sands. (One man's "fantasy trip," for example, is another's "guided daydream.") People and ideas and publications stream like protoplasm, and sorting them out and getting on top of them can result in Excedrin headache #303.

But, if I were to wait (as I've been tempted to do) until both humanistic psychology and education were more matured and settled disciplines, I'd be sitting around for a long, long time. It seems better, even at the risk of oversimplification, to take what they have to offer now—ideas that can help all of us *now*—and integrate it with the equally fast-moving discipline of religious education. Ten years from now, let's hope, both religious education and education in general will be very different than today, thanks in large part to the people whose work is referred to all through this volume, people who are involved in this cross-pollinating.

Some thank-yous, of course. Two big ones: first, to Father Louis Savary, S.J., a pioneer in the marriage between the psychology of growth and church-type growth, and a very patient friend and source of ideas. Please look at his "Afterword for Ruffled Believers" at the end of this book, even if you are unruffled, and at the several references to Father Lou's work which are scattered throughout the experiments.

Second, a thank-you to the Very Reverend Fred Jelly, O.P. Father Fred has filled the slot of theological consultant in charge of questions the author couldn't answer and has marshaled the resources of the members of the Dominican House of Studies in Washington, D.C. (where he is prior) and generously shared them with all of us.

Of course, neither of these helpers is responsible for the opinions (and any possible errors) in this book.

A third giant-sized thank-you has to go to the administrators at St. Joseph's High School in Pittsfield, Massachusetts: Father Richard Sniezyk, director, and Sister Louise Thomas, S.S.J., principal. Many of the ideas here were tested, with Father's and Sister's support, by me with students at this school. I hope you have the same sort of freedom to experiment with religious education methodology that I've had. (If you don't have it, hang in there anyway.)

A very special thanks has to go to the wonderful students I've been lucky enough to work with at St. Joe's; most of them are members of the class of 1976. Every so often teachers strike it rich, and get one of *those* classes—classes with eager, knowledgeable students who really want to grow spiritually and are not ashamed to say so. Although this is the ideal and not the norm (unfortunately), it helps a teacher realize what is possible under optimum conditions. If you can keep this vision in your head when faced with a sea of blank faces, it really helps.

In this book, there are growth ideas from students Dennis Bates, Bob Loehr and Christine Quallen, and examples of "getting high naturally" (in Chapter One) from my

10

friends Mark Harris, Tim Snyder and Chuck Steak and my daughters Sarah, Cecelia and Julie. Many thanks to all of them and to the many young people who have shared their profound experiences and thoughts with me.

To complete the record, I have to list at least the following people, all of whose lives have spilled over into *Experiments in Growth.* Thanks to Jack Canfield of Amherst, Massachusetts, my graduate adviser and a mentor, too; to Sister Natalie Cain of Texas, a glowing teacher; to Sheila Crean and Sibylle Mayer who know about yoga and share their knowledge graciously; to John Wren-Lewis for input on dreams and religious education; to Toby McCarroll of the Humanist Institute in San Francisco for ideas and vision and encouragement; to Monsignor Robert Probst of the College of St. Thomas in St. Paul; to Father Alfred McBride; and the late Bill Geary of *Our Sunday Visitor* for more of the same; to the members of our local prayer group and my fellow religion teachers, friends and idea-bouncers at the grass-roots level: Sister Mary Teresa Salafia, M.P.V., Teresa Giardina, Gretchen Caprio, Gwen Sears, Ann McGaharn, Sister Kathleen Keough, S.S.J., Joe Hould, Ed Butterworth, Vinnie Marinaro, Father Constantine Mangos of the Greek Orthodox Church and my husband, Al, for his translation of scientific concepts into lay language. The reference and music librarians of Pittsfield, Massachusetts' public library deserve a special bouquet.

A few of the ideas here have already appeared in seed form in my small book for Argus Communications, *Poster Ideas for Personalized Learning,* and I thank Argus for permission to repeat myself. By now, the pool of humanistic education strategies is so large that people borrow and cross-borrow from one another with little awareness of the original sources of their methods and exercises. Wherever possible, I've tried to give credit as due and welcome any corrections and additions on that count.

Ave Maria editor Gene Geissler and book designer Charlie Jones, both fine authors in their own right, won't give themselves any credit, I know, so I'll have to do that for them and tell you what fun they are to work with. And, to make things complete, I guess a thank-you must be added to the writers and actors of *Search for Tomorrow,* who helped keep this book light (and damp).

who me ?

A MINI-QUIZ FOR TEACHERS

If you'll fill out this work sheet thoughtfully before reading *Experiments in Growth,* it will make the book a better tool for you. Fill in your answers to each question, and then look at the author's thoughts. Do we agree? (Maybe not.) Then go on . . .

1. Each May or June my religion students leave me—usually, forever. What *one* difference do I hope to have made in their lives? In other words, what is **my** goal in teaching religion? Why am I doing it? _____

_____

_____

_____

Does your answer say something about helping young people come in touch with God, fall more and more in love with Him so they might say "our hearts were burning within us"? Or is your answer concerned with helping students learn more facts about their religion?

My answer would have to be the former, which is the much broader answer. I see the religion teacher's task as helping the student meet God personally and learn how to build a one-to-one relationship with Him that will last all his life, and motivate all his actions.

2. How can I help my students build a personal relationship with God?

_____

_____

_____

Apparently, if the disinterest/dropout rate among young people from their churches is a reliable indicator, the approach of learning information about God and religion (bible stories, church rules and history, moral teachings, etc.) doesn't do the job. People have not only heads, but hearts as well. Both have to be involved in any relationship. Think for a minute of our human friendships: We have information or facts about our friends, but that's not the same as "knowing" them, is it? The real knowing is based on the information and facts *plus* the experience or "feel" we have of them, isn't it? In the same way, religious education that hopes to create life-long student/God friendships has to include food for thoughts about God and food for feelings about God. Most of us accept this educational principle readily; accepting it isn't the same as implementing it. So, these next three questions . . .

3. Are my students offered plenty of head/thinking/factual information about

    God? _____

    _____

    _____

    _____

If you run through a typical class of yours in your mind, chances are that between 75 percent and 100 percent of what's offered the students is in the head category—factual information about God and religion. This has been the pattern of religious education since the 1500's, and we've gotten pretty good at it. We've gone from memorization of questions and answers to more effective learning-through-experiencing methods like role-playing and arts and crafts, with audiovisual aids and all sorts of personal involvement of the students. This is fine. Head learning is the simpler type of learning to facilitate and then to measure.

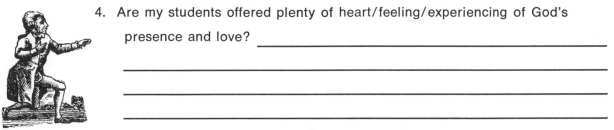

4. Are my students offered plenty of heart/feeling/experiencing of God's

    presence and love? _____

    _____

    _____

    _____

A much harder question to answer and implement! Again, think through a typical religion class as you teach it. How often are students asked to reflect upon the ways God touches their lives? to relive some of those experiences? to talk about them? to pray about them? Are classroom prayers just words said in unison—or encounters with Someone who lives? Are your students learning any simple skills for their own spiritual growth which they can carry with them the rest of their lives? Are you using a text that has a strong streak of the "He touched me" theme woven among the factual material? Do you believe this is as important as names and places and authoritative teachings and bible quotations—or do you skip the personal angles? (Some texts never touch on the I/Thou relationship; do they think the kids are already there? or incapable of having this sort of relationship? What do you think?)

Most important of all, are you a person "alive with the Spirit," so that students have a living, breathing example of what the life of man with God can be? We know that the best way to motivate others toward spirituality is to help them catch it, like the flu, from people who have already been "seized." (Those of us who don't meet this description, author included, don't have to give up. We just have to keep growing.)

Let me tell you my story, in hopes that it may help to crystallize yours. I started teaching religion by a very traditional format of lecture and discussion questions (which were rarely answered). Finding how blah that was, I moved on to "process learning" or "discovery learning" through experiential methods—thinking that was the new day, both the Alpha and the Omega. Only several years later did I realize that even though my classes had improved greatly and the kids didn't fall asleep anymore, *my goal was still a head-type goal:* to get the students to know more *about* God, to help them learn information *about* Him rather than to help them *know* Him. For some time I had equated this religious-learning-by-experience (experiential methodology) with the experience of God Himself, which is quite a different thing.

It took still another step to try to incorporate the experience of Him into my classes, so that I could help my students have both the head and the heart ingredients they needed to build a lifelong relationship with Him. I really resisted adding that one last step, the heart ingredient ("I can't even cover what I've got now"). Expanding the contents of a course meant more work and also implied a presumption on my part (who, me?) that the textbook writer had left something out. The missing ingredient was added, however—the "what" as well as the "how"—and my own experience has been that students' lives have been changed because of it.

5. If I don't have a pretty even balance between religious facts and religious

experiencing (or between what you've got and Who's got you) in my classes,

what can I do to get it? _____

_____

_____

_____

This leads us to . . .

WHAT THIS BOOK IS ABOUT

This book has nine chapters with a total of 31 experiments (and many more follow-up ideas and references) which will all give students skills to begin—or continue—to build an intimate one-to-one relationship with their God. Since the feeling, intuiting, experiencing food for that relationship is less often offered to young people than the thinking, reasoning, remembering ingredients, these exercises in spiritual growth are, primarily, heart-type exercises. There's head-type matter here too, though, and together these two sorts of learning help the whole person grow closer to God.

My suggestion —if you agree with the goal of religious education and the means to reach it described in the mini-quiz—is that you add to your classes as many or as few of these experiments as you feel is necessary to create the religious facts/ religious experiencing balance we've been talking about. Start wherever you sense there's something for *your* students, perhaps using the many suggested curriculum tie-ins to find an experiment which you can zipper into your present course of study. You might then move on to setting aside a small portion of each class time just for spiritual growth experimenting (see below). Some church schools may even want to design an entire course on spiritual growing, using this book as a text. Or, perhaps you will want to start by using *Experiments in Growth* as a personal workbook for yourself (or with a small growth group); in that case, the fruits of your contemplation and experimenting will spill over into your classroom. Do whatever feels right, and see if you can end up designing more experiments especially for your own students. Here are

SOME SUGGESTIONS

● It's really helpful to find a set time for these exercises. Perhaps the first five or ten minutes of a weekly class can be spent doing a growth experiment (some are longer). Or, for classes that meet more than once a week, how about having the first or last meeting of the week become a special time for exploring God's presence in the lives of both teacher and students? Most of the experiments end with more ideas and leads for further exploration; the references give additional avenues to examine. If an experiment really clicks with your kids, you will want to make the most of it and keep going in that vein.

- Some experiments may not work with some classes, or they may work with only a few students. That's OK; no need for a mini-trauma. Some take time—like years —to work, and neither the teacher nor the students will know when they're first tried if anything has happened. That's OK too, and is the reason why all these exercises are called "experiments." The teacher's role is to present them as well as possible and remain open-ended and flexible about results, leaving the worries about the end product to the God who sent these kids our way. (Some students may not want to grow spiritually and should surely be given the freedom to read the latest *Mad*—or anything else—while the teacher and other students move along their own paths.)

  An unhappy mistake (not uncommon) is the pill-popping mentality about teaching exercises, the "Well, folks, step right up and just take these easy little molds and pour the kids into 'em—and you'll be there" sort of instant enlightenment programming by teacher-as-technician types. We really need a more fluid, more artistic approach (see Chapter Eight for more thoughts on this).

- If you are able to have a regular time for growth experiments, how about giving it some suitable name? Little children like the idea of a "Growing Time"— themselves as the plants and God as the gardener (a theme which, of course, would reinforce all sorts of lessons on creation). Older children respond to the same image in more adult language, maybe using something like the "bloom where you are planted" quote, with appropriate visual devices, or Jeremiah's ". . . (your) soul shall be like a watered garden," or Joni Mitchell's "we've got to get ourselves back to the garden. . . ." (Therese of Lisieux, of course, built a whole spirituality—not always appreciated today—on the idea of herself as a little flower.) John 15:1 and 1 Corinthians 3:6-9 pick up the God-as-gardener theme again; teachers are His helpers, says Paul.

- Many of the growth experiments use pencil and paper. Can students set aside a special section of their religion notebooks for their growth record? Or, if their text has blank space or wide margins, can this be used to keep some sort of log? A simple title like "Ways People Grow Closer to God" or just "Ways People Grow" and a number for each experiment would do. Better still, if there's time and opportunity, the experiments could be made the basis for workbooks or journals, with space to keep track of growing efforts (see Chapter Nine for more details on keeping records and journals). Journals can include all sorts of other things, like favorite quotes, diary-type entries, pictures and artwork and so on. A journal, however, unlike a regular notebook, just has to be considered as personal and private property, looked at only upon invitation by its owner.

- The language and vocabulary of each experiment here may be too sophisticated or too simplistic for your students, depending upon their ages and where you live. At any rate, the words in the left-hand column of each experiment are just a suggested script for the teacher to take off and ad lib from. The right-hand columns are for notes and stage directions. At the end of each experiment is space for evaluation, asking "how did it go?" "how much time did it take?" "do I want to repeat this?" and "what else could I do?"

- It's a good idea to try different categories of growth experiments and then zero in on the few categories that work best with each class. The teacher can then design more of what works best, or even use the same ideas over. Since we're all growing all the time, an exercise used in September may have a different and deeper meaning in March. (We should just be sure to say that something's a repeat, if it is, so our students won't think we're becoming senile and forgetting what we've done.) Some experiments (like those in Chapter Two) are especially designed to be repeated regularly.

- Most of the experiments deal with students' feelings and personal experiences. We care about these things—and that's great. But students complain as bitterly about the teacher who cares "too much" (interpret: "is snoopy") as about the teacher who doesn't care enough. Unfortunately, religion teachers seem to be especially vulnerable to this pitfall of *over*concern—and understandably so, because we *do* care. Probably the best rule of thumb for all of us on this is to let sharing come from students' initiative rather than from teacher-triggered probing. We can also give students plenty of opportunity for anonymous feedback, rather than peeling layers off their souls more publicly.

- Often, the most we can do with a growth experiment in a classroom (a place not particularly conducive to religious experiencing) is to have a dry run of a technique which students can practice better on their own, later, in private. This is especially true of the physical things-to-do in Chapter Four. When this is so, it's good to follow up with a repeat mention of the way of growth at a future class.

- Somewhere along the line, toward the end of a school year, you'll want to pull things together. If we each know 50 ways to grow and can only find time for two or three, it can be confusing. Each student might choose one or two or three things to add to his or her life, and to work on over the summer. What we've presented in *Experiments in Growth* is enough for half a dozen lifetimes; no one can do it all!

- Most of all, spiritual growing should be fun, both for teacher and students. The good gardener (here comes that example again) not only helps his plants to grow, but enjoys them and learns from them, doesn't he? He loves each plant for its uniqueness, and doesn't try to make daisies look like roses or cucumbers taste like strawberries. He values his plants, no matter what stage of growth they're at and prizes them for what they may someday become, never hurrying them along but respecting each one's rate of growth. He weeds gently. Most of all, he sees his gardening and his garden as a means of helping himself be all *he* can be, *his* best self.

Now, the chapter which follows is a theory chapter, if you like that sort of thing. Chapters Two through Eight contain the seven categories of growth experiments, which can be used in any order that feels right. Chapter Nine takes a look at the future of spiritual growth ideas, and goes into more detail about how each of us can put these ideas on and live with them. It is especially written for those readers who might be using *Experiments in Growth* as a spiritual workbook for themselves, as well as a source of classroom exercises. If some of your students have taken this work very seriously, refer them to this chapter for additional help in planting seeds. "An

Afterword for Ruffled Believers" is for those among us who are really concerned that religious education is going to the dogs. (If you work with teachers or pastors or parents—or students?—who wish the Baltimore Catechism would return, maybe they'd appreciate reading these comments by a widely acclaimed authority and author.) There are also an index, and an invitation to all readers. Happy reading, gardening, whatever!

Am I making the most of what I've got?

chapter 1
THE ROOTS OF THIS BOOK

HUMAN POTENTIAL

Religion and psychology have been friendly enemies since the days of Sigmund Freud, with assorted churchpeople recognizing the help psychology could lend to their ministries—but at the same time bristling at many psychologists' view of man as nothing more than an animal.

Fur has especially flown over statements like Freud's that nothing is so completely at variance with human nature as the command to love one's neighbor,[1] or B. F. Skinner's saying that the only difference he expects to discover between the behavior of rats and men is that men can talk.[2]

In the past decade, a different sort of psychology has come into prominence. It's called "humanistic psychology," or "Third Force psychology," to distinguish it from the other two main schools of psychological thought (Freudian and behaviorist). Humanistic psychology is concerned with man as much more than an animal—it's concerned with his hopes and dreams and, most of all, his potential. Humanistic psychologists ask the question "How far can man go?" and "How terrific can he really be?" and, more practically, "How can we help him get there?" They are concerned with man not as sick or "normal" (whatever that is), but as "self-actualized," "enlightened," "expanded" and other such idealistic descriptions. One of the key themes of humanistic psychology is the often-quoted statement that most people are using only about two to five percent of their potential![3]

Another theme stressed in the literature of the human potential movement (which is the putting-it-into-practice end of humanistic psychology) is that all of man must be studied and worked with if we are to have good psychology; that is, we can't deal just with a person's emotions or childhood experiences or his behavior, but we have to consider the total person, have a holistic (yes, like the word "holy") picture of humans . . . and this includes, of course, man's spiritual nature as well as his physical, mental and emotional facets.

---

[1] Sigmund Freud, *New Introductory Lectures on Psychoanalysis* (New York: W. W. Norton, 1933).

[2] Quoted in *The Broken Image* by Floyd Matson (New York: Doubleday, 1966).

[3] Herbert A. Otto is one of the pioneers of the human potential movement. He writes about how little of our potential we use in *Guide to Developing Your Potential* (New York: Scribners, 1967) echoing William James's earlier work.

It's tempting to go on at length about this fascinating field of study and about the key people in it,[4] but that will keep us from getting to our focus, which is

HUMAN POTENTIAL AND RELIGIOUS EDUCATION

The important question for us is: What's the connection between the human potential ideas and our field, religious education? Already you can see from the above that there's a big connection: God surely wants us to use what He's given us, to develop our talents, to be all we can be. If He's made us "little less than the angels," "other Christs," we just know he wants us to uncover and use that potential we all have. But how do we do this?

There are church-related means, of course, but over the past 10 years or so, bookstores have also had to add whole new "selfy-helpy" sections to handle the deluge of books on how to tap our potential. You've seen them, haven't you, with titles like *Passages: A Guide for Pilgrims of the Mind*[5] and *Expanding the Self*[6]? These books are different from earlier help-yourself-and-influence-people books and courses. The best of the human potential works are solidly rooted in experimental psychological research being done in classrooms, growth centers, homes and offices and factories and other places where people grow. They're much more than the *Gee, You're a Beautiful Guy and You Should Really Feel Good About Yourself* item, or even the circuit preacher's positive-self-image/pop psych approach.

The interesting thing about the trend in these books is that, more and more, they tend to be *spiritual* growth manuals, not just "develop your emotional responses" or "teach your mind to relax" writings. As time passes, human potential researchers are finding that a holistic view of man shows him tending toward the spiritual, putting his physical, mental and emotional natures together and transcending all three.[7]

---

[4] Perhaps the best introduction to humanistic psychology is Frank G. Goble's *The Third Force* (New York: Grossman Publishers, Inc., 1970), which is also in a Pocket Book edition ($1.25). This book has a foreword by Abraham Maslow, whose own work would be the next logical step for readers who want to pursue the theory behind the practical growth exercises. *The Farther Reaches of Human Nature* (New York: The Viking Press, 1971), Maslow's last writings, is an exciting place to start. The word "humanistic" in connection with religion can stand church-type fur on edge. It can imply atheism to Christians and even eradication of their culture to Jews. But in *Experiments in Growth* it's used in the sense that Maritain or any of the Christian humanists of any age would have used it.

[5] See Experiment No. 11.

[6] *Expanding the Self: Personal Growth for Teachers,* Angelo V. Boy and Gerald J. Pine (Dubuque, IA: Wm. C. Brown, Co., 1971).

[7] In the January 1971 *Newsletter* of the Association for Humanistic Psychology, Michael Murphy of Esalen, the trend-setting growth center in California, wrote about his institute's growing emphasis on the transpersonal dimension of human experience. The catalogues from Esalen (which are sort of a weather vane of direction in the human potential movement) are, with each issue, increasingly concerned with matters church-oriented people would label "religious." See also the introduction to William Schutz's book *Here Comes Everybody* (New York: Harper and Row, 1971): This well-known author and encounter group leader writes that all his experience with body and mind and group has

transpersonal ?

Psychological research is confirming what we already know from religious sources—that it's man's nature to stretch out to the beyond. Psychologists call the study of man's spiritual nature "transpersonal psychology," and it is a distinct branch of study in its own right.

Well, religious educators have been talking about spiritual growth for centuries, right? We've talked about it in terms of attending church, worshiping, receiving sacraments, praying, doing penance, spiritual reading and so forth, all of which are good ways to grow spiritually. One big problem, however, is that many of the students we enthusiastically share these ideas with don't buy them (the "my father dragged me to church on Sunday . . . I might as well be in jail" mentality).

Today, we also have available to us ways of spiritual growth which have sprung from the researches of humanistic and transpersonal psychology. Some are very old and some are quite new, but all work! What's more, these methods are usually attractive to our students because they come from a world which speaks their language, the so-called world of "new consciousness." (True, that is a pretentious phrase, and the humorless, intense seeker of enlightenment is an easy person to satirize, as are the not-infrequent excesses of the human potential movement.) Learning from psychology today (as the Church of the 13th century learned from ancient philosophy and the Church of the Renaissance plugged into secular art), we can integrate these ways of growth into our religion classes along with traditional church-centered ways of growth. Together, they can mean a real difference in fostering for our students the "love affair with God" we were talking about a few pages earlier, a union based both on facts about, and experience of the sacred.

GETTING HIGH (ON GOD?)

There's one special aspect of psychological research we should really spend a little more time thinking about: It's what is called the "physiology of consciousness"—what happens in the body in terms of brain-wave activity, the nervous system, body chemicals and so forth during *differing* states of consciousness. This research, in particular, has very significant implications for religious education (as well as for many other fields of study).

We're all familiar with at least three different states of consciousness—sleeping, dreaming, and being awake, as you are now while reading this book (I hope!). Scientific research is being done in many places today on other states of consciousness, nonordinary consciousness . . . or in more simple terms, "getting high" or "turning on." (The vocabulary is from drugland, but is used—by young people especially—for similar nonordinary consciousness experiences that have nothing to do with drinking or drugs.)

led him to feel (even though he doesn't yet understand it well) that the "spiritual element is central" to human growth. There is a counterpart to the idea of man's psychological drive to wholeness in the physical and biological sciences: Double Nobel Prize winner, biologist Albert Szent-Gyoergyi, writes (in *The Graduate Faculty Newsletter* of Columbia University) of an "innate drive in living matter to perfect itself." He calls this principle syntropy, the opposite of entropy.

Perhaps you're familiar with some of this investigation,[8] through books, courses, magazine articles and TV reports. Interestingly, our students probably know more about nonordinary consciousness than we do. They wouldn't call it that, though. They would use the language about being high or call it "getting psyched" or "spacing out" or "freaking out," depending upon how old they are and where they live. Here are some reports from young people about their highs:

● In very typical language, a 13-year-old girl tells about being beside herself: "I thought I was really in love. Mike was my first boyfriend and I had been going with him for six months. The most we had ever done was hold hands, and this on very rare occasions. This was enough to put me in heaven.

"One evening in April, my mother was expecting me home right after a C.C.D. class. I asked her if I could walk home with Mike, but she insisted that I get a ride home with her (so I wouldn't get mugged). Well, I went home with Mike anyway, because it was such a beautiful night and I had the feeling that he was going to make the most of this occasion.

"We got to my back door and Mike was very nervous—as I was, because I knew that any minute my mother would come barreling down the driveway by the back door with her high beams shining. Finally, I said, 'Mike, I really have to go in' and was just turning to go when he reached out and kissed me. That minute, in drove Mom. Off went Mike. I went in. Mom followed and announced, 'You're grounded for a week!'

"Well, it didn't bother me at all. I was so happy I hardly heard her. Her death sentence didn't even touch me. All night long I didn't even know where I was— I was so happy I could have died."

(The reader will be discreet enough not to linger on this story to wonder who the real-life villainess was. The point, of course, is the supranormal state of consciousness of the daughter.)

● Now, the same psychological happening, but under very different circumstances, as reported by a star pitcher of 15 who has learned how to get himself psyched before a ball game:

"When I'm going to pitch, I get dressed—a certain way. Then I go to a spot on the hill by the baseball field, about an hour before the game. I try to picture in my mind just what's going to happen: who's going to be up, how each one hits, what sort of pitches I want to throw them, how I'll look pitching (like Tom Seaver,

---

[8] If you've been to lectures on Silva Mind Control or Transcendental Meditation or read about alpha brain waves, this territory is somewhat familiar ground. An excellent synthesis of this research and religious traditions from all over the world is Father William Johnston's *Silent Music: The Science of Meditation* (New York: Harper and Row, 1974). See Experiment No. 11. There's also *Transpersonal Psychologies,* edited by Charles Tart (New York: Harper and Row, 1975), a study of mystical traditions, including Christian mysticism.

usually). I run through the whole game, like a movie. Most of the time, the things I concentrate on happen later, just like I thought of them.

"Usually, I don't notice anything that's going on around me. The only one who knows what I'm doing is the catcher—otherwise, I try to stay by myself. One time I had to stop thinking because this kid I hadn't seen for a long time came along and started to talk. He used up all my thinking time, and guess what happened? The other team clobbered me."

(Apparently, this concentration technique which the pitcher devised for himself works; his record at the end of his last Babe Ruth season was 10 and 2. You'll notice that, while thinking on the hill, he's not in the same everyday frame of mind typical of most of us most of the time.)

● Here's another nonordinary consciousness experience that could be called a double-psych! It happened to a nine-year-old and her 14-year-old sister, who tells the story:

"My father had this idea of planting a half acre of potatoes—not a small garden like most people plant, but a half an acre. He thought it would save us money. When September came, here were all these potatoes that had to be dug, and guess who got elected to do it?

"One miserable day (it was raining and had been raining all the night before) he took my sister and me up on this mountainside where the potatoes were and we started digging for them. Some of the potatoes had little reddish-orange potato worms in them—here we were down on our hands and knees in the mud and the rain. It was horrible.

"Finally, my father said, 'Why don't we turn on the car radio?' That was a great idea, so we did and after that the two of us picked right along with him and it seemed to get much easier. We both got so wrapped up in the music that we forgot what we were doing, and finally we were just gone on 'Rock 99' (the name of the station), right in the middle of the rain and the potato worms.

"But I never want to do that again, and neither does my sister. To top it off, guess what was the *one* thing that went down in price that winter? Right, potatoes!"

(It wasn't love, nor sports concentration, but music that acted as the catalyst here. Result: an altered state of consciousness, worms and all.)

● Finally, here's a story of part of a simple day in the life of a 17-year-old about to go in the Navy. See what he's learned about being high, and about enjoying life:

"One morning in September, just before I left for the service, I had to get some records from my old high school, so I got up early and thumbed into town. At school, I met a lot of people I hadn't seen in a long time: kids I had gone to school with and a teacher I really liked. We just talked about what was happening —nothing special.

23

"Then I met Sandra. She and her family were on my old paper route about three or four years ago. I used to stick my puppy in my paper bag while I delivered. We started talking about Sandra's mother, who is someone I like very much and hadn't seen in a while. Finally, she suggested that I call her mother, so I did and we made plans to get together later.

"I had lunch with an old girlfriend in the cafeteria and we just compared notes on what we were doing, and then I visited for about an hour with Sandra's mother at her house and caught up on their family and *their* dog.

"Well, it was just great, seeing all these people and floating with them and being one with them. This is a high, about the best one I know, I believe. I go drinking with my friends, but this is much better. I've been getting psyched on people since I was 13."

(The simplicity of this story is what makes it so special. We all do the same sort of things this young man does, but how many of us do them in this beautiful supraconscious way? Think what this could do to the U.S. Navy!)

Now, all these young people know what it is to be in a state of nonordinary consciousness where they are out of themselves, stretched beyond their everyday selves. They have had experience in focusing totally on one thing or one person or one feeling. Our students do this too and, what's more, have it happen fairly often through the same means as the kids in our stories (love, sports, music, people) or through tuning in to nature, being part of a spirited crowd, daydreaming, dancing, getting lost in a game or book, or even communing with a pet.[9] (Compare this sort of living to the average adult's. Most people over 25 might get high (naturally high, that is) a couple of times a year—when our team wins, or when we welcome in the New Year—but it's certainly not something that happens to us often, is it?)

Interestingly enough, another little piece of this picture is that kids sense

---

[9] Researchers into the physiology of consciousness make fine distinctions between differing states of nonordinary consciousness, often depending upon the trigger or elevator which takes the subject there. Our lumping of all these "highs" together isn't meant as a bypassing of the finer points made by the researchers, but is done as a means of helping us get a handle on this enormous subject. For further insight, you might read Claudio Naranjo's *The One Quest* (New York: Ballantine Books, Inc., 1973) for general background and the beginning of *Music and Your Mind* by Louis M. Savary and Helen L. Bonny (New York: Harper and Row, 1973). The definitive research on altered states of consciousness is often associated with the more scholarly writings of Robert E. Ornstein, whose *The Psychology of Consciousness* (San Francisco: W. H. Freeman and Co., 1972) is well worth serious study by anyone interested in the implications of this field for the future.

Readers familiar with the left cerebral hemisphere-right cerebral hemisphere research will recognize *Experiments in Growth* as an attempt to effect a balance in religious education between the two types of brain functioning. Robert Samples and others point out that the most essential ingredient for facilitating right hemisphere activities (feeling, imagining, intuiting, etc.) in the classroom is a high-trust environment. The kids, that is, must feel good about following their hunches and non-fearful of not having the "correct" answer. Intuition and creativity must not be seen as having second-class status if the right-left balance is to be achieved.

(although they might not be able to explain it) that spending time in the "psyched" condition carries good things over to the ordinary conscious state. One reason athletes are usually big guns in high school or junior high is *not only* because they can kick a ball into a goal or smear the opposing tackle, but also because they *often* (not always) carry with them a certain "something": a put-togetherness, an awareness of the ordinary little things of life, and an inner calmness that can often be the result of having spent time in a nonordinary state of consciousness. A popular song calls it knowing "how to leave myself behind."

People who meditate usually have this same quality, because they too have learned to focus or flow into a singleness of attention. People who pray really well often have this together quality too. Who are the "expanded people" you know? What do you think helped make them this way? Can you guess, from what you know of them, whether they spend much time in some sort of "natural high" state? Can you find out?[10]

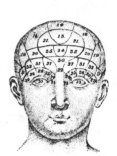

Yes, now at last we're getting around to some connection of all this to religion—and, specifically, to religious education. The psyched space in our minds is also the prayer space; prayer is a form of nonordinary consciousness when you're praying in a way that takes you out of yourself. The Jesus People know this. They talk about "getting high on God" or "tripping out with the Lord." For the first time, the encountering of God (that is, the religious experience) is being studied by scientific means and we're learning what happens to us physically and psychologically when we're caught up in prayer.

A word should go in here about our definition of the word "prayer." You'd hardly expect that the prayers we sometimes rattle off before a class or during church would be very conducive of nonordinary consciousness! That sort of praying (which may be the only sort of prayer your students know—why not ask them for their definition of the word?) isn't what we're talking about here. Throughout this book, "prayer" is used in a broader sense, meaning walking with God, the awareness of being with Him, of experiencing His presence (and His love), of being able to say, "He touched me." *This sort of prayer is the trademark of that one-to-one relationship we were talking*

---

[10] Maslow, mentioned above, called this lasting "certain something" the plateau experience, as contrasted with peak experiences that come and go. In fact, he saw "Third Force" psychology as only a preparation for a higher or "Fourth Force" psychology—or transpersonal psychology. Other scholars call the plateau the "fifth state of consciousness," or a similar term, depending on their typology of consciousness. (If you can dig it up, see the article on states of consciousness by Daniel Goleman in the 1972, #2 issue of *The Journal of Transpersonal Psychology*. This gives an idea of how many people have cared about this experience in so many different times and places.)

The older textbooks of ascetic theology spoke of the distinction between "sensible consolations" (peaks) and the unitive state between man and God (the plateau), which would be a religious interpretation of the same phenomena.

A still unresolved question remains to be argued in the professional journals about *how to measure* the presence of this fifth state of consciousness, the "something special" characteristic of the expanded person. Brain-wave measurement, researchers say, may be less useful at this point than some as yet undevised measurement of how much the person loves! (This will hardly be news to any of the religions of the world, will it?)

about earlier as being the goal of religious education and of all our efforts.[11]

Now, we're working with boys and girls who may not be the least bit interested in relationships with God, or in religious experience. They may not have any thought at all about trying to find Him or in going where He is. Yet, many of them (like the young people quoted above) have already been there—where He is—without knowing it, in that altered state of consciousness which is the home base of religious experience just as it is of sports involvement or music listening or of being in love. Or, if they haven't been there, they know there's something special, and desirable, about the other kids who have spent time in that space . . . even if they can't quite put a finger on what that specialness is or where it came from.

We can use our students' experiences in being high or observing those who know how to get high naturally (that is, not with pills or drink) to help them become familiar with their "God space." Several of the experiments in this book are slanted along these lines, as you'll see, and one (Experiment No. 6) deals directly with the ideas in these last few paragraphs. (None of this should imply that there's *no difference* between, say, the music or the sports highs and the God experience. Here we're concerned with building on the *similarities* between religious and nonreligious highs.[12])

So, we find ourselves at the end of all this floaty thinking the inheritors of not one but two sources which will help us reach our goal of building relationships of love with God. Traditional religion gives us information about Him, and it teaches us about religious experience which comes both from Him immediately (grace, powerful enough to knock some people off their horses, like Paul) and from our own graced

---

[11] Again, the older texts warn against reaching out for "spiritual experience," stressing that contemplative states are a gift. Well, yes, of course—and yet, surely we might do all we can to prepare ourselves to receive that gift. Why continue to let students (and nonstudents) in on types of praying which may bore them silly and never tell them about the best sort? In *The Living Light* for Winter, 1974, Father Berard Marthaler rephrases for our time what has been said for 2,000 years: ". . . a (even, *the*) basic task of all religious education is to give the learner some feel for religious experience" . . . the "highly personal encounter (with God) that touches a man at the marrow of his being."

[12] For good insights into the distinctions between the experience of God and the peak experience, see Thomas Merton's *Zen and the Birds of Appetite* (New York: New Directions, 1968, pp. 71-72). Paul Hinnebusch, O.P., among many other writers, points out that while the profound experience may be *one* way in which God communicates Himself, it is just a faint reflection and reminder of Him (see *Friendship in the Lord;* Notre Dame, IN: Ave Maria Press, 1973). If our students were tuned in to the religious experience, there would be no need to try to expose them to it by starting with "secular highs"; unfortunately, many of them *aren't* tuned in to the presence of God in their lives— so, we start with what they know.

A fully Christian viewpoint on religious experience must, of course, allow for both the action of God and the psychology of the grace-receiver. (Richard Hauser, S.J. of Creighton University has explored this in an unpublished doctoral thesis dealing with both Maslow and Merton.) With the "Hartford Eighteen," we affirm that realizing one's potential and being true to oneself is certainly not the whole meaning of salvation (as some would have it). In early 1975, this group of Christian thinkers of nine denominations met to affirm the separateness of God and His kingdom, and to condemn pervasive contemporary ideas which have filtered into Christian theology and seem to undermine the transcendence of God. One of these is the idea that we can make it on our own, that we can— by solely human means—become our best selves.

efforts (the practice of tuning in to His presence through any of a wide variety of types of soul-searching and prayer).

Humanistic psychology teaches us that people who begin to make the most of their human selves (with or without acknowledgment of God's role in this work) tend automatically toward transpersonal or matter-transcending experience.[13] These two approaches to spiritual growth—the religious and the psychological—are separate, but complementary. Marrying them gives us the following experiments in growth.[14]

---

[13] Followers of some schools of spirituality may react to the humanistic "work-on-your-potential" theme with distaste; working on yourself means thinking about yourself, just the opposite of selflessness. "Death to self" and mortification are more their cup of tea. A couple of questions for them: Doesn't the idea of "losing yourself" or "surrendering to God" imply that one has a self to lose? a self to surrender? Doesn't "I live, now not I; but Christ lives in me" or "I must decrease . . ." suggest that there was, once, an "I"?

Is asking God to fill a void where nothing has ever been really the highest form of spirituality?— or even a very good form? Does He really want us to stay emotional children with big human gaps that we ask Him to satisfy? Or, isn't the idea of a mature self freely given up a much richer sort of selflessness?

Numerous fine writers on the psychology plus religion front have tackled this matter in depth and have also pointed out (with appropriate horror stories) the damage done by an imposed spirituality that denies the person a chance to work out his own identity before freely turning it over—or, better, transcending it. The point is mentioned here just for the record. (Many psychiatrists would add that the "noble" person who never thinks of himself is caught up in the neurotic role of "Rescuer" or "Mr. Nice Guy," and is of little help either to those he rescues or to himself.)

[14] Carl Jung, the great Swiss psychiatrist, would approve. In 1933, he wrote (in *Modern Man in Search of a Soul,* New York: Harcourt, Brace and World, Inc.) that religions ought to contain expressions of man's psychological life, but had unfortunately been reduced to concern for things of the outer world only. On the other face of the coin is Jung's famous statement (from the same source) that not one of his patients in the second half of life had been healed without regaining his religious outlook (". . . with the decline of religious life, the neuroses grow noticeably more frequent. . . "). Much of the human potential movement has roots in Jungian psychology; see especially the chapter in this book on "Stories and Symbols."

Interestingly, Father Andrew Greeley and William C. McCready found in a survey that, although 40 percent of their interviewees had experienced what could be called a "mystical experience of a powerful spiritual force which seemed to lift them out of themselves," very few associated this experience with formal religion and (worse yet) that their clergymen would be the last people with whom they would discuss this experience. Let's hope this separateness will not always be the case. See *The New York Times Magazine,* January 26, 1975, and also Father Greeley's book, *Ecstasy, A Way of Knowing* (Englewood Cliffs, N.J.: Prentice-Hall, Inc., 1974).

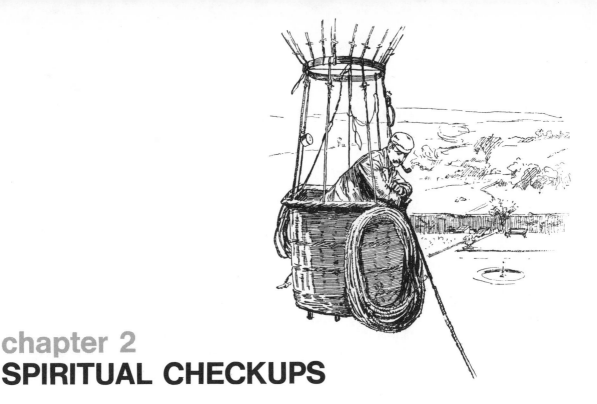

chapter 2
SPIRITUAL CHECKUPS

Here are the simplest growth experiments in this book—three ways of checking up on

- where we've been (spiritually)
- where we're at (spiritually)
- where we're going (spiritually)
- how we're going to get there.

These first three experiments are easy introductions to the whole idea of spiritual growing and our responsibility toward ourselves in that department. Because they're short and sweet, they're simple to grasp and simple to do. These same qualities make these three experiments good for encores, so that you might keep going back to one or more of these checkups during a school year. You'll find two experiments on human relations here, and one on values.

As you do this sort of self-evaluation with a class and begin to see results (sometimes students will say things like "I used to groan when you nagged us about how we were doing, but it really does help," or "I don't have enough willpower to keep after myself, so I really am glad you're asking these questions") you can devise your own ways of self-rating. Take a look at the values clarification references at the end of Experiment No. 3 for sources of similar ideas you can adapt to the religion class, or just make up your own self-inventory exercises to fit the needs of your students. Here are some of the simplest ways of rating one's self:

- letter or number grades, as on a report card
- a scale or continuum from zero to one hundred
- multiple choice from Excellent/Very Good/Good/Fair/Poor (or 1/2/3/4)
- a graph with a line showing highs and lows
- stars or checks (none through three) next to a list.

Just a reminder: Have you read the earlier pages that tell what this book is about? There are many suggestions there for implementing all the growth experiments, suggestions which will help everything sprout smoothly.

How's Your Love Life?

EXPERIMENT NUMBER 1

BACKGROUND:

Here's a good place to start with the growth experimenting. This is a very simple introduction to three key ideas:

1) We can grow.
2) Growth doesn't "just happen," but has to be worked on by each of us.
3) God helps with this growth—if we ask Him.

You might try this experiment at the beginning of a school year, then repeat it in Advent and Lent, the seasons of soul-tending. It could be used again to wrap up the year, "as is" or with variations of your own. If this is the first growth experiment you're using with a class, you'll want to preface it with some introductory comments about the purpose of experiments in spiritual growth (see "What This Book Is About").

MATERIALS:

Paper and pencil (preferably, a log or journal).

CURRICULUM TIE-IN:

Life with God, prayer, other people.

"We're going to be doing some thinking about how people grow, especially about how people's souls grow. One thing we can do to help ourselves with this is to check up on our relationships with other people. Let's do that today, OK? . . .

(The . . .'s indicate a pause so students can think and/or contribute.)

"On your papers would you please list, in a column on the left-hand side, all the people in your family who are now living with you at home. . . .

(Can you do this on the board or a flip-chart as you go? And, yes, the dog is a member of the family.)

"Now, after each name, will you draw a scale like this:

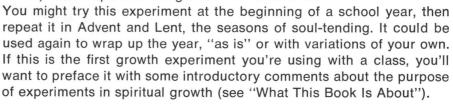

"At one end of each scale, put a zero, and at the other end, the number 100. . . .

0   100

"Now, let's see if we can rate ourselves as to how we're doing with each person on our lists, using the scale next to each one's name. For instance, perhaps you and your father are on pretty good terms right now because you've been mending fences and smoothing paths

(Use whatever examples are suitable for your age group.)

30

for the day you get your license. You might rate your relationship with him at about 75—or three-quarters of what it could be—and you'd put an "x" at that spot on the scale for your Dad. . . .

Dad: 0 ⎣————————————————×————————⎦ 100

"Maybe you and your sister Lucy are having some not-so-good times lately because she's always taking your clothes without asking. (Of course, you never do it to her.) That rating might be about 25 or so. . . .

"Now, go ahead and work down your list. . . .

"All set? Here's something else to add to each scale. Try asking yourself this question about each relationship: 'Which way is it going?' . . . that is, are Dad and I, for instance, improving in the way we get along, or is our relationship going backwards? . . .

"On each scale, put an arrow to indicate the direction in which the relationship between you and that person is going. Sometimes you can tell this best by thinking back to how you got along with that person a year ago. Your scales will look like this:

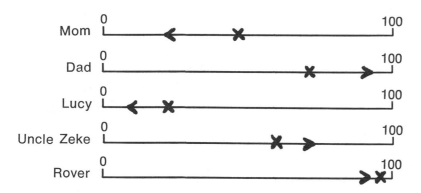

(Keep using the board or chart to illustrate.)

"Now, take a look at what you've got. It's a picture of you and everyone you live with and where you're at. How do you feel about it? . . . What's your batting average? . . . Are things generally moving uphill, or are they all going down? . . . Is there *no one* you're doing well with at home? . . . Is the dog the only one who loves you? . . . Why are some of these relationships good and others not? . . . Did you ever stop before to appreciate the ones that *are* pretty good? . . .

(These are thinking questions, not discussion questions.)

31

"Here's the next question: Of all the relationships you've charted, which one is most in need of being improved—that is, which one is in worst shape? . . . Circle that person's name. . . .

"And think: What one thing could I do to improve the relationship with that person? . . . If the person is your mother, for example, would one small action, like taking out the garbage without being asked, help to improve that relationship just a little? . . . Would it help to move the mark on her line up a few points? . . . Would it help to turn the arrow around? . . .

(Suggestion: Could you also throw in some example from your own life at this point, letting the kids see that you too — oh, wonder of wonders—are in need of improvement?)

"So, think of one small thing you *could* do for the circled person and write it down over the scale next to that person's name. . . .

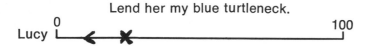

Lend her my blue turtleneck.

Lucy   0 ⊢─◄──✕──────────────── 100

(Don't forget.)

"Now, I'd like to suggest that some time this week you try to do this one thing for that person. Could you do it more than once? . . . Really try to remember, and I'll remind you when I see you again.

"There's one more relationship we haven't checked up on. What would that be? . . .

"Right, how are you doing with God? . . . Let's draw one last scale:

God   0 ⊢────────────────── 100

"First of all, how can you judge how you're doing with God? . . .

(What ideas do students have?)

"One measure might be how much you are aware of Him, of His presence throughout the day. A very unusual person *might* go through the day with a sort of lingering sense of God being around, and might rate himself in the last tenth of the scale. Where would you put yourself according to that standard? . . .

"Another test might be what Jesus said to the apostles at the Last Supper, '. . . you are my friends if you do what I command.' What commandments was He talking about? . . .

(John 15:14)
(The two commandments of the New Testament: love God, and love your neighbor as you love yourself; Mt 22:37-39.)

"Let's add three more 'x's' to this scale now. Where would you rate yourself on loving God? . . . on loving yourself? . . . on loving others? (Look back to the family scales for the answer to that one.) . . .

"Now, will you average out the four 'x's' on the scale for God and put a big 'X' where they all meet? . . .

"What next? . . . Right, what direction is your relationship with the Lord going? Let's say, in the past year have you become closer to Him, or do you seem to be less aware that He's part of your life? Think back to this time last year and compare . . . and then let's put an arrow on our scales to indicate direction. . . .

"And next? . . . Yes, what could you do to improve that relationship with God? Let's list on the board some general ideas that might be helpful. What, for instance, might help a person walk more closely with God? . . .

"Is there one item you would be willing to pick from our list—or from your own ideas—that you could try to practice for at least a week? Is it worthwhile trying to improve your relationship with God? . . . If it seems too difficult, how about asking Him for some help? . . .

"In a week, I'll ask you to think again about the two things you wrote down, the things that would help two of your relationships improve—one with someone at home, and one with God Himself. Will you save your papers until that time? No one, of course, is obligated to work on his or her friendships like this, but if we don't take definite steps once in a while, love has a way of drying up, like a stream that's not fed. See what you feel like doing with these ideas, OK?"

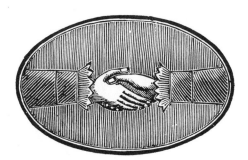

(If you have time, you may want to hash over the idea of the right kind of self-love, a fresh stumbling block for each generation.)

(If students have come up with other norms of judging one's relationship with God, factor these in, too.)

(Praying, trying to tune in to the ways He speaks to us, receiving the sacraments, reading scripture, looking for signs of Him in our world, church-going with thought, and — of course — paying careful attention in this class.)

(You can see the value of logs.)
(When it's time for follow-up, no one has to talk about how things are, but can just answer mentally to "How am I doing with the circled person?" and "How am I doing with God?")

DATE TRIED: **TIME:**   **REPEAT?:**

RESULTS:

MORE IDEAS:

This experiment could obviously be expanded if you wanted to spend more time on it, or were having an intensive (Lenten?) self-evaluation, or were using it in a non-classroom setting where you don't always have to play Beat the Clock. You could:

1) add groups of scales to cover the other people in students' lives—relatives, teachers, neighbors, youth leaders and coaches, friends, probation officers.

2) have regular how're-you-doing? times each week, asking students to record in their log the progress in their resolutions. The practices could be changed each week, so that one week might be seven days of trying to share small things with Lucy and the next week might be seven days of keeping your own paws off her things. Small, bite-sized resolutions are best and easiest to keep. Students need to be reminded, too, that progress in human relations is slow, as in s-n-a-i-l.

The self-portrait that results at the end of a whole year of this kind of self-inventory would be very helpful. Remember too: Logs are private. If students are afraid that others will sneak looks at what they've written, help them devise some sort of code or shorthand so only they will know the meaning of their markings.

REFERENCES:

Why Am I Afraid to Tell You Who I Am?, John Powell, S.J. (Niles, IL: Argus Communications, 1969)

Of all the many, many books on how to improve human relations, this very popular synthesis of the best of several schools of psychology is a good, readable choice. There are also cards available that amusingly illustrate the last chapter, "Catalog of Games and Roles." See, too, the same author's *Why Am I Afraid to Love?*

Parent Effectiveness Training (P.E.T.), Thomas Gordon (New York: Peter H. Wyden, Inc., 1970)

    If you are working with adults rather than with students, many of them will be parents rating themselves on how they're doing with Dick and Jane at home—and maybe Puff and Spot too. Such an inventory usually produces a lot of teeth-gnashing over one or two children on totally different wavelengths from Mom or Dad. P.E.T. gives concrete, practical skills for parenting; it is similar to Haim Ginott's work, but even easier to apply. See also Gordon's *Teacher Effectiveness Training (T.E.T.)*

Scriptural Checklists

EXPERIMENT NUMBER 2

BACKGROUND:

The bible has several sets of instructions on "how to make it," from as early in its pages as the Ten Commandments in the Book of Exodus. These various listings have been growth guidelines for centuries and are just as useful today. Here's an experiment in evaluating ourselves, using the scattered teachings of Jesus known as the Spiritual Works of Mercy. Just as useful would be self-ratings based on the Beatitudes, the Corporal Works of Mercy, the Gifts of the Holy Spirit or the other listings at the end of this experiment.

MATERIALS:

Paper and pencil.

CURRICULUM TIE-IN:

Spiritual works of mercy, bible, other people, service, suffering, forgiveness, prayer.

"There are many ways we can check up on how we're doing in our lives as believers. One way is to use the so-called checklists that are in the bible, rating ourselves by them. Let's do that using the list called the Spiritual Works of Mercy. Did anyone ever hear of it, or know what's on it? . . .

"First of all, how many spiritual works of mercy are there?

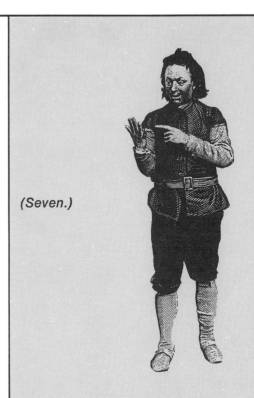

(Seven.)

"Why don't you make two small columns at the right-hand side of your paper? . . . At the left, in the large space, we'll list the seven spiritual works of mercy and in the first right-hand column you can grade yourself on how you're doing in that quality. The second column is for later. You could use letter grades as some report cards have, or do it any other way you'd like.

"Before we begin, let me ask if anyone knows from where in the bible this list comes? . . .

(It's not in any one place, but is scattered through the gospels.)

36

"Let's wait until we have it written down, and then I'll ask you again. . . .

"Although these items can be listed in any order, they're usually put down like this: The first spiritual work of mercy is

WARN THE SINNER.

"Will you write that after a number one on your paper? . . .

"Right away we've hit the toughest one of the seven. Why is warning the sinner a hard thing to do? . . .

"Right! You can see the possibilities for making people hate you if you go around practicing this advice. Yet, it is the advice of Jesus and Christians down through the ages have tried to follow it. Can you think of an example of some time when you might be able to warn someone who's obviously taken a downward path, in hopes of helping him or her turn around? . . .

"And, most important, is there some way you know to help turn someone around so he won't resent it? How can you be a help rather than a pain? . . .

(Unless someone knew.)

(While you do it on the board.)

(It implies that we have to judge who's sinning, and then know how to correct him so he'll change. Very hard!)

(Mt 18:15-17)
(Even if your students are young, they may have a brother or sister who keeps messing up his or her life.)

(A good start: Speak from the heart, not from "your throne.")

"Finally, give yourself some sort of mark in the first right-hand column as to how you think you're doing in following this advice of Jesus. Have you ever tried to pull someone back from a wrong path? . . . Have you done it gently? . . . and effectively? . . . Did it work? . . . for long? . . . Take all of this into consideration, and grade yourself . . .

"Well, the other six spiritual works of mercy are easier to do—we started off with the hardest. Here's the second for you to write down:

INSTRUCT THE IGNORANT.

. . . and here, 'ignorant' suggests people who don't know why they're here on earth. Who are the ignorant? . . .

(Children, sometimes; people of all ages whose lives are completely secular.)

"How can you personally instruct these people? . . . First, how about the children? . . .

(Many ideas possible; does your religious education program use older students as classroom aides with younger? If not, can you do anything to get this started?)

"Next, how can you, at your age, instruct adults who are obviously ignorant of any meaning to life, who plainly don't see higher things or God or spirituality as having any importance for them? . . .

(By your example of how happy a life filled with God can be; other ideas?)

"Some church members even sell or hand out literature on the street or door to door, as you know. They are trying to perform the second spiritual work of mercy by doing this. What do you think about this way of instructing? . . .

(Answers will range from great to awful, depending upon your denomination —but the "awfuls" might be led to admiration for the zeal of street preachers.)

"Now, let's each rate ourselves on this quality in the first column on the right. Do you ever 'instruct the ignorant'? . . .

"The third spiritual work of mercy is

COUNSEL THE DOUBTFUL.

If you'll write that down. . . . How do we do that? . . .

(By giving good advice, from a believer's frame of reference.)

"But, again, what's the pitfall in this teaching of Jesus? He tells us to counsel, to advise—but what can go wrong here? . . .

(People who give unsolicited advice or who play God are not very popular —or very helpful.)

"Think of whether or not you have been able to advise people well when they were in doubt about which way to go, or what to do . . . and give yourself a grade for how you're doing in this department. . . .

"The fourth spiritual work of mercy is

COMFORT THE SORROWFUL.

That's certainly easy to understand, isn't it? . . . do we need to talk about this one? . . .

(Perhaps only to acknowledge the frustration of not always being able to comfort. Often all we can do is share sadness.)

"Will you rate yourself on this quality now? How often and how well do you comfort someone who is unhappy? . . . Or do you turn the other way from people who are sad so you won't be made unhappy by them? . . . Do people come to you when they're down? . . .

"The fifth spiritual work of mercy is a hard one. It's

BEAR WRONGS PATIENTLY.

"When someone has done something wrong that hurts you, how do you react? Think about the last time that happened . . . and give yourself a grade. . . .

(Examples? No names, please.)

"The sixth teaching on our list may be even harder than the fifth. It's

FORGIVE ALL INJURIES.

"Think now about the people who have hurt you recently. . . . Have you forgiven them for doing this? . . . Or do you still hold grudges against them? . . . Are you not speaking to someone like this? . . . Rate yourself on this difficult, difficult work of mercy. . . .

"Finally we are told in the seventh spiritual work of mercy to

PRAY FOR THE LIVING AND THE DEAD.

None of us would mind doing that, I guess, but still it can be hard to do. Why? . . .

(We forget.)

"Which 'living' are especially hard to pray for? . . .

(The ones on the giving end in numbers five and six, above.)

"One way to help ourselves remember to pray for the living and the dead is to make a list of all the people we want to pray for, and stick it up somewhere at home where we'll see it. Take a couple of people from the list each day—maybe one living person and one who's dead—and try to remember to pray for just these two. The next day, pick two more, and so on. Keep adding to your list as new people come to your attention, or new groups of people. Give yourself a grade on this last quality now, OK? . . .

(Or put up their pictures.)

"Now, take a look at your grades. How are you doing? . . . Could you pick one of the seven spiritual works of mercy that you think you could improve in? . . . It might be the one you're doing least of, or it might be the one in which you're doing only so-so, but in which you think you could do much better.

"Circle that one. And can you write now, on the other side of the paper, some specific things you could do to carry out this work of mercy in your life? . . .

40

"I'd like to suggest that, for the next week, you make a real effort to improve in just this one spiritual work of mercy. See if you can do one or two of the things you listed on your paper—you might put this up on your bulletin board or by your bed at home so you'll see it. See what other ideas you can come up with to make it happen.

"You don't have to do this, of course, but if you're really interested in growing closer to God and living the life He talks about, this will help. If you're not really interested in doing that, please understand that I wouldn't try to force you to care—I couldn't do that if I wanted to.

"A couple of last questions for you: Now that we've listed the seven spiritual works of mercy, can anyone tell me where they come from in the bible? . . .

(Unless this was answered earlier—the gospels, but not in one spot.)

"Which of the seven teachings comes from a part of the gospels which we all know very well? . . .

("Forgive all injuries" comes from the Lord's Prayer, and other spots as well.)

"Next week, we'll check back and see how everyone's doing, using the last column on the papers. Can you hang onto them for that long? . . ."

(Be sure to do this — teacher as nag again. After that, you could concentrate on another work of mercy until the whole list is covered.)

DATE TRIED:　　　　　　　　　　　**TIME:**　　　　　　　　　**REPEAT?:**

RESULTS:

MORE IDEAS:

1) Go on to design similar check-yourself experiments using other lists from scripture or tradition. Be sure to explain terms that are vague to today's kids—words like "meekness" and "fortitude" and "piety"; always give examples for the qualities you're listing. Here are some possible checklists. Which fit in best with your subject matter?

- The Ten Commandments (Exodus 20:1-17) and the shortest of checklists, The Two Commandments of the New Testament (Matthew 22:37-40)

- The Eight Beatitudes (Matthew 5:1-12)

- The Qualities of Love (1 Corinthians 13:4-8)

patient	kind
not jealous	not conceited
not proud	not ill-mannered
not selfish	not irritable
doesn't keep a	not happy with evil
record of wrongs	happy with the truth
never fails	never gives up
eternal	

- The Gifts of the Holy Spirit (Isaiah 11:2-3 and tradition)

fear of the Lord	piety
knowledge	counsel
fortitude	understanding
wisdom	

- The Fruits of the Holy Spirit (nine are in Galatians 5:22)

charity	peace	joy
patience	kindness	goodness
faith	mildness	long-suffering
modesty	continency	chastity

- The Corporal Works of Mercy (six are in Matthew 25:41-46)

feed the hungry	clothe the naked
give drink to the thirsty	shelter the homeless
visit and ransom the captive	visit the sick
bury the dead	

- The Capital Sins or Vices—and their opposites—the Cardinal Virtues

pride	humility
lust	chastity
anger	meekness
gluttony	temperance
greed	charity
sloth	industry
envy	justice

  (These come to us from St. Gregory the Great and other Fathers of the Church via the medieval theologians.)

2) Other religions and systems of growth have their own checklists. These often parallel the Judaeo-Christian ones above, saying the same thing in a different way. Students are usually interested in seeing that the virtues we're pushing are universal—not just something dreamed up by their own Church to make life harder. Here are some checklists from the East which could be the source of some comparative study:

● From the yoga of India, we have
   The Five Restraints (or Yamas):
      refrain from violence, lying, stealing, wasting or self-indulgence, and possessiveness

   and *The Five Observances (or Niyamas):*
      observe purity, contentment, simplification of life, self-study and the study of sacred books, and the remembrance of God.

   (If you have a yoga text, look up the gentle Sanskrit names for these; often used in English is "ahimsa," meaning nonviolence.)

● From Buddhism, we have
   The Noble Eightfold Path:

right knowledge	right intention
right speech	right conduct
right means of livelihood	right effort
right mindfulness	right concentration

   and *The Four Exalted States:*
      loving kindness
      compassion
      joy in another's joy
      equanimity

REFERENCES:

Beginnings, Lyman Coleman (Waco, TX: Word, Inc., 1974)

The last of the 12 *Serendipity* books, and one of the best—subtitled "a mini-course in personal growth." It has the Coleman self-evaluation using the Beatitudes, also found in his *Rap.*

Remember Man, Charles E. Jones (Notre Dame, IN: Ave Maria Press, 1971)

This "Lenten coffee table reader for people who seldom find time for Lenten reading" has two good scripture-based self-examinations. There's "The Way of the Cross Today" by Ronald Luka and Charles Jones' "The Way of the Cross Today for Children." All sorts of possible uses for both of these; other fine reading and graphics too.

The Wheel

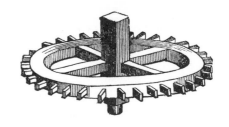

EXPERIMENT NUMBER 3

BACKGROUND:

This consciousness-raising experiment could be given some pretentious title like "Finding Your Philosophy of Life," but that would insure its sudden death in most classes. It attempts to help students discover the value(s) at the heart of their lives. "The Wheel" offers a circular image of life, in contrast to other experiments in this book which describe life in typically Western, linear fashion. A secondary feature of this experiment, in fact, is its use of the ancient circle or mandala symbol (see "More Ideas").

MATERIALS:

Paper and pencil (logs/journals?).

CURRICULUM TIE-IN:

Purpose of life, values, everyday activities.

"On your papers today, how about drawing a circle—a pie or a wheel, like the one I'm drawing on the board? . . .

"Leave a hub or small circle in the center of it, and then make 12 pie-shaped wedges in the big circle, like this. . . .

(See sketch at the end of this experiment.)

"OK. That circle represents your life.

(And only if you have the most adoring of classes can you add this awful pun: "If your life is a circle, you'll never be square.")

"In the outer wedges, let's put 12 different things—the things that make up your daily life, the way you spend your time. For instance, one large chunk of most kids' lives is school. Let's put 'school' in one of our wedges. . . .

(Keep using the board.)

"You probably spend a lot of time at home, so let's put 'home' in another of the sections. . . .

"What else could we add? . . .

(Here are 10 other things — but if students have more good ideas, use theirs first: work, homework, sleep, entertainment, hobbies, sports, church, eating, seeing friends, dating.)

"Now the point of all this is to take a look at our lives. All we have to do is fill in the center circle, the hub of the wheel. In here we'll put the central value of our life, the core thing that holds all the other parts together, the desire or belief that rules all our daily activities.

"Let's make a list on the board of some of the values that could go in the center. What are the 'gods' in some peoples' lives? . . .

(A list for the board: power, money, romance, status, fun, knowledge, God, service, comfort, etc.)

"Let's see how some of these operate. I'll put the word 'power' at the center of the wheel. Can you think of anyone whose life was ruled by the desire for power? . . .

(Dictators and autocrats from all times, Attila to Napoleon to Hitler.)

"If power is the most important thing in your life, how does that make you feel about the other things on the wheel? . . . about school, for instance? . . .

(Education is one road to power — you'd probably study hard.)

"Who'd like to be the teacher for a few minutes and ask the class about power and some of the other parts of the wheel? . . .

(Select someone you won't have to prompt; be a student and ask questions of "the teacher" if necessary.)

"Good. Let's have another teacher now—who'd like a turn? . . . And we'll erase 'power' and put 'fun' in the center of our wheel. Teacher, will you ask your class how this new core makes the parts of life look now? . . .

(E.g.: "If fun is the central thing in your life, how will you probably feel about your work?" — more than one possible answer here.)

"And now, a third teacher please. Who'll try this time? . . .

"Teacher, will you please erase 'fun' and put 'God' in the center? . . . and will you go around the whole wheel this time, asking how each of these daily life activities will be seen by the person who puts God at the center of his or her life? . . .

(You may want to think in advance about some of the catchier connections, like God and eating, and God and sleep.)

"Thanks very much. I'd like to ask you now to look at the list of core values we have on the board. Can you decide which one is at the core or hub or center of your life? . . . Has it always been there? . . . Which others were there before this time? . . . How long has today's central value been the core value of your life? . . . Do you think this is it for the rest of your life, or can you foresee some other value being at the heart of things in the future? . . . Those are just some questions to sleep on."

(Along these lines, two good books are William Stringfellow's Imposters of God, *Pflaum,* and J. B. Phillips' Your God Is Too Small, *Macmillan.*)

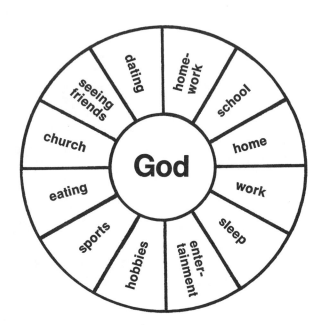

DATE TRIED: **TIME:**   **REPEAT?:**

RESULTS:

MORE IDEAS:

1) The points in "The Wheel" could, of course, be amplified upon. With God at the center, each section of the wheel could be the basis of a week's efforts. For instance, one week could be a time for students to try to become more aware of God's presence and activity in their homes; another week, to become more tuned in to the implications of a God-centered life for entertainment. (You can use the old observe-judge-act approach, with some mini-project to work on each week.) Again, logs and nagging teachers are very helpful temporary crutches.

2) If you like to do things with slides, this experiment lends itself beautifully to that treatment. One way: do the experiment as described, then reinforce it by putting together a bunch of slides illustrating the sections of the wheel—slides of kids in school, families at home, people at work and so forth. Remind students of the wheel with God at the center, then run through the slides asking questions such as "And what does He have to do with these scenes?" etc.

3) Somewhere during the course of their years in religion classes, let's hope your students have been asked to stand back and ask explicitly the big questions: not only "What's at the center of my life?" (as in the experiment), but also the other *Alfie* questions:

    — "What's it all about?"
    — "What am I doing here?"
    — "Where am I going?" and "How do I get there?"
    — "What are people for?"

These are really the questions of pre-evangelization, which many students never are asked to ponder. If you think that's the case with your kids, be sure to work them into your curriculum somehow—otherwise your students may find you giving answers to questions they never asked.

A second group of basic questions we may never think to ask but just take for granted might go:
Do I believe in God? (Some students aren't sure they do.)

Is it important to me to belong to a Church in order to worship God?
If so, which Church?

(Your curriculum may cover these questions, of course; but if not, it's risky to assume that all your students are happily settled in their commitment to Catholicism/Christianity—or whatever faith they have been reared in.)

4) Chapter Eight goes into detail about the value of symbols and signs to spiritual growth. As noted above, "The Wheel" makes use of an ancient symbol, the circle, associated in Christian tradition with eternity and the basis of many wreaths, rings, haloes and sanctuaries (or entire churches). Older students may be intrigued enough with symbolism to research other manifestations of the circle or mandala archetype (especially religious examples). Here are some leads for them—or you:

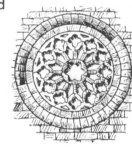

- sacred round or circle dances, typical of many primitive peoples, and also wheeling, whirling sacred dances such as those of the American Shakers and Muslim whirling dervishes, also various winding religious processions of many cultures. See *Sacred Dance, Encounter with the Gods,* Maria-Gabriele Wosien (New York: Avon Books, 1974)

- the Heavenly City of Jerusalem is often pictured in circular form, surrounded by concentric rings of the blessed doing their own circle dance (and maybe singing *Will The Circle Be Unbroken?).* God Himself is often at the hub of a wheel of angels, or ranks of angels. Cherubim, especially, seem to come in winged wheels. See art of the late Middle Ages, especially Florentine and Siennese works.

- Ezechiel's vision of the wheels with eyes and faces (Ezechiel 1:15-21) and Elias' fiery-wheeled chariot (4 Kings 2:11) are compelling biblical images, as is the scriptural image of God at His potter's wheel, forming man from the clay and shaping his life (Sirach 33:13-14). How about the Negro spirituals which go with these Old Testament wheels, like "Ezechiel Saw the Wheel"?

- the beautiful rose windows of cathedrals all over Europe (and America—how about your hometown?) Can you find pictures of the most beautiful of all, Chartres?

- the solar system/cosmos/zodiac/calendar sort of wheel is another recurring circle image, one which crosses boundaries of time and space and pops up in dozens of cultures. In some illuminated manuscripts, angels are shown turning the wheel that is the universe. There are, too, primitive circular sites such as Stonehenge that are connected in various ways to the movements of the heavens.

- from Oriental cultures, we have the Wheel of Law and the Wheel of Life.

- the circle as a symbol of man's highest, most integrated psychological state—or, in Jung's language, of "individuation." The psyche was a sphere to Plato, and many other explorers of the mind of man have seen the closed circle or orb as representative of a whole self.

Research on any or all of these round ideas could lead to the creation of one's own mandala, or to questions about ways in which our lives are circular and are filled with circle images. Two fine references:

Mandala, Jose and Miriam Arguelles (Berkeley, CA: Shambala Publications, 1972)

Mandala Symbolism, Carl Jung (Princeton, NJ: Princeton University Press, 1972)

REFERENCES:

Meeting Yourself Halfway, Sidney B. Simon (Niles, IL: Argus Communications, 1974)

The latest and simplest of Simon's values clarification books, any or all of which are of great help to religion teachers. Values clarification exercises, like the one in this experiment, help us take a look at what we "sort of" know; they help our values to be "freely chosen," to use one of Simon's touchstones. A note: values clarification is great, but not an end in itself for religion teachers. For instance, if a student decides that the core value of his life is having fun, we still have a ways to go. Can we offer him something better, without manipulating him into the "right" (i.e., our) answer?

Integrating Values, Louis M. Savary, S.J. (Dayton, OH: Pflaum Publishing, 1974)

Specific application of values clarification theory and techniques to clarification and integration of *religious* values, against a backdrop of Bernard Lonergan's theological method. This is just the first of several fine Savary books suggested as references. Their trademark: down-to-earth, practical help from a fellow pilgrim who has the broad scholarly background so many of us lack.

Making Sense of Our Lives, Merrill Harmin (Niles, IL: Argus Communications, 1973)

An excellent series of values clarification exercises, complete with good Argus posters and spirit masters for classroom handouts. Dr. Harmin has the common touch, is emphatically non-ivory tower.

Self-Actualization, Robert Valett (Niles, IL: Argus Communications, 1974)

A compendium of exercises, quotes and food for thought about this topic, borrowing Maslow's (and Kurt Goldstein's) famous label as a title. Several "What's running your life?" exercises.

Experiments in Prayer, Betsy Caprio (Notre Dame, IN: Ave Maria Press, 1973)

In this, the companion book to the present volume, there's a "Super-Prayer Experiment," the last of 46. A fantasy trip to music, it's designed for the same purpose as "The Wheel": to help students see that life can be guided by one or several of many "gods," so that they can choose intelligently among the possibilities.

chapter 3
SPIRITUAL AUTOBIOGRAPHY

"The more you use the pronoun 'I', the less Christian you are. . ."
—advice from a minor seminary manual of the 1960's.

1960 was just yesterday, and many of us have been trained according to the sentiment above: Do *not* refer to yourself in conversation or writing (or, if you must, apologize for the "personal reference"); use the editorial "we" even when sending strong I-messages, and in all ways make yourself small and insignificant. This school of spirituality has led to some confining bonds and some strange sorts of humility, all in the name of self-denial.

There is, however, another equally strong tradition in Christianity which runs parallel to the self-negation thread. That is the tradition of giving personal testimony as to how God has worked in one's life, as Paul does in his epistles:

"I toil and struggle, using the mighty strength that Christ supplies, which is at work in me." (Colossians 1:29) (Doesn't he sound like us when he goes on in the next verse, "Let me tell you how hard I have worked for you. . . ."?)

We find this approach in the *Confessions* of St. Augustine, the autobiographies of Cardinal Newman, Sts. Teresa of Avila and Therese of Lisieux, of Pope John XXIII and of many others. We hear it today on Billy Graham's (and others') TV-cast crusades, when sports personalities, entertainers and "just folks" stand up before thousands to speak of God's action in their lives. Keith Miller, the popular author, writes in this style too.

This chapter springs from that second tradition, the tradition of "telling your story" (to use Sam Keen's phrase). Some call it autobiographical theology and Martin Marty points out how deeply rooted this tradition is in scripture. Each of us has a special story to tell of the continuing adventure between our own soul and God, and although most of our stories aren't as dramatic as the famous ones mentioned above, each is unique and interesting. Here are some of the ways in which this storytelling can help people grow spiritually:

●   All of us have the need to see abstract theological concepts (like grace and faith and "the inspiration of the Spirit") in concrete form. For young people, especially, specific illustrations from the lives of real people are needed to make doctrines come alive. Only then can these same abstractions be recognized in *their* lives. In *The Seduction of the Spirit,* theologian Harvey Cox tells his story. He writes that *not* to do so leads, by omission, to the implication that "divinity can be severed from flesh."

● While each person's story is, indeed, unique, at the same time it is universal. Men and women of all times and places really are much more alike than different. Hearing another's story helps one see how one's own story reads, and it also helps a person experience unity with the rest of one's own people/ God's people.

● If we neglect to tell our stories, we imply that our own history and our life are unimportant. That isn't true—at least, we've been teaching that our students and ourselves are of great worth just because we are here and because God wanted us as we are. Do we really believe what we say? If so, our stories are very important.

● Today is lived better when yesterday and tomorrow frame it. The people with total views of their lives, who see them as having a beginning and an end, seem to do more with those lives, don't they? They are less likely to let time sift past them unmarked and unused; they are more aware that they "only go around once."

The following four experiments are designed to help students and others tell their stories. The first two give us an overview of our lives; the other two pick up specific strands in those lives—the good times and the bad times, the natural highs and the natural lows. The experiments really can be used in any order, so do what feels right with them. Just a caution or two. . . .

The facilitator or teacher should have in his or her mind the understanding that spiritual autobiography means just that—the story of someone's "spirit." We're talking here about how God has worked in the lives of each of us, and it can be tempting for some people when given the floor to wander. "Let me tell you my spiritual story (or a piece of it)" is not at all the same as "Let me pour out my entire life history, A to Z." The former is much more specific. For instance, a tale of "My Appendectomy" could, of course, be the story of how someone felt close to the Lord in a time of emergency and pain—but it could also be just a rambling about a hectic 24 hours with no hook-up to that person's soul-story. The leader must keep that distinction in mind and help spoken witness (including our own, please!) move along the higher path. Otherwise a whole class can be wiped out when Joe gets the floor and has a chance to orate.

A variation on this theme is provided by the *True Confessions* addict who, if given the chance, can't wait to tell everyone that he or she is a rat (beast, skunk). That may be true, and perhaps even enlightening to others, but it can also be a see-how-humble-I-am-you-peasants trip. If you don't hit some sort of gentle median level that excludes gut-spilling, people can end up feeling they have to tiptoe out of the room because someone's insides are all over the floor.

One other dead end, at least with most young people, is the adult who talks

52

in the ecstatic God-zapped-me idiom. Yes, maybe He did clobber you and your life has since turned around and you are constantly burning with love for Him, love that overflows and oh! wow!! gee whiz!!!, etc., etc.—but this volcanic eruption approach is not so hot for those who haven't been hit in the same way. Watch Sunday morning TV for some examples of very sincere people telling their stories in a style that is almost guaranteed to turn kids off royally—then do the opposite. Different strokes for different folks, as they say.

The material in this chapter is probably the most basic in this book, and for that reason the most valuable. See what happens with it if you give it some time.

He Touched Me

EXPERIMENT NUMBER 4

BACKGROUND:

Here's a simple time-line experiment to familiarize students with the idea of spiritual autobiography. Be sure to allow everyone time to think as you go through the exercise; without that time, the whole strategy can become manipulative and people just end up putting down any old thing that comes to mind. (Which of us could remember "my happiest moments" in 10 seconds?) The aim of this experiment—in churchy language: the sanctification of everyday life; in non-churchy language: the sacralization of the normal. The greatest barrier all of us may have to growth along this line is our prejudice that the touch of the holy is reserved for some special elite few. It's not.

MATERIALS:

Pencil and paper (journals?).

CURRICULUM TIE-IN:

Everyday life, the future, saints.

"On your papers, would you please draw a line across the center? Now, at the left-hand side of it, just at the edge of your paper, put the year in which you were born. . . .

"Now, at the other end, on the right, put the year in which you will be 80 years old. . . .

(Do all this on the board.)

"OK., now if you are —— years old today, put this year's date at about the right place on your time-line, and then divide up the first segment of your line into as many pieces as you have years.

(This will look like a scale—see the chart which follows.)

"Good. These lines, of course, stand for. . . ? Here's what we're going to do with them.

(Our lives; some may protest that they'll live more than 80 years— fine!)

"We're going to chart on the lines the times when God was especially active in our lives. Of course, He's part of those lives all the time—you remember that He said, 'I am with you always.' But there are times when He seems especially to be with us, when we can really say, 'He touched me.' Sometimes when this happens, we are aware of it, and other times we don't realize until much later that He was especially close to us. What is one sort of situation you can think of when God is very much a part of our lives? . . .

"How about very happy times, like birthdays or holidays or vacations or surprises or ———————? Do you think God celebrates those good times with us, even if we don't think to remember that He's around? . . .

"Why don't you put a few 'x's' on your time-line for two or three of the happiest times in your life, and label the marks. For instance, the first Christmas you really remember well might have been when you were four, and you got the tricycle you had been asking for. That could go on your time-line. Try to think of the very best happy times in your life and record them. . . .

"All right. Now, what other sort of situations are times when God is doing something for us or with us or is especially close to us? . . . How about His coming to us at Baptism or in the other sacraments? Let's put these down, even though we might not have been very aware of Him when these events took place. . . .

"How about times of trouble or sorrow or sickness? . . . Let's chart a few of those on our time-lines . . . and you might ask yourself, when they happened were you in touch with God? . . . Was He there? . . . Did you recall that He was there? . . .

"Then, for each of us, there are times of real success, times when we accomplish something that's important to us. What marks could you put on your line that show achievements? . . . Some of these may already be listed under happy moments, right? . . .

"Do you think God played a part in those times? . . . At the time, were you conscious of His part? . . .

(Matthew 28:20)

(Students will have ideas; take them as suggested by the class rather than in the order here.)

(Your doing this on the board or a large chart will make it simple; how about using examples from your own life?)

(Note the distinction between God's being with us and our awareness of His presence.)

"Is your paper getting crowded? . . . One more set of occasions we can add are times when we come to some sort of crossroads in our lives, times of change and of making decisions, turning points. What would be some possible examples? . . .

(a family's move, grad-uations, a new school, the decision to break up with someone, a refusal to take a wrong turn.)

"Finally, let's add any other times when God seemed very real to us, times when we felt very close to Him. Perhaps, for some of us, it might have been when listening to music, or we might have been especially in touch with God some night on looking up at a starry sky or the moon. Can you remember any particular moments when you could almost say, 'He touched me' ? . . . Some people call these "religious highs."

(The "Natural Highs" Experiment zeros in on this point.)

"Now, let's take a look at what we've got before us. These are special times when God was particularly active in our lives. There are lots of them, aren't there? Can you guess, very roughly, what percentage of them were also times when you were *aware* that He was there? . . .

"That is, did all these things happen to you without your ever once realizing that He was in on them? . . . Or, about half the time did you realize that He was present and responsible for a lot that was going on? . . . Or all the time? . . . If your answer is the last, you're rather an unusual person—and a very fortunate one! . . .

"Also, what are the patterns here: Were you more aware that God was involved in your life when you were younger? . . . Or are you getting more aware of this as you get older? . . .

(This could be shown in a zig-zagging graph line over the time-line.)

"Here's another pattern to look for. Have you been more tuned in to God in times of trouble and crisis? . . . Do you have what's called 'fire-engine religion'? . . . Or are you as conscious of the Lord in good and happy times as in bad? . . .

"Now, finally, let's look at all the blank space left on our lines. Are there any definite "He touched me" times coming up which you could fill in now? . . .

(Turning points? Celebrations? Trials?)

"How do you think your 'awareness line' will look in the future? . . . The purpose of this experiment is to help us spot special 'He touched me' times as they come up in our lives, and become more aware of the fact that they are special moments with God *as they're happening.*

"You might keep your time-lines and add to them as you recall other such times. Why not keep on recording these moments as they happen? What are the six types of events we've defined so far as possible 'He touched me' times? . . .

(happy times, sad times, reception of sacraments, successes, turning points, "religious highs")

"Some people draw much more spacious lifelong time-lines in a diary or journal, divided by months or seasons rather than by years, as we have done. They put aside a little time each week to record the stories of their life with God. Would that be something you'd like to try? . . ."

Awareness Line:

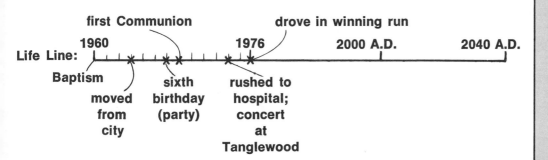

Life Line:

first Communion — drove in winning run

1960 — 1976 — 2000 A.D. — 2040 A.D.

Baptism — sixth birthday (party) — rushed to hospital; concert at Tanglewood

moved from city

57

DATE TRIED: **TIME:** **REPEAT?:**

RESULTS:

MORE IDEAS:

1) A natural follow-up, flowing from the time-line charts, would be to have students share their testimony to God's action in their lives. It could be done in small groups, in witness talks to the whole class ("once upon a time") and/or in writing. This would emphasize the value of telling our stories. Each student should, of course, be free to pass so that no one will feel pried open. However, *not* to tell one's story might be to deprive someone else of a chance to clarify his or her story—the Lord uses each of us to teach others, doesn't He?

2) How about prefacing (or following) this experiment with excerpts from the auto-biographies of any of the many people who have shared the stories of their souls throughout the centuries? Can you find someone who wrote about God in his or her childhood? Girls usually like St. Therese of Lisieux's stories about what a brat she was when little, and how God pulled her out of her brattiness (see her *Autobiography* in the Ronald Knox translation; N.Y.: P. J. Kenedy and Sons, 1962). Father John Powell, mentioned at the end of Experiment No. 1, has even titled his story *He Touched Me,* borrowing—as we have here— the phrase from popular music and perfume commercials (Niles, Illinois: Argus Communications, 1974).

REFERENCES:

Acts Alive and *Discovery,* Lyman Coleman (Waco, TX: Word, Inc., 1972)

Two of the *Serendipity* books, with good spiritual pilgrimage/what's-my-relationship-with-God? graph exercises. Throughout the entire series, many excellent exercises in history-giving that can be hooked in with the theme of spiritual autobiography.

My Book

EXPERIMENT NUMBER 5

BACKGROUND:

The child really is the father of the man. Having a sense of "our stories" is one way we can get a feel for our lives in their totalities, which in turn helps us make the most of those lives. This is one reason people of all times and places keep diaries and scrapbooks and photo albums. A life overview is especially important to those of us whose past has been dismal; rejecting that past or burying it can leave us with gaps and black holes in our stories, can make us feel incomplete. (A thought, though: If you have even one student whose background is really horrible, you might skip this sort of unearthing of the past— or wait to experiment on a day when that student is absent.) The image of God as author is, of course, drawn from God as author of scripture.

MATERIALS:

Pencil and paper for those who want them.

CURRICULUM TIE-IN:

Everyday life, the future, death, life after death, saints.

"We believe that God is always with us and that He loved us and cared about us from the beginning of time, even before we were born. But how many of us can remember, as we go through our days, that God is right here with us all the time? . . . How many of us are aware of His presence most of the time? . . .

(Have you one saint in your class? Two? Congratulations!)

(Give people time either to get settled or to get out pencil and paper.)

"Most of us have a very hard time remembering that God is around— or that He has been around ever since we began our lives. Here's a little experiment designed to help us become more aware of this. There are a couple of ways you can do this exercise: One way is to get settled very comfortably in your seat, close your eyes and try to picture the things I'm speaking about; another way is to listen carefully and sketch or doodle as I speak. Decide which way you want to follow along, OK? . . .

"Here we go. Can you picture, in front of you, a very large book? Maybe the cover is fancy leather, or even velvet. . . . Picture the color of it, and on the front (in gold letters) it reads *The Story of* (fill in your name). . . .

(Slow down; allow time for the picturing.)

59

"Open the book now. See the title page, with the same words as on the cover. This is a picture book, and the first chapter is titled *Baby Is Born.* Can you fill in the details of the picture under this title? What is the setting . . . a hospital? a home? a taxicab? . . . Who's there, along with you and your mother? . . . What do you look like? . . .

"Next picture: the exterior of the baby's birthplace. How does this look? . . . What sort of weather is it? . . . What does the setting or surrounding land look like? . . .

(Again, be sure to pause long enough for students to come up with both answers and the mental pictures.)

"The next chapter has the title *Baby Is Three Months Old.* What does the picture for this chapter look like? . . . What would you be wearing? . . . Are you able to smile? . . . Who's in the picture with you? brothers? . . . sisters? . . . How old are they? . . . How are they dressed? . . . Can you work in an invisible ingredient? God is also present in this picture: How can you represent His presence? . . .

(If you form your own mental pictures as you go, you'll be able to gauge the amount of time to allow between questions.)

"Chapter Three is titled *Baby's Home.* The picture is of the place you lived when you were first born. Fill in the details of the picture in your mind. . . .

"Were there other homes that came afterwards? . . . Pick one of these that you think of most when you hear the word 'home'—perhaps it's where you live now—and add that picture to your book. At what season was the picture painted? . . . Is there anyone in front of your house? . . . Who is there? . . . Are you there? . . . How is everyone dressed? . . . Is God in the picture? . . .

"Turn the page and find a floor plan diagram of this house. How does it look? . . . How are the rooms laid out? . . . Is there a plan for a first floor and a second floor? . . .

(Yes, a long silence— not the worst thing in the rush of a school day.)

"The next two chapters are yours to design as you will. You might give them titles like *Friends* or *Pets* or *Playing* or *School* or *The Family Grows Up,* or anything you like. Choose a couple of titles that sound interesting to you, and create the pictures that illustrate them. I'll stop talking for a couple of minutes. . . .

"There are three more important things to look at in our books. Can you picture a chapter headed *Today?* . . . What pictures of you would be in that chapter? . . . What are the things you do most often, and how would an artist draw you doing them? . . . Take another minute to imagine the pictures in this chapter. . . . Is God in these scenes? . . . How can that be shown? . . .

"Now, try to imagine at least two-thirds or more of your book as blank pages. Maybe they even have gold edges. These, of course, are the pages yet to be written. What are the chapter headings and the pictures going to be for the rest of your life? . . . Is the answer all up to you? . . . Is it all up to God? . . . Who's writing your story anyway? . . .

"Finally, two last chapters at the very back of the book have the titles *The End,* where you picture a possible end to your life. . . . Is God there? . . . And *The Beginning,* where you add a picture of what you think comes next. . . . Is God *there?* . . . In what form? . . . Take a couple of extra minutes to illustrate this last part of your story in any way you like. . . .

"I'd like to suggest that you take this book in your head home with you. Tonight as you're lying in bed, before you fall asleep, try to sketch in some of the titles for the future chapters and some of the pictures that will go there. Again, see if there's some way God will be in the pictures. Or, perhaps, go back to the early pages of the book and look more closely at the pictures we went by in a hurry today. Add some more details to them.

"Why don't we all stretch and open our eyes and come back from our mental libraries to this room? . . . Is there anything anyone would like to share from his or her book? . . .

"Did anyone have any especially interesting pictures? . . . I'm wondering how you worked God into your illustrations. . . .

(Some possible answers: God as artist painting or as author writing, a glow or light, Jesus in human form, a breeze that blows through the scene.)

"We can each keep our books and work on them and enjoy them for the rest of our lives. I'd like to know of any further experiences you have with them."

DATE TRIED: TIME: REPEAT?:

RESULTS:

MORE IDEAS:

1) If the imaginary books seem to be popular, why not go back and look through them again? Design more chapters and pictures from the past or sketch out more fully the clear pages of the future. The books, of course, could actually be written and illustrated. Many students will have sources of picture-material at home—baby photos and parents' memories. Some won't, however, so be cautious with suggestions like "Ask your mother. . . ." A beautiful gift from older students to other members of their families would be a book for anyone titled *The Story of——————*. If you try making books either for students themselves or as gifts for others, see how gracefully the image of God can be woven into the natural events.

2) The next-to-the-last chapter of each mental book is about death. How this is handled depends entirely upon your students and their past experiences with death, which you will want to explore before killing them off any more vividly than above. Ideally, however, the books could be a jumping-off point for extended consideration of death and dying. (See *Experiments in Prayer,* below, for dying ideas in the three "This Is Your Life" experiments and in one called "My Tombstone.")

   You can also ask students to write their own obituaries, if they seem open to death discussions. (Would they want flowers, or something "in lieu of"?) Be sure to tackle various aspects of the American way of death, including talk of freezing the seriously ill until such time as cures are found for their maladies, and artificially prolonged life. Have students heard of cemeteries with tapes of the "inmates'" voices on file?

Relatedly, what is the reason for the great appeal of horror films and death and

violence on TV? Why do so many people enjoy watching Count Dracula sink his fangs into a neck? Does watching help us come to grips with death and violence in our own lives?

As always, what are the religious implications of our acceptance of death on film and our avoidance of the fact of death when it really happens (corpses with make-up on them, euphemisms like "passing away," etc.)? How spiritually mature is someone who hasn't thought about the end of life and who can't bear to face either his own or other people's deaths?

Every religion teacher will want to have a few questions and experiments on tap for those times when events in students' lives or in the newspapers make the subject of death a natural.

REFERENCES:

Born to Love, Muriel James (Reading, MA: Addison-Wesley Publishing Co., 1973)

A T.A. (Transactional Analysis) book, like *I'm O.K.—You're O.K.,* with many leads for personal history awareness. Reverend James applies T.A. to church situations and gives specific questions that help people tell their stories.

The Seduction of the Spirit, Harvey Cox (New York: Simon and Schuster, 1973)

The famous theologian writes "his book" and our own stories become clearer as a result. Good reading.

Telling Your Story, Sam Keen and Anne Valley Fox (New York: Doubleday and Co., 1973)

More pop than most of Sam Keen's work, and filled with good exercises along "My Book" lines that you could use as supplements to this experiment. A little too much of the it's-so-easy tone for your author's taste; getting a handle on our lives *isn't* easy! Nevertheless, good.

Experiments in Prayer, Betsy Caprio (Notre Dame, IN: Ave Maria Press, 1973)

This earlier companion book to the one you're holding has three experiments with the title "This Is Your Life." Each is designed to help the student get that overview of his or her life that is so hard to come by. In this book, the prayer ingredient is added.

Natural Highs

EXPERIMENT NUMBER 6

BACKGROUND:

In Chapter One we talked about getting high naturally, and how examination of the common "natural highs" (to use language understood by our students) can lead us to familiarity with the "God high." This experiment attempts to do that; it spins off the "He Touched Me" ideas of Experiment No. 4. The example used here—communication with an animal—is one familiar to lots of boys and girls, as well as the medicine men or shamans of many primitive cultures where animals are thought to "know" something we don't. You could, however, substitute one or more of the stories in Chapter One (getting high on music, sports, love and people) for the dog story below. In many ways, this is the grounding, base experiment of this book.

MATERIALS:

Pencils and paper (again, a reminder that journals are the best aid for many of these experiments).

CURRICULUM TIE-IN:

Saints-and-animals stories, prayer, drugs/drinking.

"Today I'd like to share with you a short story which was told by a boy of six. Who would like to read it from this book? . . .

(An easy chance to include someone not very active in class.)

'I have a dog. He is big and he is sort of gold or yellow. He has white paws and a white mark on his forehead. He's got a furry tail that sticks up and floppy ears and big eyes. My mother says they're caramel colored. Under his snout he's soft and mushy.

'I talk to my dog. We sit in the yard and I tell him how I feel and he listens. Sometimes I can almost hear him talking back to me—he doesn't say things but he knows what I'm saying and he would answer me if he could. He talks with his eyes. He's like my brother and he loves me and trusts me.

'Sometimes when we're talking I feel like we're the only two people in the world. It's like there's nobody else—just him and me. When we get like this I don't even hear my mother call me for dinner.'

"Well, how about that little story? Does it sound possible? . . . Did anything like that ever happen to you and an animal? . . .

(Maybe you can collect a few more stories; the point here is the loss of touch with his surroundings triggered in the little boy by his intense involvement with his dog.)

"Can you think of any stories of people who were as close to an animal as the little boy is? . . .

(Timmie and Lassie, St. Anthony and the fish, the Lone Ranger and Silver, many others.)

"Some of the stories of the saints even tell about people who tamed ferocious wild animals and communicated with them. There's one about St. Francis and a wolf, and others too.

(Adam in the garden.)

"How about someone in the bible who lived with all kinds of animals, and, probably, had some way of communicating with them which was what we would call 'beyond normal'? . . .

"The ability to relate in that special way to animals has, in many times and places, been considered a sign of a higher spiritual level, such as man might have had in paradise.

"Now, the important part of the little boy's story for us is that he could get so 'lost' in talking to his dog that he didn't hear his mother call him to dinner. His normal time and space boundaries seemed to fade, and some of his senses tuned out while others were sharpened. Being 'out of it' like that is a very special state of mind —some people call it being high, others call it being spaced out or psyched, and psychologists call it being in an altered state of consciousness. They even have conferences on it at the Smithsonian Institute in Washington, D.C., and at other places.

"Lots of things can get people high, some of them good things and some not so good. What can you think of that sometimes brings this state of mind about? . . . Let's make a list on the board:

(Collect as many ideas as possible from the kids before turning to this listing.)

Drugs, including alcohol
Music—making it and listening to it
Movies/TV (sometimes)
Driving
Fantasizing, daydreaming
Sports—both for spectators and players
Dancing/twirling around
Nature
Food (sometimes)
Learning (for some people, as in 'aha!' when a light dawns)
Happenings: Christmas morning, weddings, etc.
Art—both creating and looking at
Fighting, making war

"These things we've listed are catalysts that help us focus our entire selves so completely on one thing that we get lost in it and somewhat separated from the rest of our world. Any other ideas? . . . How about being in love? . . . And how about just getting high on people? . . .

"Now, on your papers, why don't you write down very briefly one story of a specific 'high' in your life. It doesn't have to be a fancy story. You can just write three or four sentences. Your title for it might be 'A Natural High.' . . .

"Do your stories add any other triggers to our list of things that help someone 'leave himself behind'? . . .

"Now, our next question is this: What has all this got to do with religion? . . .

(If no answers—which is very likely!) "Or, to put it another way, do you know of any 'religious highs'? . . . Maybe you've had the experience of one, or maybe you've read or heard about something like that or seen something that might be called a 'God-high' on TV or in a movie. . . .

(Maybe someone has read The Inner Game of Tennis *or other "transpersonal sports" books.)*

(Again, if you have time for them, the young people's stories in Chapter One may help make these experiences more real to your class.)

(After writing, if there's time for sharing with a partner, that would be just fine.)

(Add to list on board.)

("Jesus People" intoxicated with the Spirit; the experience of being lost in prayer; martyrs so wrapt in God that they can face wild beasts or flames or stone-throwers, etc.)

"Next, would you choose one of these two topics to write a few lines about now:

> 'A God-High I've Had'
> or 'What I Think a God-High Would Be Like.'

(You'll probably want to apologize for the term "God-high"—maybe your students have a better phrase for the phenomenon.)

"Will you take a few minutes to jot down your story? . . .

(Again, sharing is a great help.)

"Getting high on God is a very common experience. If you've ever had 'natural highs' then this 'high space' is familiar territory to you. Many people get there by praying well. Can you think, though, what difference there is between the 'God-high' and the 'natural high'? . . .

(When God is directly involved, He helps — i.e., the idea of grace, which helps us be in His presence, as contrasted with the human roots of "natural highs.")

"If someone said to you today, 'I'd like to learn how to get excited about God,' or 'Could you help me learn how to get high on God?' what would you say to him? . . .

(All the experiments in this book are designed to help people come in touch with God and experience Him in their lives. The most obvious way you could recommend is that the person learn to pray from the heart.)

"You might want to keep track of highs in your life as they come along, of times you enter that particular space where you're lifted out of your everyday self—as the little boy was with his dog. Note what triggers the highs, and whether or not they seem to have any religious meaning for you. Usually, what happens is that we naturally keep going back to the things that give us this kind of experience. Unfortunately, people who use alcohol or other drugs to get high often don't realize that that same experience can be arrived at in many other ways.

(Here's a chance for your 2¢ on a couple of abuses: the decidedly unnatural life-style which is based on the pursuit of highs of all sorts, as opposed to just enjoying them off the cuff AND abuse of drinking/drugs. Kids listen better when we don't preach, don't they?—go easy!)

"Ideally, as we become more and more familiar with this other 'space' of ours, we move from off-and-on highs (or 'peaks') to living at that level where all of life and each person we meet seem wonderful, where every day is rich and filled with the presence of God. If you get there, please let the rest of us know what it's like!"

(See note 10 in Chapter One on the "plateau experience.")

(Reminder: The teacher/ facilitator is also a student/learner. Our students appreciate knowing that we feel this way and that we can learn from them.)

DATE TRIED: **TIME:**   **REPEAT?:**

RESULTS:

MORE IDEAS:

This experiment began with a story of human and animal communication, one of life's simplest joys. Just watching chickadees from the kitchen window is, for some people, a way of getting out of one's self. Those who have pets know what it is to enter into that animal's gentle space regularly and emerge refreshed; they follow the advice in the Book of Job to ". . . ask now the beasts, and they shall teach thee. . . ." There's even a little book called *Prayers of the Animals* by "Captain Noah" (Philadelphia: Captain Noah, Inc., The Kenilworth - Suite 1405, 1974), for those who don't feel ridiculous with anthropomorphism. Wouldn't you like to read "The Prayer of the Bat"?

There are other ways of becoming one with God's created world—cloud-watching, soaking in sun or water, swimming, caring for even one plant (talking to it?). For most of us, these nature experiences can be powerfully sacramental catalysts to communion with the Creator. Since they are so easily available, perhaps they should be explored more fully and encouraged even more strongly than in the experiment. Can students report in detail on some of their experiences with "nature highs"? Can each add one new living thing to his or her life? Spend time with it? Contact God through His creature? (See *I and Thou,* below.) Report back to the class on any effects of this experimenting? (See also Experiment No. 28, "My Tree," where we go one step further. A natural object is used in a symbolic way to lead to spiritual growth. Paul Tillich and others used the coined word "panentheism"—not pantheism—to describe the idea and experience of God in all and all in God.)

Each of the triggers listed in the experiment can be explored in depth; several (art, music, sports, celebrations) are examined in detail in later experiments.

REFERENCES:
— On animals as triggers of transcendent moments, as in our dog tale:

I and Thou, Martin Buber (New York: Scribner's, 1970)

In this famous work, originally published in 1923, Buber writes about separate "dialogic spheres" (two of which are dialogue with nature and with animals) as arenas for spiritual encounters, into which God may also enter. He seems more of a cat man than a dog lover.

Myth and Mythmaking, Henry A. Murray, ed. (New York: George Braziller, 1960)

A collection of essays. Religion historian Mircea Eliade writes on the paradise myth and has some valuable insights on animals as teachers of the transcendent. Also, background for Experiment No. 28 ("My Tree").

— On nonordinary consciousness:

The Varieties of Religious Experience, William James (New York: New American Library, Inc., 1958)

The pioneer work (1902) in the psychology of religious experience, from a scientist-philosopher's approach. James found "the religious *appetites* even more numerous than the creeds."

Religions, Values and Peak-Experiences, Abraham H. Maslow (New York: The Viking Press, 1970)

The modern counterpart of James's work. Maslow affirms, in scientific terms, a species-wide need for spiritual expression. Believers in God will want to add their own dimension to the work of both these giants who studied religious experience from the ground up.

Getting High Naturally, Louis M. Savary, S.J., ed. (New York: Association Press, 1971)

A photo-meditation book with sections on the many catalysts that get people "there." See also the introduction and appendix to Father Savary's *Music and Your Mind* (with Helen L. Bonny), referred to in Experiment No. 25, for basic background in ASC (altered states of consciousness).

The Book of Highs, Edward Rosenfeld (New York: Quadrangle/The New York Times Book Co., 1973)

Recommended with reservations. A catalogue of over 250 triggers to nonordinary consciousness—several of them open to question. The last trigger listed is "Living"; the space under that title is left blank! Good background material in an introduction by Andrew Weil.

Pain and Healing

BACKGROUND:

Our past can hold us back. Old heartaches and pain (some from the time of our earliest childhood) still cause bitterness and hurt today—crippling us because we live them over and over or just because they're there, festering away. Much is being written and done today about healing, and about the healing ministry. Here is a simple and relatively nonthreatening experiment in emotional and spiritual (but not physical) healing. A spin-off of the "He Touched Me" experiment, it's just a small introduction to the complex and beautiful theme of being healed, and could just as well be in the chapter on prayer. (See also Experiment No. 25 for some ideas on preventing more pain in our lives, and Experiment No. 15 for thoughts on the necessity of the Cross.)

MATERIALS:

Pencil and paper (or journals).

CURRICULUM TIE-IN:

Suffering, the Cross, prayer, the sacrament of Penance.

"Our experiment today is about pain and sorrow and suffering and hurt, things we've all experienced in the past and will go through again in the future. Do you know of anyone whose life is free from these things? . . .

"Probably not. In fact, there has been the idea, through the centuries, that suffering is a mark of God's favor. Why would anyone think that? . . .

(Because so much growth can come from pain; because it gives us a chance to imitate the Lord and share in His redemptive work; because a person who has suffered is often more in touch with others' pain.)

"Can you think of anyone you'd call 'a friend of God' who had or is having a lot of troubles—either physical or mental or emotional or all of these put together? . . .

(Job, of course, and other people of the bible; many sufferers among the saints; and, undoubtedly, personal friends of each of us.)

"Even though everyone goes through life with pain and hurt, still you'd agree, I'm sure, that there's a lot of difference in what people do with their pain, isn't there? Jesus shows us one way to handle pain, both through His teachings and through His life and death. What examples of His approach to suffering can you remember from the gospels? . . .

(The Beatitudes, the grain of wheat, etc. Jesus' sufferings are often thought of by young people as physical only—you might mention some of His heartaches too: over Lazarus, the faithlessness of His friends, the rejection by His own people.)

"Let's make a list on the board—and you might copy it as we make it up—that shows all the different types of suffering we average people are likely to meet in our lifetimes. We'll leave out things like violent deaths and martyrdom and towering-inferno-type disasters. Afterwards we'll talk more about what to do with these hurts. What are some types of suffering? . . .

(If students suggest a different order or breakdown, go along with them —it'll all be there in the end.)

1) *Physical sickness,* physical handicaps or shortcomings, injuries, birth defects, etc.
2) *Mental or emotional suffering,* such as that caused by loneliness, lack of love, painful shyness, feelings of worthlessness ('I'm no good'), fears, despair and hopelessness, anger, doubt, etc.
3) *Failure* to achieve something (not making the team, not getting a part in the play, striking out with the bases loaded) and *mistakes* we fall into because of our own weaknesses, with resulting senses of sin, guilt and shame.
4) *Loss*—of people we love, of things, of respect and position, of God in our lives, of pets and friends, of security.
5) *Injustices* from others—ridicule, neglect, unkindness, misunderstanding, being used, being put down, false accusations, manipulation, betrayal, insults, lack of trust, abandonment.
6) *Embarrassing moments.*

"That's quite a list, isn't it? We've all experienced some of these things too, haven't we? . . .

(Can you give an especially pertinent story from your own life?)

72

"Let's act out a few of these pains, making up some examples that are typical for kids your age. For instance, will a few of you come up now and act out this situation: A boy is in school with kids who don't like him and who aren't very careful about hiding it. Who would like to be the boy? . . . Who would like to be in the 'in group' of three or four? . . . OK, let's see now how the scene looks in action. . . .

"Next, how about a monologue by someone who's looking in the mirror and really suffering over how he or she looks? . . .

"How about a short scene on the pain involved in feeling shy? We could go to a dance; someone can't think of a thing to say. Who wants to come to the dance? . . . Who'll be the couple? . . . Which one is the shy member of the pair? . . .

"Now, back to what we can do about the pain that we all feel from time to time, for one reason or another. We were talking earlier about Jesus and His thinking on being hurt or suffering. He told us we'd have to face it sooner or later, but did He *want* us to suffer? . . .

(The role-playing can be omitted if you're pressed for time, but it has two things going for it: 1) seeing suffering depicted makes it a little easier to face it in our lives; 2) seeing others act out pains and hurts helps take away that "nobody but me ever had that happen to him" feeling. Role-playing keeps the pain at a safe distance.)

(These need only be a minute or so long.)
(Girls might be surprised to hear a boy do this agonizing.)

(Or, for younger boys and girls, how about a moving-into-a-new-neighborhood skit?)
(Often, two girls will do this better than a girl and a boy—one girl takes the role of the boy.)

(Important: The Lord is not a sadist and Christians aren't called to masochism)

"If you recall, Jesus is shown throughout the gospels as a healer. He healed people of all sorts of pain and Christians believe He's still doing that today. What do we say just before we receive Holy Communion? . . .

(E.g., Matthew 8 and 9.) (". . . only say the word and I shall be healed.")

"Well, many of us are still being hurt today by the memories of past sufferings and pains, like those on our list. This keeps us from being our happiest selves, doesn't it? Is there some example you can think of that shows how past pain or leftover pain can get in the way of someone's life in the present? . . .

(How about in your life?)

"If this is happening to any of us, if we are being crippled in our lives by memories of things that have hurt us in the past, we can turn the pain of that memory over to Jesus, the healer. We can ask Him to cure our suffering just as He cured the suffering of so many of the people who actually lived alongside Him. This is called 'inner healing.'

"Take a look at our list. Leaving out the things under number one, the physical sufferings (which usually don't come under the heading of 'memories') see if you can think of one painful memory from your past which still hurts you today. I suggest that you start with just a small hurt, rather than something extremely painful. After you've decided on one memory, let's take a minute to ourselves and ask God to heal us of the pain we still feel when we think of that memory. . . .

("The healing of the memories" is Agnes Sanford's term, in particular. Note how all of this could be tied into the healing power of the sacrament of Penance.)

"If you like this idea, keep working on that one memory that has caused you recurring pain by reliving it a little bit at a time, and asking the Lord to heal your hurt until you can recall it without sadness. Healing is usually gradual, but it does happen. Remember that Jesus said, 'My peace I give to you.'

"After that, you can start working on a second hurting memory. Your copy of our list will be a help in deciding what to work on.

"One last thing: you might also want to include some prayer for the strength to forgive those who have caused any of these pains. Unless we have that forgiveness, we often can't be healed. I wish you very good luck in this work—it's most important to all of us."

(John 14:27; James 5:13 reads: "Is any one of you sad? Let him pray.")

DATE TRIED: **TIME:**   **REPEAT?:**

RESULTS:

MORE IDEAS:

If you feel qualified to open up the subject of physical healing, starting with scriptural examples, that would be an excellent follow-up to this experiment. However, proceed with caution. . . . Are you prepared with informed answers to questions such as "My grandfather prayed for God to cure him of cancer, but he died anyway. Why?" or "If you pray to be healed and you're not, does it mean you're not good enough? What *does* it mean?"

Despite the honored heritage of physical healing in the history of the Church, it's often a subject far removed from the lives of typical American young people. They may associate physical healing with the throw-away-your-crutches programs on TV, may be put off by the thought of laying on of hands, may find the simple faith necessary for such healing too simple for them to grasp (our children aren't "childlike").

It would be a shame to prejudice them against the very simple to apply guidelines for inner healing by hooking that up too soon with the much harder to handle physical healing. Of course, your own church tradition and even region of the country may have made the latter subject commonplace to your students, in which case you have a freer rein.

REFERENCES:

Healing, Francis MacNutt, O.P. (Notre Dame, IN: Ave Maria Press, 1974)

Father MacNutt is well known for his involvement in the healing ministry, and is one of the most readable and on-target writers on contemporary spirituality. His book is especially good on the distinction between the acceptance of suffering and the need for healing it, a fine but important point. He's been there.

Inner Healing, Michael Scanlan (Paramus, NJ: Paulist Press, 1974)

Equally inspiring, Father Scanlan writes with strength and gentleness on the fine points of inner healing: trust in the Lord's healing power, holding on to hurts for negative reasons, forgiving those who hurt us, pain that won't go away, cautions in the healing ministry and, generally, how to do it. He's been there too.

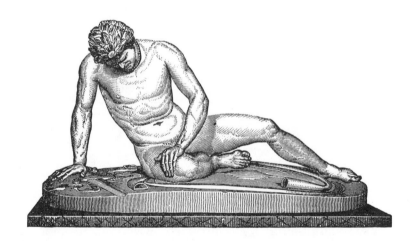

chapter 4
PHYSICAL THINGS-TO-DO

Raise your hand if you were tempted to skip this chapter! (If so, you have lots of company.)

Bodies are very convenient things to skip over, aren't they? We've each been inside our particular skin for so long that most of us pass right over it when asked to think about "ourselves"—that word takes on the meaning of "our personalities," or "our thoughts," or maybe "our souls." Not only do we take the old frame for granted, but as it gets older, as wrinkles etch in and hairlines recede, it's just so much easier to leave it behind and move on to "higher things": lofty thoughts, intellectual trips, various head games and the like. After all, The Real Me is just temporarily tied to this bunch of cells, and they'll turn to dust before too much longer anyway.

One of the best contributions of the human potential movement (see the comments about that umbrella phrase in Chapter One) has been a re-emphasizing of the importance of the body to the spirit. We are being taught again not to split ourselves down the middle, between body and soul, but to approach ourselves and our growth in terms of our whole selves, body and spirit interacting and working together.

This is really a very Christian approach, isn't it? After all, we believe in a God who took on a human body (literally, "incarnated" Himself) and healed human bodies, too. We believe that our bodies, as well as our souls, will be resurrected. In the words of the beautiful song, ". . . and I will raise him up on the last day." Nevertheless, physical things-to-do have seldom been part of the religious education curriculum.

Unfortunately, we reflect (in our negation and/or neglect of our bodies) a 2,000-year-old heresy which, church efforts to the contrary, just hasn't been squelched. Paul wrote about how the flesh opposed the spirit (Galatians 5:16-21, for instance), and with good reason. But one step more brought people to the heresy which split man into body (matter, therefore evil or, at best, an illusion) and spirit (good, noble and holy). The church history books tell the tales of battles against various forms of this thinking, best illustrated by a man climbing a ladder from the (evil) material world up, up and away to the (good) spiritual world. There has been war against Manichees and Albigensians, against Jansenists and Puritans all these years, each group—and others—in turn propounding its version of gnosticism (knowledge/spirit being all and things/flesh/matter opposing it).

Unfortunately, despite conciliar documents and official pronouncements, popular spirituality has reflected a lot of this dualistic partitioning of man. Weren't many of us, as kids, led to believe that if you enjoyed a physical sensation (of any kind) a great deal, it probably came close to being sinful? Weren't we brought up to "mortify the senses," not as Paul would have us do it, but as though there were something wicked about them? Practice in "feeling nothing" was, for many of us, part of our Puritan/American heritage, part of our religious tradition. After all (the thinking went), if you "allowed" a person to open up to his feelings and senses, he might run to all sorts of horrible excesses. His reason and will might be buried forever under an onrush of fleshy-squooshy-wallowy sensations (mostly sexual, of course) . . . and then where would he be? Better by far to train him to keep that stiff upper lip, admit to as little contact as possible with his body and its normal functions and, in short, pretend that he's really a spirit just visiting earth for a short while (using a set of muscles and bones and nerves while he's here). In *The Transformation: A Guide to the Inevitable Changes in Humankind* (New York: Dell Publishing Co., 1972), George Leonard gives all kinds of interesting background on our "flight from the flesh" in the name of faith—recommended reading.

Fortunately, many "bodywork" people and thoughtful religious educators over the past few decades have been helping us get over our lopsidedness about things physical. Sensory awareness trainers, psychosomatic medicine researchers, natural food enthusiasts, Gestalt therapists, yoga teachers, kung fu TV programs, bioenergetic analysts and young people in general have been reminding us again (well, we *did* know it) that all of man's self, body and soul, works as one whole entity—and that we neglect the former at the expense of the latter. Another way of saying it is that human beings function in three ways: innerpersonally or intrapersonally (what's going on inside), interpersonally (what's happening between us and other people), and transpersonally (what's going on between a person and the ineffable). Helping ourselves and others grow, then, means to concern ourselves with all three of these areas, not just the last two.

Well, maybe you're too pooped to think about physical things. It's just easier to sit back and read and think about growing than it is to flex a muscle in the cause. But, as you may have noticed, our students aren't pooped—and each class that comes along seems more tuned in to the physical than the one before.

Fewer students today are willing to surrender that childlike enjoyment of wholesome physical pleasure which we, due to either our sophistication or our brainwashing, have often outgrown. To them, it makes sense to do breathing exercises to help themselves pray better, and to avoid the foods which make us too sluggish to tune in to our neighbor, and to take the time to sense and marvel at "eternity in a grain of sand."

Here are some comments from high school freshmen who were asked to test some of the following physical experiments in their religion class. They are from both

boys and girls, ranging from very athletic to completely sedentary, from enthusiastic about religion to blah about it, and (according to their own self-descriptions) from stuffy to very receptive in their openness to new ideas:

- "Interesting, but tough."
- "Fun. Something new—really different from anything I've ever done."
- "Relaxing, peaceful . . . gives you a sense of realization within."
- "I like this. It not only helps me with God, but with myself. It gives me a sort of freedom and more control over myself."
- "They help me spiritually. I think at one moment I could almost feel God's presence."
- "I could feel love and wanted to give love. I think it is God's love."

Feedback from younger children has been in the same vein.

You'll see that Experiment No. 8 is a how-am-I-doing? checklist on good health (just like we had in those old hygiene classes), and the next three experiments are experiential physical exercises of the simplest sort. If you want to go on, there are many more ideas in the references and additional-ideas sections after each experiment; an entire course could be planned just around physical-things-to-do that have spiritual effects. See what happens with these.

Back to Basics

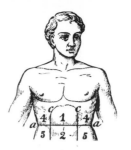

EXPERIMENT NUMBER 8

BACKGROUND:
Nothing could be simpler than this easy checklist, designed to help experimenters realize the necessity for a solid physical foundation for spiritual growth. But, nothing can be harder for many people than putting resolutions about keeping in good physical shape into effect.

MATERIALS:
Pencils and paper.

CURRICULUM TIE-IN:
Stewardship.

"Today, we have a very easy experiment. Would you take your papers and make a narrow column—about two inches wide—down the left-hand side, please? . . .

"Now, pretend that it's 10 or 20 years from now and that you are the mother or father of a brand-new baby. You've just brought the baby home from the hospital, and you're thinking about the things you want to do to help him—or her—grow strong and healthy.

"In the left-hand column of your paper, list the things you, as a parent, will want to make sure of so that baby grows up in as good a physical condition as possible. For now, we're talking just about his physical health, not mental or emotional health (which is a whole separate topic). You might start off with 'Get enough sleep,' for instance. . . .

"Leave a couple of lines between each thing you write. . . .

(Give class a few minutes for this.)

"All right. Now, let's see how many ideas you 'parents' came up with. What are some things on your lists? . . .

"Sounds sort of familiar, doesn't it? . . .

"Would you add anything else? . . .

"Now, in the space to the right of each item for building good physical health, how about evaluating *yourself* in that department? . . . Be honest now—give yourself some sort of grade as to how well you're doing in eating the right foods and all the other things on your list. Then, write down a few comments after each item that tell how you could raise your grade. . . .

"I'll let you have a few minutes to do this. No one will see your papers. . . .

"Well, how does your evaluation look? . . .

"Now, all these growth experiments we're doing are supposed to be about growing *spiritually*. Why, then, am I asking you if you're getting enough sleep, or if you're getting enough exercise? . . .

(The baby should get enough sleep, eat nutritious food, get plenty of sunshine and fresh air, have some exercise every day, have any health problems solved as quickly as possible, have preventive health care — checkups and shots, safe environment, be taught health and safety rules, etc.)

(Just like Mom's always telling it.)

(No one may answer, with good reason!)

(Be surprised if your students aren't very aware that a strong body makes soul growth much easier.)

"Have you ever heard the expression, 'The spirit is willing, but the flesh is weak'? . . . Where is that from? . . .

(Jesus to His friends who could not stay awake with Him in the garden on Holy Thursday; Matthew 26:41.)

"A lot of people say that, and with good reason. They'd *like* to take time to help someone else—but, oh, they're so nervous that they just can't do one more thing. Or, they would *like* to pray more—but, oh, they're so worn out that they can only drop in their tracks at the end of the day.

(Can you fill in with a personal story here if no one else connects?)

"Does that sound familiar? . . . Can you think of any time in your own life when a stronger, healthier body would have helped you to live a little better, a little more fully, to have taken an extra step spiritually? . . .

(Making good use of what God's given us.)

"Well, this short list—which was really about you more than about your child-of-the-future—is to nudge each of us to think a little about the spiritual reasons behind all those old physical health rules. Taking good care of our bodies is really a way of helping ourselves grow spiritually; some people call it 'stewardship'—what does that mean? . . .

(How about nagging on this every so often?)

"For the next few months, you might want to work on improving in just one of the things on your list."

DATE TRIED:　　　　　　　　**TIME:**　　　　　　　　**REPEAT?:**

RESULTS:

82

MORE IDEAS:

The experiment has given a start for helping students get a handle on their physical selves (or improving whatever handle they already had). Nevertheless, the simple physical things mentioned above may just make the difference between people being walking zombies and becoming not yet dead. A step further is toward vibrant, radiant good health—and this is directly connected to a person's use of his energy (also, stewardship).

Why not suggest that one or a few students research various aspects of human energy, especially along the lines of making the most of it, in the light of the view that we have a responsibility to ourselves to use whatever gifts God has given us as well as possible. Here are some of the several avenues such research could go down:

- The expansion of biophysics as a science. Of particular interest is research being done by Semyon Kirlian of the Soviet Union, whose photographs show a "bioplasmic field of energy" surrounding the human body and other living things. A person who thinks of himself as part of a plane of energy rather than as a material unit is going to have a unique self-concept (and life). (There are those of us who don't experience ourselves at all, neither matter nor energy.)

- The work of Alexander Lowen (bioenergetics).

- Practical, on-the-spot ways to increase energy when the blahs hit. Ideas here could range from the athlete's quick intake of sugar (and why that is or is not a good idea) to yoga breathing, to forming mental pictures of an energetic self.

- Suggestions for nonwasting of energy or conservation of one's energy. These could range from reducing the amount of fidgeting and nervous habits we all have to not brooding over depressing thoughts, waiting for phones to ring and the like (the famous "Serenity Prayer" is a good motto for energy expenditure).

- The transmutation of energy—that is, how emotional energy is turned into physical manifestations, how spiritual energy (like prayer) can be converted into healing power, how negative energy (like anger) can be made positive, and other such transferring of energy at one level to energy at another. What does it mean, specifically, to pick up another's vibrations? Is there a literal meaning to Francis of Assisi's "Lord, make me a channel . . ."?

A fine book to live with and work with, human-energy-wise, is Laura Huxley's *You Are Not the Target,* referred to in Experiment No. 25. World fuel shortages and higher electric rates may add up to energy crises we are unable to affect (much), but each person can live in charge of his or her own energy crises. As with everything else in *Experiments in Growth,* keep coming back to the specific connection this research has to the life of faith . . . here, of course, it is that the pooped person just can't do as effective a job of serving the Lord as the alive person.

REFERENCES:

Any of the zillion books and pamphlets and magazine articles to be found everywhere from supermarket to beauty parlor. How about digging-in in depth on one or two things (nutrition, exercise) that you really want to learn more about?

Christian Yoga, Jean-Marie Dechanet, O.S.B. (New York: Harper and Row, 1960)

This now classic text by a Belgian Benedictine is a favorite of body and soul people (i.e., those who experience the body as the "temple of the soul"). Whether or not one is interested in yoga, the background given by Father Dechanet on the synthesis of the whole person is extremely helpful. Prayer and meditation as springing from the physical are discussed at length. His own devout and charming personality shines through his words. Sane cautions too, very middle-of-the-road.

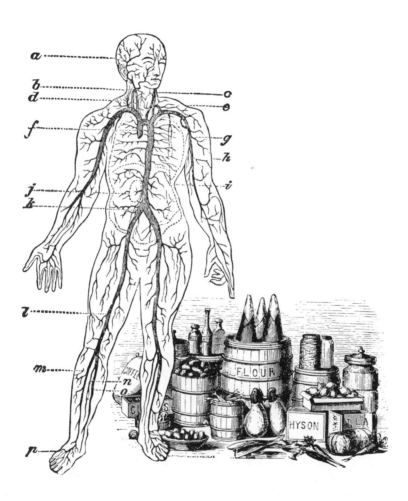

The Bubble

EXPERIMENT NUMBER 8

BACKGROUND:

This experiment is about the phenomenon known as "centering," a term which means different things to different people, but which usually has the connotation of being "together" or integrated or in balance, of having one's body and spirit in equilibrium. Monks of the Orthodox churches talk about finding the "place of the heart," and John of the Cross wrote about his soul's "deepest center," concepts which come about as a result of getting centered. (Experiment No. 16 asks students to represent this concept in a drawing.)

With imagination games like this one, build in the option of sitting it out so no student feels pressured to participate. Expect a little silliness at first—often, just standing next to a student who is about to crack up provides nonverbal control of giggles.

MATERIALS:
None.

CURRICULUM TIE-IN:
Prayer, the presence of God.

"I'd like to start this experiment by asking if one of you can tell the rest of us about a time in your life when you've had the physical feeling of coming unglued, or of falling apart at the seams, or just going to pieces. Does anyone have such an experience that he or she would be willing to share with us? . . . What we'd like to know, briefly, is what the circumstances were and, more important, how it felt. . . .

("Torn-to-pieces-hood," said William James)
(If no one responds, be ready with some example from your life, with emphasis on how it felt.)

"Thanks. Well, lots of us have had that feeling. A famous poem describes it with the words 'Things fall apart: the center cannot hold.'

(Yeats' The Second Coming)

"OK. Now, today, we're going to try an experiment that may help us get a little more 'together' and a little less unglued. If you'd rather watch quietly than experiment, that's OK—but why not try?

"First of all, sit as straight as you can in your seat; really get squared off with your feet flat on the floor and your back and shoulders up tall. Be comfortable though, not stiff.

(Or, if you are doing things on the floor these days, sitting cross-legged will also work.)

"Now, close your eyes and see if you can follow the directions I'll give you. Try to imagine the following spots:

- one just above your head. . . .
- one just under your feet. . . .
- one on each side of your elbows. . . .
- one just in front of your waist. . . .
- one just behind the middle of your back. . . .

"Now, connect these imaginary dots with imaginary arches. . . .

(Pause a few seconds after each.)
(Go slowly.)

"You have the framework here for a make-believe bubble. Can you also imagine some sort of covering on the frame, so that you are inside the sphere? . . . It can be a transparent covering of soap-bubble-like material, or it can be solid, such as dress fabric or even metal. . . .

"Now, here you are all collected inside your bubble. Can you find one more spot, this one inside yourself? See if you can find your center. . . . This will be a spot of spiritual quiet . . . a place where it's silent and calm and where you seem to come together . . . a 'still point'. . . .

(T. S. Eliot's good phrase, and if you're looking for quotes, Browning wrote, "There is an inmost center in us all, where truth abides in fullness.")

"You may want to stop with this step, or if you've found what seems to be your center, you may want to add another step. The calmness and unity we feel in our centers can be thought of as God's presence. The Kingdom of God really is within us.

"Without creating anything that isn't there, see if you can imagine that God is at this place in yourself. . . .

"And, if that idea appeals to you, see if you can let this peace that comes from Him spread throughout all of you from the center spot, like ink spreading through a blotter. . . . Try to picture it spreading to your legs . . . your arms . . . your brain . . . and all through you, into every cell, just like blood goes to all parts of the body. . . .

(Go slowly.)
(A good pause, which you can time by doing this exercise yourself — slowly.)

"When you're ready, let your bubble dissolve into the air, or let the pieces fall away like an eggshell does when the chicken hatches, and come back to the classroom. . . .

(Note: There's a thin line between suggesting possible experiences, as we've done here, and pouring kids into molds. You would not want your language to get any more suggestive than what's above.)

"When we all get back, let's compare notes on bubbles and on centers. Does anyone have anything to report? . . .

(If no response, perhaps you can ask how many were able to construct a bubble. And of what sort of material? And how many were more or less able to find their center? Where? Different people have different spots.)

"Some call this centering 'coming home and quietly resting.' Some compare the center spot in themselves to the eye of a tornado— especially if they live very hectic lives.

"Can you remember any time in the past when you have felt especially together and centered? . . . when 'the center comes clear'? . . .

"Think for a minute about babies and very small children. Their whole beings—body, emotions, thoughts—are very unified, aren't they? . . . Whatever they do, they do with their whole selves. They are very centered. As we get older, we lose that quality and begin to get tugged in different directions. Who's ever noticed that quality in the very young? . . . Can you remember being that way? . . .

"Well, this is a difficult experiment to do at first try. If you have trouble with it, or feel like you're not very centered, you might want to try it again on your own until you get the feeling that all the parts of you—physical and spiritual—are working in harmony.

"There's another way you can keep practicing centering too. Let's just do it together now, and then maybe you'll decide to use this idea on your own. Instead of imagining that you're in a bubble, just try to find your center where you're sitting right now. . . .

"Now, stand up and get yourself lined up inside . . . and see if you still have that center. . . . Try to get a sense of yourself as a whole person, a person put together. . . .

"And now, walk anywhere around the classroom doing anything you like and see if you can keep that experience of being centered. . . .

"OK, let's sit down again. . . .

"How'd you do? . . .

(Times often mentioned are when doing art or craft projects, making music or — for students who have studied the oriental martial arts, like karate — while engaged in combat or self-defense, playing sports. Cf. Experiment No. 6, "Natural Highs." What's the connection?)

(Elton John's ". . . never, never, never leaving harmony.")

(the kinesthetic sense)

(Let this last as long as you choose.)

"This is something you can do any time and place, isn't it? . . . I think you'll find that taking a second to stop and get centered helps everything in life flow more happily and smoothly, including things like praying. . . .

"The Quakers talk about 'peace at the center' and 'centering down.' That's what we're after—it's like coming home."

(How would you feel about asking students to get centered every so often? Before each class? After each class? Before a quiz?)

DATE TRIED:　　　　　　　　**TIME:**　　　　　　　　**REPEAT?:**

RESULTS:

MORE IDEAS:

1) Some students may find they are absolutely unable to locate anything resembling a center spot in themselves. If you get more than a few who have this sort of reaction, you might ask the class to try a simple set of balancing exercises which will tell something about their centeredness. They go like this:

- Ask everyone to stand.
- First, all stand on right foot, left foot raised behind. Can they balance for 30 seconds without wavering?
- Next, try it on the left foot with the right foot raised. How's the balance this time?
- Repeat the above, first on the right foot and then on the left, but this time with the opposite arm raised in the air each time. How's the balance this way?
- If you want to go on, repeat the set with these variations:
    1) Instead of just raising the foot behind, catch in the hand of the same side
    2) with foot held in one hand and other hand raised, bend forward slowly, as far as possible (without landing on face), and then come up slowly.

89

You can ask: "How many find balancing easy? . . . hard? How many are more balanced on one side than on the other?" The point of adding balancing postures to a class (in addition to the obvious value of providing a seventh-inning stretch during the day) is that they can show us strikingly how *un*balanced we are. If our bodies aren't working harmoniously, it's no wonder that we can't find some spot inside where everything seems to come together. The body's natural tendency is to maintain balance (homeostasis), but this naturalness—like so many others—has been bred out of us.

You can suggest that those who found themselves very unbalanced physically might practice the balancing postures at home. As they improve bodily, they should find it easier to zero in on the spiritual balance or centering described in the experiment. This, in turn, carries over to better living, better studying, better praying and better all kinds of things.

2) If you've gotten as far as getting students up on their feet for the balancing postures above, perhaps you can take them one step further (depending on their age and degree of coolness). You might try eurythmics, or moving the body in rhythm or patterns to represent the mood or meaning of words. This approach, often taught to young children with great success, comes from Rudolf Steiner's work (the Waldorf Schools) and is practiced both for therapeutic and artistic purposes.

Perhaps your text has some eurythmic prayers—the Lord's Prayer is often given hand and body gestures. If not, make up "gestured prayers" (as Father Lucien Deiss terms them) yourself or collectively with your class. A start: "Our Father" would seem to call for eyes and/or hands raised, "Who art in heaven," a raising of the arms, and so on. Once the motions have been decided upon and listed on the board where all can see them, have someone lead the class in this prayer with motions. (Yes, David can sit it out if it's just too embarrassing for him.)

One more step takes us to dance in the liturgy, a specialized art for those with a little more background, which they could get from Father Deiss' new book with Gloria Weyman, *Dance for the Lord* (Cincinnati: World Library Publications, 1975) and Carla DeSola's *Learning Through Dance* (Paramus, N.J.: Paulist Press, 1974.) How about someone researching sacred dance history? (See reference in Experiment No. 3.) The Islamic tradition is especially rich in movement as spiritual facilitation—the whirling dervishes, and the Sufi walks and dances whose purpose is to create a path of joyous movement toward God.

Students are probably familiar with the popular "Lord of the Dance." Can you dig up the late medieval English carol, "Tomorrow Shall Be My Dancing Day"? In each, the dance referred to is a symbol of Christ's life of love. Nothing new here!

3) And still one more step takes us to a discussion of prayer postures. Surprisingly, many students still think that prayer and dropping to the knees are inseparable, which is OK except that it rules out (for them) prayer while walking, standing, sitting, lying down, leaping, toe dancing or scuba diving. Why not discuss this, and if you have a lot of down-on-your-knees-to-pray kids, work in some of the experiments that call for prayer in various postures? (See, for instance, Experi-

ments No. 23 and 28.) Ask students to try praying in different settings and positions and report back. For classes that are very free and creative (especially with little children), you might quietly try this slowly done, on-the-floor prayer called "The Puddle," designed by Sibylle Mayer:

"Pretend you are a puddle on the ground . . .

The water is moving gently, with no waves—only little ripples . . .

The ripples fade away, and you are calm and still, like a mirror . . .

The sun beams into you, right to the bottom of the puddle. It's like God becoming part of a person and shining through the person. . . ."

(And, of course, bring your puddles back to normal child shape very easily and gently, at their own puddly pace. No sudden snap-to-it signals, please!) Ask students, "Is this praying?" If it works, it is—which is the point: that prayer needn't be linked to pious poses.)

REFERENCES:

The Centering Book, Gay Hendricks and Russell Wills (Englewood Cliffs, NJ: Prentice-Hall, 1974)

A collection of simple affective exercises (similar to several in this book) for use in the classroom, more than half of which are physical things-to-do. The authors use a very broad definition of the word "centering." Particularly helpful are their adaptations for classroom of the skills of the Senoi dreamwork, a few of which are similar to suggestions in Experiment No. 31, and their ideas for sidestepping negative energy, which fit in with our "Crabby People" Experiment (No. 25).

Centering, Mary C. Richards (Middletown, CT: Wesleyan University Press, 1962)

The author, a potter, begins with her experiences of centering clay on the potter's wheel, and ends with her own centering, with narrative digressions into pedagogy and poetry along the way.

New Eyes

BACKGROUND:

This is a sensory awareness and concentration exercise, which echoes a much-written-about sentiment: that, just as Jesus told us, we have eyes but do not see (Mark 8:18). It's also linked to the subject of wonder, of being aware of the "everyday miracles" around us. Chesterton wrote about trying to see the world with the eyes of Adam, experiencing it as though for the first time. This exercise helps us to do that more frequently, to facilitate our own transfigured moments.

MATERIALS:

Paper and pencils.

CURRICULUM TIE-IN:

Wonder, the world, creation.

"Have you ever had the feeling that you were missing a lot in life? . . . Specifically, did you ever have the feeling that just being alive was pretty wonderful, but that you were so busy you didn't have time to appreciate it or much of anything else? . . .

"Today, we're going to do a very simple exercise that helps us sharpen the way we look at things. First, put your books on your lap or under your seat and clear off your desk tops, except for one piece of paper and your pencil or pen. . . .

"Now, on the paper, I'd like you to draw a circle—just a small one, about the size of a dime. . . . Fill it in . . . and if you like, you can make it the center of some kind of design, such as . . .

"When I tell you to start, you're going to sit quietly and gaze at the center point you've drawn for one minute. Yes, that seems silly—but there is a reason for it.

"Those are the instructions. Any questions? . . .

(You'll have an example of this, for sure, if the kids don't.)

(A flower, an eye, some abstract design.)

(Yes, you can blink if you must — or better, rest a moment; no, don't cross your eyes.)

"Please sit up straight so you're looking down on the circle instead of from an angle. . . .

"All right—start. . . .

(Time 60 seconds.)

"Now, look away from your circle and at one of your hands. . . . You can bend and move it. . . . Does it look the same as always? . . .

(Possibly!)

"A lot of people find that concentrating for a short time on some focal point, like the circle, causes things looked at just afterward to look new and more 'real.' Your hands haven't changed, have they? . . . But it's as if you have put on a sharper pair of glasses or been given a new pair of eyes. People say they see things as though for the first time. . . .

(Or, in the jargon, have raised their level of awareness.)

"Would this new way of seeing be a good thing to have all the time? . . . Why? . . .

(It gives us greater appreciation of the world around us, helps us enjoy life more.)

"Let's try it one more time, now that you know the reason behind this concentration exercise. You can use your circle to focus on again, or you can find something else that is a good focal point— either on you or on your desk, or something in the room that stands out. Any suggestions? . . .

(The tip or eraser of a pencil, a button on clothing, a clip in someone's hair, some design you may have drawn on the board — see if your dictionary has a picture of a mandala or yantra, focusing designs.)

"Just for the record, if you were outside, what could you use as a focusing object to help you get that one-pointedness of sight? . . .

(A pebble, a blade of grass, a leaf, a flower, a spot of light, a knot in a tree trunk.)

"What might be in a home that could be a good point of concentration? . . .

(A spot or design on a rug or in the wallpaper, a point in a picture, a ceiling fixture.)

"And if you were waiting for the dentist or the bus, or anything else, what could you use? . . .

(A coin, a ring you wear.)

"OK, stare at whatever you're going to use for the second trial run of this experiment. Don't try to make anything happen. I'll time a minute. . . . Begin. . . .

"Now, look at your hand again. . . .

"Is it just the same as always? . . .

(Maybe so!)

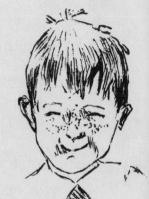

"Now look at the face of someone else in the room. . . . Seriously, ask yourself if that person looks the same as always. . . .

(Maybe so!)

"How many of you feel there is some change in your vision, in your perception, after you have gazed at some object or focal point for a minute? . . .

(Perhaps only a minority will have reacted this way; old habits of seeing change slowly.)

"If you were to practice doing this once a day or more, what—in the light of our discussion—do you think *might* happen? . . .

(The person's world, including the people in it, would really begin to be transformed; from half-seeing everything, he or she would progress to seeing fully.)

"And—tough question—what connection does that have to do with religion? . . .

(More appreciation of the world and the people in it would presumably lead to more appreciation of their Creator and more care for His world and people.)

"Now, here's a suggestion on doing this experiment in church. You might try this just once or twice, at Mass. At about the beginning of the Canon (What's that?) find a focal spot, such as a lighted candle or the center of a flower on a lady's dress or man's shirt. Focus on it, and then at the elevation (What's that?) look at the Host. It may take on a newness you've lost through seeing it so often. You can still listen to the words of the Mass while doing this.

"After a while, people who practice this concentration exercise off and on during the day get to keep their new eyes. They don't need to do the exercise as much. They really perceive, not just look . . . and although the world hasn't changed, it looks amazingly alive and wonderful to them.

"If you'd like to practice doing this, we can leave something up in the classroom to focus on, or you can keep using your design or anything else you like. See if you can work in this exercise in spare moments. Let us know what begins to happen if you do, OK?"

(Maybe someone will remember!)

("Religion Teacher Encourages Distractions During Mass"—headline of the week. Of course, that would assume the kids were paying attention to begin with.)

(Cf. the people who mirror Jesus in Experiment No. 13. They often have this quality.)

(Or, again, you might want to program it into future classes.)

DATE TRIED: **TIME:**   **REPEAT?:**

RESULTS:

MORE IDEAS:

1) A very common device used for concentration is a lighted candle. Students may suggest this, and it's fine for a follow-up; initially, however, an even more accessible/less esoteric focal point (like the student designs) is better because it can be used inconspicuously anywhere. That's the idea—to do it, over and over and over each day until our new eyes are in place.

    The main value of this experiment is that it helps us achieve a *physical* focus that sharpens vision and results in a fresh look at things; with the candle you could also add (if you wanted to) the symbolic implications of the light:

- It represents God, or—more specifically—Jesus, the "light of the world" (John 8:12).
- When you stare at the candle it almost becomes part of you, so that "you are the light of the world" (Matthew 5:14 and *Godspell).*
- It warms and irradiates you, like God's love.
- God's light in us is supposed to shine forth (Matthew 5:16), and not be covered up (Luke 8:16-17).
- We should "walk as children of the light" (Ephesians 5:8).

Adding these and other symbolic angles for a candle is good, as long as it doesn't take the main point of the experiment out of the senses and into the head. But, if you can balance off both ingredients, fine. (A second step often added to the staring exercise, which works especially well with a candle, is to close the eyes after staring and try to visualize interiorly the stared-at item. The purpose is the same—to help us get new eyes with which to see the same old world.)

2) You could devise similar experiments for each of the other senses ("new ears" could lead to more awareness of sounds we make, vocal and other. It could also include some experimenting with thinking about the mood-altering effect of music we play—intentionally or accidentally—on the radio or on records throughout the day . . . and the resultant implications of it for our spiritual selves). Psalm 113B (Are we like the pagan idols that hear, see, touch not?) could be your jumping-off point; your theme song could be the hit from *Tommy,* "See me, feel me, touch me. . . ."

Too far out for religious education? Father Carl Pfeifer has written in one of his syndicated "Know Your Faith" columns that "every Christian" must develop a "kind eye and ear that notice life's riches," because this is what it takes to become contemplative. He sees this—nurturing the capacity for contemplation—as one of the major responsibilities of religious education. We would like our students to have that tuned-in quality, wouldn't we? It's the "be here now" experience, to use the good cliche.

On the other hand, in *Gestalt Therapy Verbatim,* Fritz Perls has some scathing words for the instant "turner-onners" who are after "this quick-quick-quick thing" of instant sensory awareness, instant joy, instant everything. He says it's as dangerous to psychology as the "year-decade-century-long lying on the couch." (Maslow, too, warned of the "mystic gone wild" who wants all experience.) While the religion teacher using some very simple exercise like the one above is hardly likely to fall into this trap, still Perls's words about being techniquey and gimmicky and how this actually prevents growth make sobering reading (New York: Bantam Books, Inc., 1971).

3) More simply, everyone can be asked to appreciate more fully than usual some small thing: a picture, a photograph, an object from nature, a vegetable or fruit, a piece of candy, a pencil, anything. The object can be turned over and over in one's hands; the appreciator can smell it, taste it, eat it perhaps, notice what makes it unique in all the world from others of its specie.

This is also a form of concentration, but with more thought thrown in. It too carries over to daily living, until finally the practitioner is so finely tuned to the world in which he or she lives that even a trip to the supermarket (especially a trip to the supermarket) becomes an exciting experience in being surrounded by color and shapes and smells and textures (only to be fizzled at the check-out counter, unfortunately).

REFERENCES:

The Zen of Seeing, Frederick Franck (New York: Random House, 1973)

A beautiful book on how dead we are, sensewise, and on seeing (and drawing) as an act of contemplation and religion "by which all things are made new." Concentration exercises as a way to stop the (hectic) world and get off for a while. The artist-author of this handsome handwritten book will be remembered for his drawings of the Second Vatican Council's sessions. His growth-skill is easy to grasp and put into action even by the nonartistic.

Awareness: exploring, experimenting, experiencing, John O. Stevens (Lafayette, CA: Real People Press, 1971)

One of the best collections (and there are many, of uneven quality) of "awakening" exercises, by a Fritz Perls disciple. Many of the recipes are sensory in nature. A good section of cautions for group leaders and teachers.

Feelings: Exploring Inner Space, Jeffrey Schrank (Paramus, NJ: Paulist Press, 1973)

The author, a favorite of religious educators—for good reasons—writes on emotions and on sharpening all the senses. His chapter on the latter is titled, aptly, "Learning From Cats and Babies."

Sensory Awareness: The Study of Living as Experience, Charles V. Brooks (New York: The Viking Press, 1974)

The husband of Charlotte Selver, who brought sensory awareness training to the U.S. from Berlin in 1938, tells of the work to unfold people's innate sense-capabilties

Meditation

EXPERIMENT NUMBER 11

BACKGROUND:
When the continent of North America sinks into the seas under the weight of all the books on top of it, a very large percentage of those books will probably be about meditation. That's how prolific the literature on this subject is (well, almost . . .). This experiment is the simplest possible introduction (and, for young children, simplify even more) to a subject many spend a lifetime studying. We use the word "meditation" here not in its "thinking about" sense, but differently. (Can you spot the other experiments in this book which are also types of meditation?)

MATERIALS:
None.

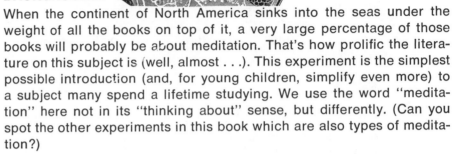

CURRICULUM TIE-IN:
Silence, stillness, stewardship.

"What do you know about meditation? Let's pool our information. . . .

(Students may know that Joe Namath and Willie Stargell and Ted Simmons and Mark Spitz meditate, or that many of the Philadelphia Phillies practice T.M.—transcendental meditation, which is one form of meditation.)

"There are many styles of meditating, but basically they can all be collected into two categories. One style is meditating or thinking about some particular idea. Can you give us an example of this type of meditating? . . .

(Thinking about your life or a scene from the life of Jesus or about the power of the Creator on a starry night, etc.)

"This is 'thinking' meditation—thinking, often in steps, about some topic or picture or story until you become very familiar with it. Have you ever done this? . . .

(Probably, especially those who have said the rosary with thought.)

"It's a good thing to do. Your thinking topic can be almost anything that you want to think about, but it's often a religious topic—and, in fact, is a way of praying or leading into prayer among the religions of the West. What are those? . . .

(Judaism and Christianity as we know them, and— more West than East— Islam.)

"The Psalms tell us about meditating in this way, and St. Paul gave his followers instructions to meditate upon the things he had taught them. You might want to set aside a little time every day or every week to meditate like this.

(See Psalm 63.)
(1 Timothy 5:15.)

"Usually, today, when we see books on 'Meditation' or hear about famous sports stars meditating, another or second style of meditation is being referred to. This kind of meditation is hinted at here and there in religious and other books of the West, but it's more often associated with the religions or ways of growth of the East. What are those? . . .

(Religions: Hinduism and its offshoot, Buddhism; way of growth: yoga.)

"The purpose of this second sort of meditation is not to think or pray, but to give both the mind and the body a little rest and inner peace that will lead to even better thinking, praying, action and everything else *after* the meditation. It's a preparation for daily living, a way of renewing yourself.

(Students as well as teachers may get hung up on this point. We can adopt methodology from another faith without adopting its theology. How "Catholic" are we?)

"As you probably know, lots of people in our own country have learned this second, more physical sort of meditation, and practice it every day. Do you think it's OK to use a technique which may be associated with another religion? . . . Or should we shy away from such things because they didn't originate with our own faith? . . .

"Well, very briefly, the main difference between the typically Western or thinking style of meditation and the typically Eastern style is that, in the latter, the mind is *emptied* of thoughts rather than being filled with them. In other words, we have one word, 'meditation,' being used to cover two opposite practices. Confusing? . . .

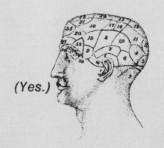

(Yes.)

"Now, what we're going to try today, if you like, is the second style of meditation in a very, very simple form. Teachers here and there across the country are beginning to ask their students to meditate in this way once or twice a day, and the reports are coming in that school becomes more pleasant as a result, and marks go up, and people seem much happier. So, it's worth a try, don't you think? . . .

(But anyone who doesn't like can just observe.)
(Watch education journals for more on these exciting first steps by creative teachers.)

"Just follow the directions. First, sit rather straight—but comfortably—in your seats. . . .

"Now, close your eyes and tune in to your breathing. . . .

"See if you can slow down the rate of your breathing a little . . . and now, just follow the breath as it comes in and goes out, nice and easy. . . .

(If students seem to be going along well, let them have two minutes or even more.)

"Don't think about anything else. Just keep following your breath for a minute or two. . . . Try to sense where it is going. . . .

"Now, when you feel ready to, open your eyes and come back to the classroom. . . .

(Wait for stragglers.)

"You've just been meditating. That's probably the easiest way there is to do the emptying-the-mind meditating. How did it go? . . . Were you able to keep with the breathing, or did other thoughts creep in? . . .

"What's the point of tuning in to the breathing? What does that do? . . .

(Keeps the mind from being pulled all different ways by its thoughts.)

"Did anyone notice any other feelings or sensations? . . .

(There may have been some "spacey" feelings—an altered state of consciousness, as described in Chapter One.)

"There are several other ways people meditate in the nonthinking way. Some are 'sitting' or 'passive' meditations, like what we just did, and some are 'moving' or 'active' meditations, to be done while working or walking or something else. How could 'following the breath' be done as an active meditation? . . . Maybe someone would like to do some research on the subject for extra credit—and you might check out the research showing the physical effects of meditation, which have been measured by doctors and scientists.

"Two last thoughts, now that we're back in our heads: First, do you think meditation could be of any use to you? . . .

"Second, since this is a religion class, let me ask you what value you think meditation might have in terms of practicing one's faith. . . .

"I'm not planning to ask you to meditate here regularly, but if you could work a few minutes of this into each day you might be very surprised and pleased with the results. Very experienced meditators aim for 15 minutes or more once or even twice a day, because the good effects pile up.

"If you do try this on your own, be patient with yourself. Remember that 'you can't push the river—it flows by itself.' "

(Just be aware of the passage of the breath while you do something else; why not stand everyone up to move around and try it—eyes open?)

(Such as change in metabolic rate, change in skin resistance which indicates decrease in stress, increased perceptual ability, faster reaction time, reduction in drug use.)

(Possibilities include increased calm and centeredness, better coping during times of stress, renewal of energy, etc.)

(It can help one open up to the Spirit, to be more receptive, to have more energy to do the good works of religion, etc.)

(Or — maybe you are! Why not?)
(Perhaps prefaced by "Let the words of my mouth and the meditation of my heart be always acceptable in your sight, O Lord" from Psalm 18.)

(The Christopher Newsletter recommends meditation as we've experimented with it.)

DATE TRIED: **TIME:**   **REPEAT?:**

RESULTS:

MORE IDEAS:

1) If you practice this meditation on the breath with students more than once, you might point out to them the spiritual significance of breathing. (Not at first, because that—again—makes the meditating a head experience, which is not the idea.)

   The breath is really what keeps us alive. It is the most basic physical function, marking our beginning and our end . . . a baby's first breath and wail mark the moment of his birth, and the lack of breath on a glass was the old pre-hospital way of identifying death. Breathing unites us with the larger universe of plants and trees sending out oxygen, and with other people, through the air we share with them.

   The Holy Spirit is, of course, often signified by breathing (as in Baptism). How about the popular folk hymn "Spirit of God," where the Spirit blows "till I be . . . breath of the Spirit blowing in me"? Then, too, throughout the Old Testament we read of the breath of God: in Job 33:4 and Isaiah 30:28,33 among other places, and there's the famous hymn "Breathe on me, Breath of God" to Bach's music.

   We breathe about 20,000 times a day—imagine how it would be if we were conscious of the spiritual implications of even a few of those breaths!

2) As mentioned above, there are several "emptying" ways to meditate. These can be taught to students, so that they have a variety from which to choose. Another style (which can be done passively while sitting quietly with the eyes closed, or actively while doing something else) is called "witnessing." The idea, simply, is to remove yourself enough from your thoughts and feelings so that you can be aware of them but not wrapped up in them (or to see yourself in action, if you do this meditation while moving around). While observing, you don't give your thoughts, feelings, or actions any labels of "good" or "bad"; you watch them as if you were a witness without evaluating them. It's something like the "unconditional positive regard" Carl Rogers describes as helpful when a therapist looks at and talks with a patient/client . . . only in meditation, there's just one person.

   You might, for example, witness yourself thinking "Oh, how I'd love another hot fudge sundae" (after you've just finished one). As witness, you wouldn't say,

judgmentally, "you cow—what do you need that for?" Your reaction would be "looks like I want another hot fudge sundae only 15 minutes after I finished my first one." Seeing yourself and your chocolate wish as an outsider would makes it very obvious that you will, indeed, look like a cow if you keep on in this way; it's a more effective way of riding herd on desires than the guilt-producing, stomach-churning struggles we often go through in trying to change a bad habit. Not all witnessing is involved with self-reform, however; you may simply just get a sense of self-observation and that is a form of meditation. It's also called "mirror consciousness"—a deliberate division of subject and object for the purpose of knowledge. Keeping a journal helps with this.

One specific application of this approach is to view yourself as you might be if you used all your potential. What would you be like? How much of a gap is there between where you're at and what could be? Can you close the gap one millimeter by doing some tiny thing as perfectly as possible, like opening that can of chicken noodle soup as well as any can was ever opened in the history of the Campbell Soup Company? Can you witness yourself doing it? Then tomorrow, open soup fantastically and add one more thing—like saying good morning to one of the people who live with you in as excellent a way as is possible. Witness that too. Self-conscious? Sure, but only at first. This might be called a God's-eye view as well as a witnessing by yourself. (There's a lengthy discussion of witnessing woven into the text of one of the favorite growth manuals, *Be Here Now* by Richard Alpert (Baba Ram Dass), a Westerner who went to the East and synthesized his learnings for Americans to practice. Read it if only to understand the thinking of "new age" people (San Cristobal, NM: Lama Foundation, 1971).

3) Of particular interest to many students will be the idea of sports—or, at least, some aspects of some sports—as a form of "emptying" meditation. This harks back to the sacred games of the Celts, of North and South American Indians, of ancient Greece, wherein (according to Socrates) "the purpose of physical exercise and games is the development of the soul."

Meditating while playing basketball or running down a soccer field is, obviously, an active meditation rather than a sitting, time-out, passive meditation. Many, many kids have experienced this and will know exactly what you are talking about, even though they most likely never labeled what was happening as "meditation." The idea is that the at-one-ness with ball, air, ground, bow, grass, water (or whatever goes with the sport indulged in) creates a focusing and merging that liberate a person from his mental activity. Getting rid of the thinking also actually improves one's performance in the sport (surely students have experienced the mischief that "trying too hard" can do to their basket-shooting or ....—just as we could tell them how "trying too hard" wrecks a lot of non-sports type things in life). The sport becomes a vehicle for spiritual expansion, just as any other form of meditation does.

Arthur Ashe, 1975 winner at Wimbledon, says about his tennis playing: "You don't try to do anything . . . (your) body already knows." No one watching his cool performance on TV could doubt that *something* different was afoot and that that something had made its mark on the man's whole life.

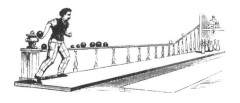

103

Other well-known sports figures meditate off the court (diamond, field, links) in longer stretches, and some (like Ashe and Al Hrabosky of the Cards) sandwich in mini-meditations between sets (pitches, innings). These long or short passive meditations complement the active meditation which occurs during the actual play. Some athletes do just one, some do both or all three. TV commentators often ridicule them, with "Oh, oh, here goes Al into his trance again—watch out, batter!"; they don't understand what's going on (meditation and trance are not the same thing).

Why not ask sports-conscious students to read up on this and then consciously try some sports as meditation for themselves? Three well-known books on the subject are *The Inner Game of Tennis* by W. Timothy Gallwey (New York: Random House, Inc., 1974), *Golf in the Kingdom* by Michael Murphy (New York: The Viking Press, 1972) and *Zen in the Art of Archery* by Eugen Herrigel (New York: Vintage Books, 1971). The application of the meditation technique to other sports can be easily made. Does the meditating improve performance in the sport? More important, does the time spent in this active meditation improve daily living? Can students devise mini passive meditations to use *before* batting (*between* halves, *in* the penalty box, etc.)? Do these improve the active meditation which takes place while actually playing? (See the baseball example in Chapter One.)

At Esalen, there is now a Sports Center devoted to the investigation of sports and physical education as media for the "transformation of humankind." One of this Center's thrusts is in developing new games that stress cooperation and coordination rather than competition and confrontation. (There are now "Infinity Ball" and "Earth Ball.") If the games and not the winning became the thing, think of the effects this could have on kids li berated from Little League parents and *mucho macho* tough-guy coaches. See George Leonard's *The Ultimate Athlete* (New York: The Viking Press, 1975).

4) Sports and religion have been good friends for a long time, as anyone who's seen a Billy Graham Crusade knows from hearing the witness of his sports friends. With students of all ages, sports can often be a vehicle for raising consciousness about religion, either in the sense of "God helps me in the ring" or, more broadly, as above in the "I meditate while I play and the whole thing helps me grow." Some well-known professional athletes hint at a combination of the two, a specifically Christianized meditation such as Stan Smith's ". . . if you open your heart, you can BE Christ—almost" (which certainly hasn't hurt his tennis game). Don't miss sports as a (physical) passageway to spiritual growth, one which is especially valuable with students of low-level spiritual enthusiasm. You can hook in with some of St. Paul's athletic references, such as the ones in 1 Corinthians 9:24-27 and Philippians 3:12-14.

REFERENCES:

How to Meditate: A Guide to Self-Discovery, Lawrence LeShan (Boston: Little, Brown and Co., 1974)

104

A psychotherapist writes the definitive, down-to-earth book on meditation in general, contrasting Eastern and Western styles, religious and nonreligious sources. No matter what the source, he reports, meditation has two major common results: "greater efficiency in everyday life and comprehension of a different view of reality." There's a good chapter on "Alluring Traps in Meditation and Mysticism," among them "The Game of Withdrawal from the World." A better start than books with pictures of human pretzel swamis and my-way-is-the-only-way teachers.

Christian Zen, William Johnston, S.J. (New York: Harper and Row, 1971)

Father Johnston is the founder of a Tokyo center where Japanese Christians can attend Mass and also meditate in Zen Buddhist style. He says that the Zen method of meditation is a usable technique for people of all faith ("Zen" is a Japanese word meaning meditation.) See also his earlier book, *The Still Point,* reflections on Zen and Christian mysticism, and his later work, *Silent Music,* on the merging evidence of science and asceticism about human consciousness.

Zen Catholicism, Dom Aelred Graham (New York: Harcourt, Brace and World, Inc., 1963)

A balanced discussion of the religious encounter of East and West by a famous master, author of the old Christian favorite, *The Love of God.* Zen meditation is explained in relation to Christianity, with plusses and minuses duly noted.

Mystics and Zen Masters, Thomas Merton (New York: Dell Publishing Co., 1961)

One of the East meets West works from the end of this favorite author's life. He, too, like the pair of authors above, seems most attracted to Zen Buddhist meditation, of all the various Eastern styles. However, there is information here on the Taoist tradition of China, and on English, Russian and Protestant mysticism from the West. Merton's work synthesizes cultures and bridges time and space; he is truly the man for all seasons.

Passages: A Guide for Pilgrims of the Mind, Marianne S. Andersen and Louis M. Savary, S.J. (New York: Harper and Row, 1972)

A must. This is a beautiful book on meditation and the exploration of inner space for "just folks." There are 43 specific exercises—some simple, like our experiment, and some more elaborate guided fantasies like those on Father Savary's records (see Experiment No. 26).

On the Psychology of Meditation, Claudio Naranjo and Robert Ornstein (New York: The Viking Press, 1971)

For those who want a scientific explanation of what happens during meditation, and what it can all mean in terms of what people can be. By two top men in the field.

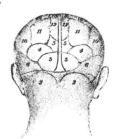

chapter 5
KNOWING JESUS

Scene: Typical religion classroom.

Teacher: ". . . and now you can see why it's so important for us to be kind to each other. Jesus *tells us* we should be . . ."

Rick (to himself): "OK. If you say so . . ."

Joe Switchblade (mumbling): "I could care . . ."

Karen (silently): "Oh, now I really get it. . . ."

Teacher: "Just open your bibles to John 15, and you'll see what Jesus wants us to do."

Christian educators find themselves falling back on "Jesus says . . ." and "Jesus tells us . . ." phrases over and over. It's as though those punch lines will be the clinchers for our students; once we share with them the information that Jesus has instructed us in a certain way all debate is settled, all problems solved.

Are we, perhaps, presuming too much here? Using the words of Christ as our final authority will be convincing to two sorts of students: Those who have never questioned the teachings of the Church or their Christian parents and teachers (Do you have a lot of students like that?) and those who have some sort of personal relationship established with Jesus and therefore care very much what He said (How many of these students have you?).

There's a big group of kids, however, who fall in the crack between the two extremes of childlike acceptance and mature faith. These are the students who have, of course, heard about Jesus since their youngest days and could answer a lot of our questions about Him—Where did He live? How long did He teach? Who were His friends? His enemies? and so forth. They have, however, outgrown buying all He says just because we quote it to them and yet have not progressed to forming any sort of working relationship with Him. They know about Him (head), but don't really know Him (heart). Even what they know about Him may have lost its flavor because of years of repetition, one too many late viewings of *King of Kings* and, possibly, over-saturation with bland pictures of a God that looks like a gal in a Breck shampoo ad.

Before we can share the teachings of Jesus with our students (the "Jesus says . . ." statements) and be confident that those teachings make a difference in their lives, we have to know where they are with Him. Here's a short questionnaire you can read to your students; ask them to choose the answer that best describes their

feelings and write the number on a piece of paper (no names). Collect them and see what you get.

Which statement best tells how you feel about Jesus?

1. I believe He was God because that's how I've been brought up.
2. I really don't care very much about His life or what He had to say.
3. I've examined the reasons people say He was God, and I accept them. For that reason, I go along with what He taught.
4. I think He was one of the best people who ever lived, and so I try to imitate Him.
5. He's my best friend, someone I walk with a lot.
6. I love Him. He's the center of my life. I can't get Him out of my mind.

These six answers constitute a continuum from our first group of young people, who have never questioned the teachings of their childhood, to the last ultimate answer to the "Who do you say I am?" question. We could even add a seventh answer along the lines of "loving Him to distraction" or being "God-struck" or the Lord being "a kind of light, and melody, and fragrance, and food." You never know where you'll meet someone graced that way.

Those of us who answered with a five or a six (or a seven) for ourselves know that that oneness with Jesus is the hub of our spiritual lives, and that without it a Christian isn't going to do much spiritual growing. This is what we want for our students too, but we really dare not assume that they *already are* captivated by Him and that the "Jesus says . . ." comments we toss around will affect them as they might affect us.

This chapter has four experiments designed to help students who may not have thought a great deal about Jesus and their lives do some thinking—and feeling—about Him. The first experiment, a "putting on" of the New Testament, will be home territory to lots of teachers. The second and third expose students to Jesus in other people and to other people's views of Jesus. The fourth tackles that aspect of Jesus' life we must all inevitably come to terms with—the Cross.

A side thought: We should carry in our minds the distinction between "love of God" and "love of Jesus." Many people may describe themselves as being "very close to God," either as Father or Spirit or both, yet not much aware of Jesus the Son in their lives. And they may be (probably are) doing fine; we'd like to think that knowing Jesus intimately helps us all do even better.

Francois Mauriac wrote, "One is never cured of God when one has known Him," and we can assume the great novelist would not mind our substituting the name of Jesus for the word "God" in his sentence. The goal of these four experiments is to help stimulate in our students that hunger for Christ that can never be cured.

107

The Personalized Bible

BACKGROUND:

Our first source for knowing Jesus better is, of course, the bible. Most students can feed us back a lot of information about the bible and what goes on in it; fewer of them would say it's a personal book that they want to hold close and live by. The technique of scripture-experiencing known formally as "relational bible study," wherein we are helped to learn—through the bible—about the relationships in our lives (with each other, with ourselves, with Jesus), can fill this gap. It's a style of bible study as old as the Judaic tradition and the apostles and St. Ignatius and as new as the *Serendipity* growth groups. Here's a New Testament passage explored in this subjective style, which is a complement to our more academic bible study approaches.

MATERIALS:

Bibles, or copies of the scripture passage you're using (here, Matthew 11:28-30, the "Come unto me . . . my yoke is easy . . ." verses). The verses could be copied on the board if you prefer.

CURRICULUM TIE-IN:

Bible, Jesus, the Cross, strengths, gifts.

"Let's arrange ourselves in small groups of three or four. . . .

(If this might become a major production, you do the dividing.)

"We're going to take a short piece from the bible today and see if we can do more than just read it and try to understand what it means. We're going to see if we can fit our lives into the words about Jesus, and then see if we can turn them around and bring the words about Him to fit into our lives.

"The passage is in the Gospel of St. Matthew. Jesus is talking to His disciples early in His public life, and He has just given a good scolding to the towns where He had performed many miracles and yet seen little turning from sin on the part of the people.

"Now, before we listen, try to put yourself in a small town in Galilee in the first century A.D. How do you imagine it to be? . . .

(Take time to stay with this and the following sense impressions.)

"What smells are there? . . .

"What sounds? . . .

"How do you think Jesus and the disciples would have looked? . . .

(Dusty, as though on the road, rugged.)

"And how would they have felt? . . .

(Tired, discouraged.)

"OK, we've set the scene. Now, who would like to read the words that Jesus said on that day? . . .

(Try to pick someone who says little.)

"And everyone else, while .... is reading, pretend that you are in a town in Galilee listening to Jesus, and also follow along with the words in your bible. The verses to be read are Matthew 11:28-30. . . .

(Or on papers or the board.)
(When all have found passage, reader begins.)

"Now, I have a few questions to ask you to think about in connection with that very beautiful bible reading. As I ask each of them, think about your answer and then share it with the other people in your group. You may not finish each time, so start with a different person after each question so all will have a chance. Please listen very carefully to what everyone has to say.

"Here's the first question:

1) Jesus tells the people to take up a yoke and carry a burden. What is He comparing them to? . . .

(Animals. This is not the discussion question.)

If you had been there, how would you have felt at being compared to an animal? . . .

(Purpose of this question: to intensify the feeling that Jesus was speaking to each of us, that we might have been there. Call time when a majority have finished.)

109

2) Was there ever a time in your life when you had the sort of 'heavy load' Jesus talks about, and then found rest with Him? (This is a rather personal question; just share what you care to.) . . .

(Purpose: history-giving. Note: if you phrased it in the present it would be too snoopy.)

3) Jesus tells the people He's talking to: 'I am meek and humble of heart.' Would you feel comfortable saying that— or anything good and true about yourself—to your friends? . . . Why or why not? . . .

(Use whatever words are in your translation. If "meek" and "humble" need defining, take care of it.)

(Purpose: comparison of Jesus' openness with His friends to our own style of relating.)

4) Jesus told His friends the truth about two great strengths He knew He had: His meekness and His humility. What inner strength do you have that you feel comfortable enough about to declare to your group? Can you say 'I am kind' or 'I care about other people's feelings'? If there's a strength that's been given you that you can proclaim, do that now. . . .

(Notice the difference between these personalized feeling/heart questions and similar thinking/head questions you might be asking: e.g. "Do you think Jesus was bragging?")

(Purpose: witness to God's goodness to all of us. We certainly aren't responsible for our gifts.)

5) What strengths do you see in the other members of your group (inner strengths, now, not muscle-power)? . . . See if you can tell each person one thing you notice in him that seems to be a strength. . . .

(Purpose: to affirm each as a human being, and —again—give witness. A standard encounter group technique called "strength bombardment." Allow all to finish this time.)

"There are different ways of coming to the bible. One way is to study and analyze the meaning of Jesus' words very objectively, making them the basis for theology. What's that, by the way? . . .

(Answers should be interesting.)

"Another way to view the bible is as we've just tried to do, as if it were God's way of speaking to us about our relationships: relationships with each other and with God and with the world and even the relationship we each have with ourself. Sometimes people try this more personal approach for the first time and come up saying, 'When did they put all those new things in the bible?' What do you think they mean? . . .

(Of course, that they've been reading it for years but have never been personally moved by it.)

"What we're trying to do with all of this is discover just what importance Jesus and His teachings and the bible have for each of us. If you like what we've done today, let me know, and we can examine some other parts of the bible in this same personal way.

(If you have the hymn Come to Me *by the monks of Weston, VT, it would make a fine closing for this experiment.)*

"A reminder: Please keep whatever has been said in your group to yourself, won't you?"

DATE TRIED: **TIME:**   **REPEAT?:**

RESULTS:

MORE IDEAS:

1) You can take any scripture passage—Old or New Testament—that is pertinent to your current curriculum and go and do likewise, making up your own relational bible study. Bible stories are even easier to personalize than teaching passages like the "Come to me . . ." verses used in our experiment. In the *Serendipity* books, for instance, are memorable exercises on such scenes as Jesus walking on the water *(Discovery,* p. 44) and Jesus calming the storm on the Sea of Galilee *(Serendipity,* p. 40).

    Take a look at what others have done, and then create exercises that fit best with your classwork. The ingredients:

    ● SET THE SCENE: where the passage to be read happened, what the circumstances were. Let students add their thoughts about the setting.

● THOUGHTFUL READING of the scripture passage; suggest that all try to imagine themselves there.

● ASK QUESTIONS ABOUT THE RELATIONSHIPS IN THE PASSAGE: There are four areas we can probe in relational bible study—relationships with Jesus, with other people, with ourselves, with the surroundings or environment. Each of these can be done by taking ourselves back into the scriptural time and place, and/or bringing the scene up to our time. For example:

	"GOING BACK" QUESTIONS	"COMING FORWARD" QUESTIONS
About Jesus	"How do I think Jesus felt?" "If He had said that to me, how would I have reacted?"	"If Jesus said that to me *now,* what would it mean?"
About Others	"If I had been .... in the story, how would I have felt?"	"How are my relationships like those in the passage?" (Be specific: Are characters arguing, or cooperating, or indifferent?)
About Myself	"If I had been there. . . ." "Where am I in this story?"	"Has something like this ever happened to me?"
About the Setting	Sense questions: "What are the colors in this bible reading? the smells? the sounds?" (These are often good openers.)	"Where have I ever been that was like the place in the bible passage?" "What does it remind me of?"

If you come up with three or four questions (not eight) and write them on the board, or just read them slowly one at a time as students are ready for them, you'll have them exploring their relationships in the light of scripture.

● REFLECTION: This can be done silently—and remember, there are different ways to reflect. Some people like to write answers to questions on paper. Some like to close their eyes and visualize what they would do in a situation. Some like to draw sketches or symbols or write poems. Others just like to sit and think. Try to work in all of these opportunities over a period of time.

● SHARING REFLECTIONS with others in a small group or with a partner. This step can be omitted and must be if someone's working alone. But the community built through sharing doubles the value of the reading and reflecting, and today is considered an integral part of relational bible study. We not only need to relate to Jesus and to ourselves, but to others (and Him in those others) for the circle to be complete. Important: All should understand that they need say no more than "feels right." Equally important, anything said to group members is personal, not to be repeated outside the group.

There are guidelines in our experiment for making the groups work, the most important being that all should really listen to each person's testimony. Lyman Coleman gives "four don'ts" for good group listening:

Don't interrupt • Don't probe • Don't give advice • Don't judge.

Groups that continue off and on over a school year have, of course, a depth and community to them that the one-shot groups can't achieve. It may take a while to appreciate the many types of enabling that come about through relational bible study, and to get a handle on all its ingredients, but it's well-invested time. Harvey Cox says it nicely: "(God) won't ask whether you believed (the bible) or . . . analyzed it. He will ask whether you did it" (Letter to *Time,* January 13, 1975).

2) You might want to expand upon the popular idea of affirming each student's gifts. Each of us has many, and too often young people—if asked—will sincerely say they have none. They can learn about their gifts from others (as in the experiment), or from you in various ways (notes on papers handed back, affirmation of different students' strengths during class when the occasion arises naturally), and from themselves (by a self-inventory).

Remember that there are many categories of strengths or gifts: physical, material, intellectual, interpersonal, spiritual, emotional, strengths that come from one's family and environment, opportunities, aptitudes, and so on.

Another point: Identifying one's gifts isn't the end but the beginning. The important question, of course, is "what can I do with them?" Stewardship again—and this will take a lifetime of answering.

Some helps in the affirmation of strengths and gifts: Karl Olsson's *Come to the Party* (Waco, TX: Word, Inc., 1972) and scripture references—1 Corinthians 12:4-11 and 15:10, Romans 12:3-8, 1 Peter 4:10-11. These remind us of the Source of our gifts.

And teachers will find all sorts of excellent building exercises in *100 Ways to Enhance Self-Concept in the Classroom* by Jack Canfield and Harold Wells. (Englewood Cliffs, NJ: Prentice-Hall, 1976).

REFERENCES:

Find Your Self in the Bible: A Guide to Relational Bible Study for Small Groups, Karl A. Olsson (Minneapolis: Augsburg Publishing House, 1974)

The author is one of the *Faith at Work* gang and he does two fine things in this book: He shares his story with us, telling us of the stages he went through in learning to love and use the bible for growth, and he shows us how to do the latter. A fine example of spiritual autobiography.

Serendipity, Lyman Coleman (Waco, TX: Word, Inc., 1972-1974)

A series of 12 workbooks, for use with spiritual growth groups, which contain the best-known examples of relational bible exercises. Their success across the continent

makes familiarity with them a must for religion teachers doing any sort of bible-based teaching. If you can possibly attend a Serendipity workshop, it will be an opportunity to experience a smorgasbord of many of the ways of spiritual growing in this book: art, group games, celebration, prayer and storytelling, as well as relational bible study. There are family bible exercises too, with *Serendipity* place mats to grace (literally) your table.

Bibles, of course—old and new.

Look especially for easily handled, non-forbidding, inexpensive editions that invite marginal notes and underlining and stuffing in pockets so that they can become very personal belongings (and let students see you doing this). Among the new translations in appealing editions are several versions of Tyndale House's *The Living Bible,* a paraphrase—there's *The Way,* with contemporary photographs to fit the biblical texts and oversized pages with lots of room for notes, as well as an index of which passages to read for which needs in life; *Reach Out* and *The Jesus Book* are both the New Testament of *The Way,* and *Soul Food* is the same thing with photographs of blacks.

The other super-popular New Testament translation comes from The American Bible Society: *Good News for Modern Man.* Filled with curiously appealing, timeless line drawings, it is a good translation (not a paraphrase) which retains some of the hallowed phrases of more traditional translations. It comes in regular paperback, or wrapped in blue denim (with a jeans pocket on the cover) as *The Blue Denim Bible,* and also in a very nice paperback edition with the Psalms (also illustrated).

Alba House publishes an English version of an Italian harmony of the gospels (also in paperback). Called *The Gospel of Jesus,* it has 500 maps and lots of pictures of the Holy Land, as well as historical background and time lines and makes a good supplement to either of the above bibles.

A "curiosity" on the new bibles' shelf is *Walk With Me* (Meriden, CT: TAMPCO, 1974), a harmony of the gospels written as if Jesus were telling His own story (e.g., "My First Sign: I Change Water Into Wine . . ."). It takes liberties with orthodox scripture scholarship (the Holy Spirit is a "she"), but does a good job in making Jesus' perspective come into focus.

Don't forget children's stories from the bible, which are often perfect starting points for older students and adults as well. There are the popular *Arch Books* from Concordia (St. Louis). Pages from these, posted on bulletin boards, make excellent meditation aids.

Finally, an easy-to-overlook entry in the "contemporary skins" department: David C. Cook publishes a six-volume *Picture Bible for All Ages.* It's a well-done comic book, in paperback size and shape (the fifth volume is about Jesus), and makes the bible come very much alive.

Mirrors of Jesus

EXPERIMENT NUMBER 13

BACKGROUND:

This is a very simple sharing experiment designed to help students think about Christ-like qualities—and about how they have met and known Jesus in special "significant others," those people who really mirror Jesus. (Companion experiments: No. 24, which attempts to help students find the Lord in *everyone,* and Nos. 29 and 30, with some thoughts about heroes.)

This is also a simple introduction to the human potential theme underlying this book: How much can each of us really expand? What can God's people become?

MATERIALS:

None.

CURRICULUM TIE-IN:

Human potential, saints, Jesus.

"I'd like to go around the room and ask each of you to share something with the rest of the class. Think, first, of the person who is the most 'special person' you know personally, someone who most seems to radiate and overflow with beautiful inside stuff.

"This doesn't necessarily mean someone who's done a lot in life, and it doesn't have to be someone who does holy things. It can be someone of any age.

"Sometimes we fumble for words when trying to describe this special 'shiny' quality—but you know it when you meet it. It just reaches out and grabs you, sometimes in person and sometimes even through a letter or a photograph. Think for a moment of your person. . . .

"OK, now let's go around the room and give everyone a chance to tell us about one of these people. You don't have to name your person, but just briefly describe him or her—age, occupation, how you became acquainted—and tell us what it is that makes that person 'shiny' to you. . . .

Miss Good Temper

(Someone will probably announce, "Look no more, folks, here I am!")

(You might lead off with an example of your own. Try hard to make it a non-church-related person lest you imply that only believers are beautiful.)

115

"Who'd like to start? . . .

"While each of you is talking, I'll be making a list on the board of the qualities that seem to be special about your people, so we can put together a picture of them at the end. . . .

(Go around the class; if anyone draws a blank, try to remember to come back to that student.)

"Let's see what sort of list we've got here. . . .

"What else would you like to add that you think is typical of these special, radiating people? . . . Let's add these to our list. . . .

(Have someone read the list of common denominators.)
(By now you may have most of these qualities—there are other possibilities too. See the lists at the end of Experiment No. 2.)

"How's this? . . .

> joyfulness
> inner calm
> concern for others
> like themselves
> tuned in to others' feelings (empathy)
> simplicity
> see best in others
> accept everyone
> have few dislikes
> at home anywhere
> sense of humor
> optimism

(You may want to make explicit what is surely implicit here; that is: "How would each of us fare by such measurements?" and "What sort of mirrors of Jesus are we?")

"Are these people's lives trouble-free? . . . That is, do they have all these qualities because they have no problems in life? . . .

(Students may find their examples' lives more problem-filled than most of us.)

"Now, these super-people are people we can use as our models of what a person can be, of how terrific we could all get to be. For Christians, who is the best model of all? . . .

"The people you told us about might be called 'Christ-bearers.' His light just shines through them. They each—even if they're not followers of Jesus—have some of the qualities that He had to a huge extent. When we look at them carefully, as we've just done, we get to know Him a little better.

"Think for a minute, now. When you're with these people, what are some of your feelings? . . .

"Do you often feel when you meet someone like this that you've always known him or her, that you're 'soulmates'? . . .

"Thinking about how it is to be with these special people gives us some faint idea of what it's like to be with Jesus—but can we really be with Him in the same way, when we can't even see Him? . . .

"Two of his disciples said that when they were with Jesus, they could feel their hearts burning within them. It can still be that way for us, today. The next time you're with one of the people you've told us about, see if you can carry over the feelings to your relationship with Jesus. Pretend He's there too—or do we have to 'pretend' about that? . . .

"Another way of describing these special people would be to say that they are 'filled with the Spirit.' Whatever words you use to tell about them, they give us some idea of the difference between just being alive and making the most of ourselves as people.

117

(Jesus, of course, the most super-person ever. Why not run down the list on the board and ask for examples of how He exhibited all the qualities listed?)

(Matthew 5:16; St. Augustine and many others talk about the "God-image" in each of us.)
(A different interpretation of "When did we see you, Lord?")

(Contentment, love, affirmation, stimulation, etc.)

(Those who've been there say yes, His presence is as real as/more real than that of the people we can see and touch.)

(No, because He really is there . . . our awareness of that fact is what needs jogging.)

(No, not booze—as someone will probably suggest.)
(If students understand the word "mentor," it could fit here, although it has a somewhat more specific meaning.)

"How could being aware of the potential in all people change the way we act toward everyone? . . .

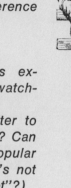

"Those of you who have the feeling that you want to work on becoming all you can be could make a point of noticing what's special about 'special people' and, also, of studying very carefully the model of humanness given us by God Himself—His Son."

(If each of us is called to "superness" — or sanctity, if the traffic will bear that word—we are bound to view others with more wonder and reverence than is usual.)

(Phyllis McGinley's expression: "saint-watching.")
(How about a poster to go with this lesson? Can you make up the popular "Be patient — God's not finished with me yet"?)

POST
NO
BILLS.

DATE TRIED: **TIME:**   **REPEAT?:**

RESULTS:

MORE IDEAS:

1) You can suggest that students keep their antennae out for descriptions of "super-people" in their reading and listening. Can they find lines describing such people in songs? (Listen to Seals and Crofts' *Robin* and Bob Dylan's *Love Minus Zero*.) Can they uncover expanded people in fiction or poetry or the comics (that's easy), among TV and movie characters (especially older films from days before the anti-hero)?

Who are the students' real-life heroes that they watch on TV or read about in the news? You could make another list of the qualities they admire in their favorite musicians, actors, sports heroes, political (?) figures, and make the connections to Jesus as in the experiment (e.g., someone may carefully follow the career of Jerry Koosman of the Mets because they admire his tremendous coolness under

pressure, and the style and elegance with which he does his thing—pitching—both when winning and losing. These are qualities shared by many "special people"; what are the parallels from Jesus' life?). Our real-life heroes are "types" of Christ, just as the Old Testament heroes were—or, said the other way, Jesus is the ultimate hero, the image of God in whose likeness we're all made, the new Adam (and wasn't the pre-tree Adam the most expanded of people, a model of what God wants for us?), who shows us what a person can be.

Do students know anything about the saints they are named for? They are fine heroes, but often (today) unknown to their namesakes who are still trying to make it. You could ask everyone to research his or her patron and find out how that person made the most of his or her potential.

2) Studying the reverse—the qualities of very unrealized people (or losers)—can help us see what we *don't* want to be. Of course, you will want to do this with love, not getting into personal examples of the crummiest people you all know. Maslow's and Harris' books, below, list the pathologies that go with *not becoming*. See also Everett Shostrom's *Man the Manipulator* (Nashville: Abingdon Press, 1967) and most of Karen Horney's work (especially good for girls and women) for other descriptions of unevolved, nonenlightened people. Can each student make up a list of "ways I don't want to be" or "masks I don't want to wear" based on personal observation and/or study? What are the religious implications (prayer, grace, etc.) once we spot these "deficiency diseases"?

3) Serious older students may also be interested in researching famous maps of growth, or ways offered to man throughout the ages to help him chart his progress from loser to winner. They can start with the traditional Christian maps of asceticism, with purgative, illuminative and unitive stages, or "many mansions," or various "nights." They might then look at comparable levels-of-consciousness maps offered by other cultures, such as the Zen "10 bulls" and the yoga chakra path of illumination. They can explore maps of growth from psychology—one is the Psychosynthesis "inverted funnel"—and fictional maps like Christian's in *Pilgrim's Progress*. Students can make up their own maps, based on the experiments in this book which are of most value to them and integrate them with one of the step-by-step outlines above. (Caution: Sometimes the young get hung up on trying to place themselves in such an outline: "Where am I?" It's tempting to overestimate, to hop lightly over the beginning stages because they're not as interesting—or ego-building. Serious pursuers of some spiritual path should look for a wise guide so their houses won't be built on sand. Spiritual paths with a lot of externals especially lend themselves to this abuse, as new followers may grab at a chance to fly before walking ("walking" in religion equalling loving God, and others, and yourself).

4) A practical action-oriented follow-up to this experiment would be for all to decide upon one specific way they could share the Christ-light in them, be better mirrors of Jesus to others. Perhaps you practice the Advent custom of *Christkindl*, where each does anonymous good things for one other member of the class throughout Advent, as though doing kindnesses for the Christ Child. How could this idea be made operative in students' homes? Could each pick a person a week from the

family and share—in one of a hundred ways—Christ's light with that person? Is this a path of spiritual growth? (For good leads along this line see *The Jesus Way* by Richard Foster, one of the excellent *Infinity* series for upper grades from Winston Press.)

REFERENCES:

The Farther Reaches of Human Nature, Abraham H. Maslow (New York: The Viking Press, 1971)

Here, in this final collection of Maslow's writings, is the whole story of his search for what makes people all they can be, a famous story which began when the young Maslow found himself analyzing the specialness of two of his own teachers. This scientific examination of the "self-actualized" people he collected, which began with his *Motivation and Personality* in 1954, developed into his life's work and a large chunk of the base of the human potential movement. He gives us a detailed picture of what the best people are like—and of what we all could become.

Winners and Losers, Sidney J. Harris (Niles, IL: Argus Communications, 1973)

A cartoon description of the self-actualized person (the winner) and the person who is nowhere near what he could be (the loser). Perfect for handing to kids (or projecting on an opaque projector or posting on a bulletin board) to illustrate the Christ-like qualities we've investigated so far. Use as a jumping-off point for Jesus-as-our-model discussions (how did He fit the descriptions of the "winners"?). Students could write short entries in their journals telling how they've won and lost, according to the text.

Called to Liberty and Greatness, Sr. M. Elizabeth Fowkes, I.H.M. and Sr. M. Johnice Cohan, I.H.M. (Boston: Allyn and Bacon, Inc., 1969)

The religion text, in four large colorful sections, built on the "how great can a person be" idea. For junior high students but useful as a reference or supplementary reading for students (and teachers) of all ages. It is outstanding and makes religion look interesting—which is certainly a good beginning.

Biographies

Biographies of people who used what they had, not to become famous or leap tall buildings in a single bound, but to enrich the lives of those they touched. Note, especially, lives of people who overcame handicaps and went on to grow. Do your students ever read saints' lives? Or did those books get packed away with scapulars and dashboard statues?

Other Lovers

EXPERIMENT NUMBER 14

BACKGROUND:

Another simple experiment, this time a two-part show-and-tell that familiarizes students with the best in Christian art and music and writing of the past and present—the witness of "other lovers" of Jesus. This part of our religious heritage is, so often, unknown to young people; too often, today's Christians are growing up in a vacuum that's disconnected from the beautiful religious testimony of the past, testimony that can help them find Jesus for themselves.

MATERIALS:

A few (three or four) examples of the work of other lovers of Jesus: reproductions of paintings and statues of Him, records of pop, folk or classical music about Him, poetry or autobiography or snatches of fiction that deal with the Lord. It would be interesting to have the full span of Church history represented—from catacomb art to today's music—if you can manage this. (Note: Try to find examples that are specifically about *Jesus,* in contrast to the broader categories of *Christian* music/art/writing inspired by Him, or *religious* works—which could reflect God-sentiments of people of any faith.) Pick selections which have immediate appeal to young people, rather than those that take time to savor (e.g., Johnny Cash on Jesus, rather than Hector Berlioz). See the end of the experiment for examples of "other lovers'" work.

CURRICULUM TIE-IN:

Jesus, sacred art, Church history.

PART I:

"Two thousand years is a long time, and in the almost 2,000 years since Jesus lived, a lot of people have loved Him very much. Many of these people were very talented, and used their 'high energy gifts' to leave behind a record of how much they loved Him. Can you think of any famous pictures of Jesus or music about Him or stories or poems of Him that have been created by people who loved Him?

"I've got a few examples of this kind of 'remembrance' of Jesus that have been left to us. Some are by famous people and some by unknown people. I'd like to share them with you today. . . .

(The gospels and epistles, naturally, but since then . . . ?)

(Folk art would be by unknown people.)
(Share your examples with a little of their background. Arrange them chronologically so you can catch the sweep of Christ-lovers spanning the centuries.)

"Now, for the rest of the time we have together this year, I'd like each of you to find some similar remembrance of Jesus that has been given to us by someone who loved Him. The person may be long gone or alive today. I can assign you turns to share your finds, or you can tell me when you're ready—which would you prefer? . . .

(The latter can mean problems though it's more democratic.)

"Where would you look for such musical or artistic or written pictures of Jesus? . . .

(Records, art and religion books, music in missalettes, artwork in students' homes, museums, libraries, Christmas cards, etc.)

"Try, now, to find a written or musical or artistic representation of Jesus that especially speaks to you. See if you can find something *you really like*—not just any old thing, but something that expresses how you feel about Him. Try too to learn a little about the artist or composer or singer or writer. See if you can discover what Jesus meant to him or her so you can share that with us too.

"If you get stuck, come to me and I'll have some ideas for you. See if you can find examples about Jesus Himself, not just 'Christian' or 'religious' music or art or writing. What we hope is that if we see how lots of other people have loved Him, it will help each of us to know and love Him more."

PART II:

Figure out some way to spread the students' showing and telling over the rest of your time with the class. Be sure each knows when his or her turn will be. If you seem to be getting a lot of one species —say, all *Godspell* or all pop-prayers—put a moratorium on that category for the remaining contributors.

Each should share what has been brought in, with a little background about its creator. Most important, students should tell why they particularly like their choice and why they selected it. Do they share the creator's feelings about Jesus? If they were to leave a remembrance of Jesus and their feelings about Him, what form would it take? How would He appear? Which of His qualities would they stress?

Then, have a vote to determine how many in the class respond favorably to the example, finding it an apt vehicle for their feelings about Jesus. Discuss the whys of this. How many *don't* care for the example? Why?

If you keep a running log of the contributions, where students found them, and class reaction to them, you'll have lots of ideas for future reference with another class.

DATE TRIED: **TIME:**   **REPEAT?:**

RESULTS:

MORE IDEAS:

1) An obvious spin-off from this experiment would be some probing into sacred art—good and not-so-hot. In case you're not sure yourself just what makes lasting religious art, two excellent catalysts for precipitating your own views are an essay, "Sacred Art and the Spiritual Life" by Thomas Merton in his *Disputed Questions* (New York: Farrar, Straus and Cudahy, 1960) and Celia Hubbard's good little book, *Let's See: The Use and Misuse of Visual Arts in Religious Education* (Paramus, NJ: Paulist Press, 1966). The main thread of each is that pictures of Jesus that make Him look like the circus bearded lady—or worse—are just short of blasphemous and certainly of no help to young people (especially boys) looking for a model.

Can you get together a collection of both good and horrible pictures of Jesus? Don't say too much about the icky ones, as they may be the same as what's hanging in Susie's living room. Just help the kids form a manly mental picture of this Man of both infinite strength and gentleness. Does each student have access to just *one* picture of Jesus he or she really likes? a picture of an adult Jesus he or she would want to follow? It may take many years to find such an image, and it may need to be replaced every so often as a person's relationship to the Lord changes. Sources: religious books and texts, calendars, art books, Easter cards. (See, also, in Experiment No. 16, the *St. Leo Bulletin*.)

2) Perhaps someone will want to research all the ways Jesus has been written about or pictured down through the centuries. You could have specialized collections of Jesus as Shepherd, as King, as Teacher (Rabbi), as Servant, as Priest, as Clown, as Brother, as Superstar, as Judge, even—mistakenly—as Superman ("strange visitor from another planet"). On this last, see *The Gospel According to Superman*

by John T. Galloway, Jr. (Philadelphia: A. J. Holman Co., 1973). Which image of Jesus does each student most respond to?

3) As an addition to selections brought in by the students, you might come up with some of the more controversial works of religious art and music. See what sort of reaction you get when students see Graham Sutherland's crucifixions or hear any of Olivier Messiaen's avant garde church music. If they *don't* like them, it will help them clarify for themselves just what they *do* like.

REFERENCES:

Images of Christ, Thomas S. Klise (Peoria: Thomas S. Klise Co., 1971)

An excellent series of eight filmstrips and four records that help students get a handle on their sense of Jesus. Even if you can only get the first filmstrip in the series *(The Many Images of Christ)* which shows many other lovers' versions of Jesus, you'll be ahead. Tom Klise, fellow seeker, has given us many fine leads for spiritual growth. (See his catalog: from P.O. Box 3418, Peoria, IL. 61614.)

He Is the Still Point of the Turning World, Mark Link (Niles, IL: Argus Communications, 1971)

One of the best and most beautiful "Jesus books," with the right questions ("Who was He, really?") and answers from many times and places. The companion books on God *(Take Off Your Shoes)* and prayer *(In the Stillness Is the Dancing)* are equally fine.

Jesus, the Son of Man, Kahlil Gibran (New York: Alfred A. Knopf, 1928)

The famous author of *The Prophet* has left us this beautifully written set of reminiscences by people who knew Jesus—as he thinks they would have remembered Him. There are 77 entries, from friends to enemies, from scriptural characters (Mary Magdalene, Peter) to passersby ("a cobbler in Jerusalem," "a Persian philosopher").

The Pearl and the Seed, Alfred McBride, O. Praem. (Boston: Allyn and Bacon, Inc., 1971)

A superb text on the history of the Church for junior high (or older) religion students. Throughout, Father McBride mixes the story of the past with the life of today's student and lards the entire synthesis with beautiful photographs of the greatest Christian art of past and present. Please go out of your way to see this text, even if you never are able to use it with a class. Superlative.

Other texts about Jesus; the revised (1975) edition of the eighth-grade Sadlier text from their "New Life" series is outstanding.

124

Some Ways Other Lovers of Jesus Have Expressed Their Love
(Use brief excerpts from the longer works.)

VISUAL ART:

Folk—ancient (catacomb paintings)
— American (Southwestern santos; Pennsylvania German fractura; needle-work (samplers, mourning pictures); Shaker spirit drawings. See the Jesus verses on these.)

— Foreign (carvings and drawings from mission countries)

Fine—paintings and mosaics and sculpture ("sermons in stone") from the earliest days of the Church (many are part of a church). Don't overlook contemporary artists (Rouault, Corita Kent, Rattner).

MUSIC:

Popular—religious songs and "rock operas" by many pop artists (Stevie Wonder, James Taylor), from country to soul to Jesus-rock to Beatle-beat to jazz.

Church—chant of various types
Masses, including mission-country Masses and Requiems (Mozart, Verdi)
hymns, including gospel songs and folk hymns
contemporary music for worship (Duke Ellington)

Folk—American (Negro spirituals and "white spirituals," Shaker songs)
— British Isles (old carols and ballads)

Classical—old (Berlioz' *L'Enfance du Christ)* and new (Poulenc's *Stabat Mater)*

WRITING:

Fiction—short stories and novels (writers like J. F. Powers are appealing to young people)

Poetry—ancient times to today (students might like Francis of Assisi, even John of the Cross, Boris Pasternak, songwriter Leonard Cohen)

Autobiography and Witness—diaries and journals of Christ-lovers (John XXIII, St. Elizabeth Seton)
— interviews (see *Jesus: Superstar or Savior?* from the St. Anthony Messenger Press)
— gravestone verses

If you eventually go on to the broader categories of Christian art and religious art, you can add examples of architecture (with pictures of the inside and outside of churches and chapels from all over), and the music and art of all faiths (such as native American Indian "eyes of God" and Navaho sand paintings). Pope Pius XII's definition of the purpose of art, "to open a window onto the infinite," is still a good one.

The Cross

EXPERIMENT NUMBER 15

BACKGROUND:

"In the cross of Christ I glory" goes the old hymn. Would many of our students say that? Or are they much more apt to run from crosses big and small? (How about each of *us?*) Experiment No. 25 is about getting rid of crosses, and Experiment No. 7 is about healing the pain crosses have caused. Here is a companion experiment for times when we must face suffering and sorrow, renewing our understanding of the cross as a way of knowing Jesus and of growing spiritually. If we help students learn to make something positive of their suffering, we give them a tool for life; sooner or later, everyone will have a share of the cross—there's really no place to go with it but to the Lord.

MATERIALS:

None.

CURRICULUM TIE-IN:

Suffering, the cross, Lent, Stations of the Cross, Jesus.

"Today we have a subject to talk about and think about that's not terrifically popular. The subject is suffering, or—as Christians might call it—the cross.

"Now, sometimes we have something go wrong in our lives and we can do something about it, or mend it, or heal it, or understand it so it doesn't hurt.

(If you've done either Experiment No. 7 or No. 25, you might refer to it.)

"But, as you know, there are plenty of times we can't do a thing about suffering in our lives. What are some examples of crosses we just can't get rid of? . . .

(Some sickness, death, some frustrations/heartaches/wants/hurts, etc. As always, an example from your own life — especially when you were your students' age—is a good bridge.)

"The cross is the ancient and foremost sign of the Christian church, of course. It makes us think of Jesus. I'd like you to do a little experiment with me now.

"Try to picture something in your mind—you can close your eyes if that helps. Picture Jesus carrying His cross up the hilly streets of Jerusalem. Fill in the details of the scene as you think it was. . . .

(Or, for young students, you can suggest the rough streets, hot sun, the people along the way.)

"Try to picture, especially, how Jesus handled the situation. Remember how tired and discouraged He must have been, and imagine as best you can what His behavior was like. . . .

(Again, you can elaborate for students too young to visualize His grace under pressure.)

"Now, another picture. The scene is the same, a man carrying a cross up the streets of Jerusalem. This time, however, imagine a very different sort of man—one who is feeling sorry for himself and trying to do things to get out of the situation, even though he knows it's hopeless. Picture in your mind how he would act. . . .

(Give the kids half a minute or so.)

"What was Jesus like in your picture? . . .

"How did the second man act? . . .

"OK. Now we're going to bring the scene up to the present and to our own lives. Think for a moment of the heaviest cross you are carrying right now—it could be one of the ones we mentioned earlier or something different. . . .

"Now, I'd like you to try another pair of mental pictures. First, try to picture someone else your age with whatever suffering or cross you've chosen as your worst trial right now. Pretend that that person is a very strong and brave young person. Picture him or her in the situation you've chosen, handling the problem with as much dignity as anyone possibly could. . . .

"Now, change the picture, and imagine the weakest possible young person handling the same problem in the worst possible way. . . .

"Finally, just to yourself, try to think whether your usual way of handling this suffering is closer to the way of the first person . . . or the second person. . . .

"I know this has been a very personal kind of thinking, but maybe there's someone here who feels free to share with the rest of us his or her problem and the mental pictures that went with it. Is there anyone? . . .

(Perhaps someone who carries no heavier cross than frizzy hair or a pesky kid brother will speak up—but this must be completely voluntary.)

"Well, where are we now? We've established that everyone has things go wrong in his or her life. And that it's OK—in fact, very good—to try to get rid of things that go wrong when and if we can. And that sometimes we just can't get rid of the things that aren't right. And that there's a good way and a rotten way to live with the crosses we can't get rid of. Anything else, so far? . . .

(This is important; otherwise people can feel Christianity advocates that "suffering was the only thing made me feel I was alive," as Carly Simon sings.)

"Let's get back to Jesus and His cross. In your mental pictures of Him, He was very brave, wasn't He? . . .

"Was He just being brave because He couldn't get away from the crucifixion? . . . Or was there some other ingredient in His courage?

(The answer you're hoping for: He saw a positive value to the pain. Stoicism isn't the point.)

"If Jesus believed that His suffering could be used to help others, and if He tells us to imitate Him in all ways, then it follows that our sufferings—much smaller than His—can have meaning and value too. Or does it? . . . What do you think? . . .

(You could get into a discussion of the redemptive value of suffering, but that really is a companion lesson, more theological, that can distract from the practical, immediate purpose of the experiment.)

"Going back to our examples at the beginning of this experiment, how could a person's sickness, for instance, be used positively rather than just endured? . . . How could it not be wasted? . . .

(It could be united with Jesus' suffering for the same purpose as His — the good of souls. And, shades of yesteryear, how about the phrase "offer it up"? Just for fun, ask how many students ever heard the expression.)

"Think about the example from your own life you pictured earlier. How could you live with it in a way that would help it have value? . . .

(As above.)

"Also, if your unhappiness comes from someone else, how would you now see them? . . . How did Jesus see such people in His life?

(With love. Whether they mean to be or not, they are instruments in our coming closer to Him.)

"Would anyone like to think out loud about all this? . . .

(Maybe not.)

"Sometimes when things are just awful, we fall into real despair and go into our dying swan routines. We can't remember all these lovely ideas. Then what? . . .

(Pray for strength to carry the cross; remember Paul's promise to the Corinthians that God never permits us to be tested beyond our strength, or allows crosses without grace enough to bear them [1 Corinthians 10:13].)

"The better we get to know Jesus as a person, and see how He handled the crosses in His life, the better we know how to live with our crosses. Another plus: We know He understands our pain because He went through it too. What would it be like to have a God who never had known pain or unhappiness? . . .

(Imagine "walking with" a gold idol or thunderbolty Zeus-type God. See Hebrews 4:15.)

"There's an old saying that's sort of hard to believe at first. It's this: 'The cross is the gift God gives to His friends.' What do you think that means? . . .

(Thanks a lot, Lord!)
(Suffering can lead to growth and, in fact, is a compliment since we are being invited to share Jesus' lot. See 1 Peter 4:12-13, and Colossians 1:24.)

"Right, by making the most of the crosses we can't get rid of, we become closer to Jesus and grow as people (our cross also helps us sympathize much more with other sufferers). This is a lot to think about, I know, but please take it home with you and see what happens, won't you? If you wear a cross or when you make the Sign of the Cross on yourself, ask if you *really* want to have it there."

(Need a poster? How about, "If you've got the love of Jesus in your heart, don't forget to notify your face.")

DATE TRIED: **TIME:**   **REPEAT?:**

RESULTS:

MORE IDEAS:

1) A companion topic to the cross—and guaranteed to be even less popular a subject—is the concept of voluntary penance, or (as we used to call it) mortification. Jesus' very direct statement is, of course, that anyone who wants to follow Him must "take up his cross" (Matthew 16:24).

Why not sound out students as to where they stand on digging up crosses to carry (in addition to those they're already shouldering)? Do they make the distinction between *taking on* new penances (like giving up TV) and mortification through *not doing* certain things they're used to doing (like snapping at a brother or sister)? One is penance through adding a hardship, the other penance through self-control—a big difference. Which is better?

Does the whole idea of penance in a you-deserve-a-break-today culture make God sound like the Giant Killjoy in the Sky? How many students can see any value in self-denials? Would they think to mention:

— it gives you something to "offer up," especially if you have a special intention in mind
— it helps you imitate Jesus and thereby draw closer to Him
— it disciplines your will so that you can really take command of yourself.

What would be some good, simple self-denials for those who have hung in

130

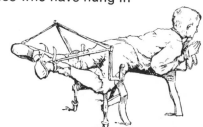

with you this far? Put together a mini-list with the class, concentrating on suggestions that have a positive side (self-discipline in cleaning one's room so that Mom doesn't have to worry about the health department condemning it), rather than "mini-punishments" (eating vile foods, going without dessert). (Teilhard de Chardin said that the first mortification of all is to work on our interior development. What could we do for our growth that is hard—but good?)

Do students know anyone homesteading in the country or living communally? Are you near Amish or Mennonite or Hutterite communities, living their simple lives? Perhaps you live near a restored Shaker village or a monastery. All these examples show us the life of simplicity and make it seem very positive and attractive, not a deprived life at all. Familiarizing students with simple living might help them see that self-denial can bear happy fruits. How could each of us simplify our lives with benefit? To what one thing or desire could we each be less attached?

2) If your curriculum lends itself to spending more time on the cross, illustrate common (and uncommon) crosses humans carry with pop songs. Students can come up with many, surely. You can have a few at hand, like *Song for Martin* (Judy Collins) and *Military Madness* (Graham Nash) and *Jesse* (Roberta Flack). If students had the sufferings of those in the songs (in these three examples, suicide of a friend, war, and desertion, respectively), how would they try to handle them—in the light of the experiment's guidelines?

3) The cross itself is a pre-Christian symbol. Older students may be interested in researching its contemporary use as a symbol of "the reconciliation of opposites" (i.e., the vertical stem of the cross representing spirit and the horizontal arm standing for matter). Thus, in the cross, instead of matter and spirit being shown in opposition (see the opening of Chapter Four), they are shown as united and in equilibrium. Jesus, of course, is the living example of this unity—as is each of us: a synthesis of two in one. (A similar symbol is the Chinese yin/yang circle, the Tai Chi.)

Much of our churchy training has led us to think in "either/or" thought patterns: Would we rather be Martha *or* Mary? Is God immanent *or* transcendent? Do we like our religion priestly *or* prophetic? Are we to be active *or* contemplative? (There are many other such dichotomies.) These neat little mental pockets may be handy, but are also an illusion. The symbol of the cross, where complementaries are united, suggests that both matter *and* spirit count, that we can be Martha *and* Mary (and so forth). The reconciliation of opposites in ourselves is a more evolved level of development than their polarization, as Jung mentioned and as nature itself shows. (Ebb and flow are both important; day and night both needed.) Maslow wrote that one of the "symptoms" of psychological growth is the shaking off of traditional artificial breakdowns so that one begins "to see the temporal and the eternal simultaneously" and " the sacred and the profane in the same object" *(The Farther Reaches of Human Nature,* p. 191 ff.).

The cross, as a symbol of two-in-oneness and as a sign of Jesus the unifier, may take on new meaning to students who let this symbolism sink into their lives.

REFERENCES:

Jesus Christ Superstar, Andrew Lloyd Webber and Tim Rice (Decca Records, 1970)

Listed here because, despite the pros and cons about *Superstar,* it certainly portrays vividly the sufferings (big and small) of Jesus: the demands made on Him, His pain at betrayal and the mockery of others, rejection by his closest friends and, finally, his despair and murder. Students who don't pick up much of the suffering of Christ from oft-repeated gospel readings can be hit very hard with His human pain by listening to portions of *Superstar.* The bridge to similar experiences of their own is an easy next step.

What Difference Does Jesus Make? Frank J. Sheed (New York: Sheed and Ward, 1971)

There are so many fine books about Jesus, but this has to be one of the best. Distilling a lifetime's encountering of Christ, well-loved guide Frank Sheed gives his answers to this basic question. He tackles suffering, as well as many other implications of the difference Jesus makes.

Man's Search for Meaning, Viktor Frankl (New York: Simon and Schuster, 1970)

A story of how good and strength can come out of terrible suffering. An adult counterpart to *The Diary of Anne Frank,* and like it a testimony to the goodness of humans in the worst of situations: the concentration camps. Helps us assess correctly the size of our crosses.

Our Many Selves: A Handbook for Self-Discovery, Elizabeth O'Connor (New York: Harper and Row, 1971)

A good growth book by a churchwoman, integrating growth from psychological sources and religious sources. The author is especially in tune with those who suffer emotional pain, and the last section of her book is titled "Creative Suffering."

EMIT, Richard O. Crane, ed. (Wheaton, IL: Tyndale House, 1970)

"Emit" is *"Time"* spelled backwards, and this facsimile of a newsmagazine that might have been published in Jerusalem during the week of Jesus' death is a powerful teaching aid. Pilate is interviewed, along with Caiaphas and Zaccheus ("I was out on a limb"), and the feature story is about a self-proclaimed "king" whose execution during Passover week caused a furor. A follow-up newsmagazine, *Emit II,* picks up the story a few months later, covering strange developments and the new religion sweeping Israel. Ads are in keeping, e.g., from the "True Light and Power Co." and the "Living Water Springs Co."

132

chapter 6
CREATION AND RE-CREATION

The wail has gone up across the country for many years now: "What's religious education coming to?" Usually the question is accompanied by remarks about foolishness and game-playing taking the place of "getting the doctrine in," and about teachers wasting time on arts and crafts activities instead of making sure the kids in their religion classes memorize their prayers. Nevertheless, the revolution in education (which has affected religious education too) moves on; we've learned that people learn best by experiencing, and experiences are now part of every good class in every subject across the board—including religion.

Experiments in Growth is largely (although certainly not exclusively) experiential, as you've noted by now. This chapter is even more deliberately so. Readers will also notice, however, that woven into all the experiences in this book are many, many old leads to spiritual growing: getting to know Jesus better, prayer, the liturgical year, the sacraments, knowing the saints and angels, singing psalms, penance, the Ten Commandments, Christian art and symbolism, bible study, and other time-tested ways of growth. As so many other recent texts for catechetics have explained in their introductions, what's happening is that the old wine is simply being served in more up-to-date bottles. Our touchstone, really, is the good old American pragmatic question, "what works?" If our students grasp and make theirs the love of God when it's presented in this way, we're on the right track; if the Baltimore Cathechism worked as well with today's students—well, that would be the way to go.

This chapter comes at the "fun and games" approaches from a slightly different angle. Here, these strategies are more than vehicles for understanding this or that way of growth, but are themselves ways of growing spiritually. Can that really be? Can playing help to stretch our souls? Two schools of thought answer "Yes" to these questions; consider their arguments and decide for yourself.

First, we have to take a (very brief) look at what's called "the theology of play." Its proponents (among them, theologians Harvey Cox, Sam Keen and Hugo Rahner (not Karl), and sociologist Peter Berger) even argue about whether to call it the "theology of play" or "play theology." Whatever they decide, the theology of play is one of several optimistic theologies which surfaced in the late '60's as a response to the "God is dead" ideas. It has much older roots, though, among them the gaming

theories found in many academic fields, and church traditions of "fools for Christ," recreation as a way of worship, and nonsense as a style of feasting.

Perhaps the most pertinent text from the bible to help us imagine such a thing as a theology of play is Jesus' teaching, "Unless you change and become like children, you will never enter the kingdom of heaven" (Matthew 18:3).

Playing helps us recapture the simplicity of our childhood, simplicity and joyfulness we may have lost on our way to Realityville, with its alarm clocks and schedules and paychecks. Play can help us once again delight in God and rejoice in the Lord, making Him the source of our joy rather than merely our resident problem-solver or need-fulfiller. Play(ful) theologians often use the dance as an image of this happy relationship between man and God (e.g., *Lord of the Dance, To a Dancing God);* the movement is, basically, a call for more balance in religion between heart and head. It needn't be labeled as worship of the Great God Experience, with resulting (heretical) implications—but, better, seen as an attempt to make the most of man's religious feelings as well as his religious thoughts.

Lots of people still feel foolish and/or guilty about seeing their lives as playful, even for theological reasons, or about calling themselves playful people *(homo ludens,* to be fancy). They might want to read more about this, and could take a look at these three sources on the theology of play. All have been published since the initial works on the subject (Cox's *Feast of Fools* being the best known of these), and their authors have had time to back off a little from the topic and show us what value a theology of play can have for our lives.

Theology of Play by Jurgen Moltmann (New York: Harper and Row, 1972) is a give-and-take between the well-known "theologian of hope" and three play theologians (Sam Keen, David L. Miller, Robert E. Neale).

Genesis 2 by Father Vincent Dwyer (Santa Monica, CA: Intermedia Foundation, 1975) is an intensive program for the renewal of spiritual life; one of its six units is "Spiritual Maturity and Play."

Gods and Games by David L. Miller (New York: Harper and Row, 1973) is especially helpful for its wealth of background material on man as a player, play and religion, and the development of play theology.

The other group of "growers" who are telling us that play can lead to spiritual growth are generally called play therapists. Much of their work is done with the disturbed, but they have much to offer our students and us for unruffled times as well. The play therapists remind us that when we create and recreate, we can get so wrapped up in our activity that we forget our outer selves (better known as masks), and open ourselves to a certain flow, or peaking, or intensity of experience that is above and beyond our ordinary state (see Chapter One and Experiment No. 6). This enjoyable experience is therapeutic, or—even a better word—re-creational, in the sense of the hymn line "Re-create in us a new spirit, Lord."

Abraham Maslow, who's referred to all through this book, wasn't a play therapist but a studier of what the best people are like and how they got that way. He lists "playfulness" as one of the qualities he found most consistently in his self-actualized

134

people. Adults have been defined as "deteriorated children" because they lack this quality.

Play is a broader category than games, of course, and recreation—or being created again—an even broader category; games are often so competitive and aggressive that they are hard work and no fun at all for the players! Also, one person's idea of a game will be another person's idea of torture. (For example, silly ice-breaker party games that can work wonderfully as openers with adults may be horrendous to teenagers for whom they seem childish; the adults have fun doing something suitable for five year olds, the teens are still too close to that age to want to revert to it, even for a moment.)

At any rate, play therapy is considered a valid way of facilitating growth by many psychologists these days, as well as by educators. If you're familiar with Maria Montessori's work, you know of her barrier-breaking play-in-the-classroom innovations. Even she had a ways to go, however; she frowned on fantasy as a "pathological tendency of early childhood." Today's play therapists would encourage both fantasy and all other kinds of play as vehicles to release the child within each of us, and to help us get out of ourselves.

(If you want to read more about all of this, and can make the necessary adaptations from therapeutic to educational settings and circumstances, the best book on the subject is probably Virginia Axline's *Play Therapy;* New York: Ballantine, 1969. For background on the seriousness of play for children, see Jean Piaget, *Play, Dreams and Imitation in Childhood;* New York: W. W. Norton, 1962.)

This chapter has six experiments that deal with play and creating things and re-creating other things. The first two give us a chance to experience the act of creation (through creating art, through creating music), so that we can better know God the Creator. The next is, simply, a game—but a growth game—which is a special sort of game. These are followed by two experiments which show us how to re-create the time in our lives. Finally, there's an opportunity for all to think about how we can use the space(s) in our lives creatively and for re-creation. None of these experiments will lead to a minor mystical experience (although, you never know . . .), but they will add to the spirit of fun and creativity in students' lives. That's growth-producing.

By now, you've undoubtedly discovered that learning through playing and creating captures students who are borderline in their interest. Fun in the religion class also has the added advantage of helping God seem more accessible, more approachable than many kids think He is. After all, if play and creative activities and games have a prominent role in church schools, maybe God Himself isn't as stony as some ancient sphinx (their thinking might go). St. Augustine was arguing for joyfulness in religious education back in the fourth century, but many of our classrooms are still wrapped in shades of black and grey.

Spiritual growing should be fun. If it's not, a lot of people will never get around to making a start on it.

135

Art: A Way of Growth

EXPERIMENT NUMBER 16

BACKGROUND:

Art experiences are a prime way of facilitating some spiritual growing. The giving of visual form to one's inner contents is growth-producing in at least four ways: 1) The creative act itself is a means of uncovering potentialities within each of us. 2) Creating and then living with the finished product, something which gives life and shape and form to previously unexpressed inner "material," helps us harness and ground our thoughts, feelings and experiences. 3) For most students, art activities are fun, and therefore good vehicles for our implementation of the "theology of play." 4) Creating our own art helps us know God the Creator better.

This is a very simple art experience, which is a visual rendering of centering (see Experiment No. 9). Several other experiments in this book have an art factor, and you could certainly add it to almost all the experiments.

MATERIALS:

Pencil and unlined paper. You could use other simple media as well. Consider colored pipe cleaners, various crayons or paints or colored pencils or chalks, clay (can get messy), and change directions to fit.

CURRICULUM TIE-IN:

Art, the arts, creation, creativity.

"I'd like you to think for a minute about the center of yourself, that place in you where everything seems to come together. . . .

(If you've done Experiment No. 9, you can refer to it.)

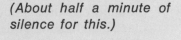

"Can you close your eyes and try to find that spot? . . .

(About half a minute of silence for this.)

"What I'd like you to try today is this: Here is some blank paper, an empty space. I have pencils if you need one. Would you please try—in any way you like—to draw or show in some way yourself and the center of you? Don't plan it too carefully. Just draw what seems to come out of you.

(Pass out paper.)

"Now, before you groan, let me add two other things: 1) this isn't an art class. Even if you can't draw at all (or think you can't), don't worry about it. And 2) you can draw a picture of yourself and somehow show your center, but you might also want to draw this with some sorts of symbols or shapes. Or you might want to draw something else, like a scene or a plant or an animal, that stands for yourself. There are no rules.

"Let's take about five minutes for this, OK? . . .

"Five minutes is up. If you're still working, how about finishing your paper at home? I wonder if there's anyone who would like to share what he or she has on paper so far. . . .

"I wonder how many found themselves just drawing something without much thought, as though the answer came up from within you. . . .

"That's a good thing. Sometimes we find the art says things we never would have thought to say in words. Maybe you'll remember this the next time you're trying to solve some problem in your life. Just sit down and start putting on paper anything that seems right; just doodle, and see what happens.

"Another thing. Can you think of any way that drawing what's inside us puts us in touch with God? . . .

(The fewer instructions the better; spontaneity is part of the creativity.)

(Watch for anyone who's really stuck in case you have to offer a suggestion. One possibility: "How about starting with a circle?" Another: "How about a building that could stand for you?")

(Don't force, but perhaps you can coax those whose work looked interesting into sharing it.)

(You'll probably get several answers. One to be sure to include: Our creating helps us tune in to God the Creator.)

137

"In the Old Testament, God told Adam to carry on His work of creating. When we use the creativity inside each of us, we're sharpening up the talent we need to do all sorts of creative things, just as God has asked us to do."

(Genesis 2:15—"Till the garden and keep it.")

DATE TRIED: **TIME:**   **REPEAT?:**

RESULTS:

 MORE IDEAS:

1) In addition to art experimenting via specific directions (as in the experiment or via any of the several techniques suggested in the references below), you might ask students to doodle aimlessly for a minute or two. When they've finished, ask them to examine their doodles for anything with spiritual significance *for them;* there might be some form that expresses where they're at in their growth right now, or some quality that is very important to them, or something they fear. There might also be symbols in the doodles—either specific symbols associated with Christianity (see Experiment No. 27), or universal symbols like the moon or the stars.

One symbol which is almost sure to appear on several papers is the spiral. Psychologists suggest that the frequent recurrence of this particular doodle is not by accident. From ancient times, the "mystic spiral" has been a symbol for the path of spiritual growth, of our "unwinding" on the way to heaven (heaven, both in the temporal and eternal sense). For the very few is the so-called "straight path," the "path of illumination"; most of us ordinary souls must wind our way more gradually—in recurring cycles, like the spiral—as we pilgrimage. (An aside: Note that the spiral must have a center, a starting point, before the unwinding on the spiritual path can begin. Cf. Experiment No. 9 and this one, on the center.) Note, too, the similarity of the word "spiral" to "spirit" and "inspiration," even though their roots are different.

If you find one of your students is spiral-happy in his or her doodling, you might pass on this list of spirals with religious associations. It will give even more insight into the spirals doodled at random, and link that student with

peoples of many other times and places. "Spiritual spirals" include:

—Spiral ascents of holy mountains, such as Dante and Virgil's climb to the summit of Mt. Purgatory, and the imitation mountains (pyramids and ziggurats, often climbed by wrap-around ramps) of the ancient peoples of both hemispheres. German children play hopscotch on a snail-shaped spiral of squares, with heaven at the center. The game is, in fact, called "heaven-hopping" and is a flattened-out climb up a holy mountain, with heaven at its peak. The idea, of course, is that ascending the holy mountain is analogous to ascending into higher planes of consciousness.

—The ancient Hebrews used the spiral as symbolic of the clinging relationship between Jehovah and His people. The Sabbath loaf was baked in a rising spiral; the rabbis wore sacred spiral side curls (and, today in Jerusalem, still do); phylacteries were wound spirally around the arm for prayers; Solomon's original temple had spiral pillars (the style of which eventually found its way to Rome and St. Peter's).

—Spiral forms from the animal kingdom, which have been incorporated into religious lore and practice (lots of sacred and not-so-holy snakes, coiling around trees in Eden and elsewhere, and also representing wisdom—"wise as serpents"; snails, that are venerated because they carry this revered symbol on their backs; Indian elephants with whorls painted on their ears for sacred rites; dragons, especially in China, guardians of temples and other holy places, whose coils symbolized "the Way" for Taoists and also for stargazers who follow the uncoiling of Draco the Dragon in the summer night sky; spiral entrails and intestines of animals used by primitive peoples for divining; the ram, or "sheep with curly horn," whose horns stand for an opening up of the mind, and who has also been a symbol for Christ).

—Church use of the spiral (bishops' crosiers, a symbol of their task of leading man on his path; whorls on the carved crosses and initial letters in illuminated manuscripts of the Celts, the latter designed as tools of meditation to prepare one for the hearing/reading of the gospel to come; spiral curls on the heads of early American gravestones, curls designed to help channel heavenly light into that dead person's soul—in the same way as the ram's horns).

—Labyrinths and spiral mazes marking off sacred territory in both primitive and more sophisticated places of worship. The most famous example is the maze on the floor of Chartres Cathedral (and many other medieval cathedrals too); walking the maze was supposed to constitute a pilgrimage to Jerusalem in miniature.

Many other whirling images are to be found in *The Mystic Spiral: Journey of the Soul,* by Jill Purce, one of the excellent *Art and Cosmos* series from Avon Books (New York: 1974).

2) From the creation of one small piece of art, as in our experiment, to the concept of creating a life that is a work of art is a big leap—but one worth discussing

139

with students. Primitive peoples have sometimes said to their more civilized (?) conquerors, "We don't have any art—we do everything as well as we can." In that sense, all of us are artists.

For a bridge from simple art experiences to "artistic living," don't overlook the domestic arts and crafts. Bread baking and other cooking, carpentry, needle-work (for men and women today), and home decorating, done as beautifully as possible, are acts of creation. What's more, the motions associated with these humble tasks, like the planing of wood or kneading of bread, help us incor-porate rhythms into our daily lives that reflect broader, lifelong ("cosmic," if you will) rhythms.

3) Relatedly, living with great art, religious or otherwise, puts us in touch with the height of creativity and, therefore, heightens our own. It also sets in motion things within us. For instance, "liking" a picture or sculpture has a content, as does "not liking." Art we like gives us a lead about ourselves (qualities we are happy with, patterns that make life meaningful), and the opposite is true with respect to art we dislike (is a picture angular and harsh? Overpowering? What does this help us see about ourselves?).

Can you rotate inexpensive reproductions of masterpieces in the class-room? You can just leave them up with no comment, hoping they will nourish creative juices, or you could discuss the like-dislike ideas above with students. Or, pick up on Kathleen Sladen's ideas from her *Are You in the Picture?* (Nash-ville: Abingdon Press, 1973); she suggests posting reproductions of master-pieces and inviting the viewer to "walk into the picture." Once there, they can look around, talk to the people present, pick up the feelings in the air. Her book has scriptural references included. (See also *Psychosynthesis,* referred to in Experiment No. 28, for a good chapter on "Pictures and Colors: Their Psychological Effects.")

Two good sources of art reproductions and suggestions for using art: Art Education, Inc., Blauvelt, New York 10913, a supplier of reproductions and publisher of some excellent books that go far beyond "art appreciation," and the St. Leo League, Box 577, Newport, Rhode Island. The latter is Ade Bethune's high-energy center for beautiful religious art (old and new), and for a small donation you can get *The St. Leo Bulletin,* full of information and things to purchase that can't be found elsewhere.

REFERENCES:

The Inward Journey: Art as Psychotherapy for You, Margaret F. Keyes (Millbrae, CA: Celestial Arts, 1974)

The subtitle is misleading—hinting at basketweaving for the disordered—until you read on and discover that the author defines therapy as "facilitating a growth and development trip." Here are several very good, simple art/growth activities (sculpting your family, drawing your lifeline, etc.) which are easily adaptable to classrooms and non-gifted students and teachers. Also, a brief but succinct summation and comparison of three humanistic (i.e., growth-producing) therapies: transactional analysis, the Gestalt approach, and Jungian depth psychology.

Exploring the Inner World: A Guidebook for Personal Growth and Renewal, Tolbert McCarroll (New York: The Julian Press, Inc., 1974)

A "whole self catalog" by the director of the Humanist Institute in San Francisco. One of the best growth manuals, by a spiritual guide whose work has taken him to the paths and writings of East and West, past and present, and led to practical applications of these for 20th-century Westerners. The illustrated chapter on art experiences as a way of growth is excellent. See, also, his chapter on the use of a journal.

The Gestalt Art Experience, Janie Rhyne (Monterey, CA: Brooks/Cole Publishing Co., 1973)

The author, like Ms. Keyes (above), is one of several educators/therapists using art experiences to facilitate growth and life-planning. Some of her concerns: "Invading Your Own Privacy," "Sensory Memories," "Using Fantasy to Find Reality," "Building a World," "Knowing Yourself Better."

Art as Experience, John Dewey (New York: G. P. Putnam's Sons, 1958. Orig. 1934.)

Heavier background reading on the philosophy of art for those so inclined. Dewey is primarily concerned with art in the eye of the beholder, aesthetics, but he also deals with the act of expression. For long winter nights. (In the same vein, the work of Ceylon and Boston's Ananda Coomaraswamy.)

The Rainbow Book, F. Lanier Graham, ed. (Berkeley: Shambhala Publishers, Inc., 1975)

A beautiful book of many colors, for those interested in either the science of color, or the effect of and need for color in our lives. Many provocative leads here for designing your own art/growth experiments.

See also references for growth games (Experiment No. 18), a broad category which can also include art activities and experiences, and *The Zen of Seeing,* referred to in Experiment No. 10.

141

Music: A Way of Growth

EXPERIMENT NUMBER 17

BACKGROUND:

Most religion teachers use music in some form in their classes. This two-part experiment focuses on one particular way of using music: When we actually compose music, we are creating (just as the previous art experiment helped us to enter into the creative process). This act of creation helps unite us with God the Creator. (See Experiments Nos. 14, 23 and 26 for other growthful/musical ideas.) A side dividend of this experiment: a mini-lesson on the Psalms.

MATERIALS:

Any simple instruments you can bring in (like an autoharp), or use of a piano—but these are not essential. Also, an example (preferably on record—but, if not, at least in print) of a simple setting of any one of the Psalms. See your parish missalette and choose one with which you think students will be familiar.

CURRICULUM TIE-IN:

Creation, creativity, the arts, the Psalms.

PART I:

"I'd like to ask you to think, today, about music—especially a certain kind of music you might hear and sing in church. What do you know about the Psalms? . . .

(Now there's an interesting question!)

"Well, the Psalms are part of the bible. (By the way, where can you find them?) . . .

(In the Old Testament.)

"When they were first written, they were written as songs or hymns to be sung. Do we always use them that way today? . . .

(More often, they're read or recited.)

"Also, by the way, who wrote the psalms? . . .

(Many are by David, but not all.)

"Can you think of any psalms? . . . How do any of them start? . . .

("The Lord is my shepherd," "All you people clap your hands," "As the deer longs for cooling streams," etc.)

"Good. Well, you may know that there are lots of composers today who have written new music for these very old words, and we use some of them in church. Can you think of any examples of psalms set to music that you know? . . .

(If you have a recorded example, play it, or at least mention an example from your parish repertory.)

"Well, there are 150 psalms, and they're all very beautiful. Between now and our next class, here's a very easy assignment. I'd like you to dig up a copy of the Book of Psalms—look in any bible that has both the Old and the New Testaments—and see if you can find a psalm that's especially meaningful to you. I'm sure you'll find more than one. Choose one and read it over several times, and come back to our next class with a copy of that psalm."

PART II:

"Now, does everyone have a copy of a psalm? . . .

(Why not have three or four copied out for those with dogs/baby sisters who eat their homework?)

"If you'll take a good look at your psalm, you'll probably find that one line in it seems to stand out for you—either because it's especially beautiful, or because it sums up the sense of the whole psalm. Try to find that line—it's often the first verse—and underline it. . . .

"In the example we listened to at our last class, you may remember that the composer had found one line of the psalm that stood out for him, and that he kept going back to it. Does anyone remember what this was in our example? . . .

(Or talked about.)
(If you have the record, play a bit of it again, pointing out the antiphon, or read your example over.)

"This one line which is repeated after every three or four verses of the psalm is called the 'antiphon.' Do you all have a possible antiphon from your psalms? . . .

"Can you guess by now what I'm about to ask you to do? . . .

(Probably.)

"Right. We're each going to set our own psalm to music. And we're going to compose the music. Does that sound hard? . . .

(Probably.)

"It's really not so hard. How would you suggest we start on this project? . . .

"For a start, how about reading the antiphon line you've chosen several times. Get the feel of it. Does it seem to go up in tone . . . or down? . . . Is it happy . . . or sad? . . . Does it seem to be quick . . . or slow? . . . Jot down some notes next to the antiphon line about how it feels to you. . . .

"Now, sit back comfortably, and let the antiphon go through your mind a few more times. See if some sort of tune for it begins to take shape in your head . . . and change the tune around until you get it some way that you like. You might even use a tune from some favorite song, if you can't come up with an original tune. When you have a tune just sit up and look bright-eyed so I'll know you've gotten something. . . .

"Good. Now if you know how to notate music, see if you can put your tune on paper. If you don't know how to do this, here's an easy way to fake it. Just put black circles going up or down the way your tune goes up or down; if any of your notes are held longer than others, just leave the circles empty—don't fill them in. You don't need the staff lines. This isn't very correct musical notation, but it will be good enough to remind you of your tune. So, why don't you try that now? . . . Sketch out the tune you've hit upon for your antiphon, or if you're still thinking about the tune—well, keep thinking. . . .

"I wonder if there's anyone who'd like to share what he or she has so far with us. You could just tell us your words and hum the tune, or sing it for us. . . .

"Why don't you take your compositions home? Keep humming the short verse you've set to music to yourself, and then see if, gradually, a longer tune or series of notes doesn't seem to suggest itself for the verses of your psalm. You'll remember that the example we used had, first, the antiphon, and then two or three verses of the psalm to a longer tune, and then the antiphon again, repeated every few verses.

144

(Work student ideas in with the following:)

(You may want to slide around the classroom and help—or, you could walk.)

(From Leonard Bernstein's Mass: "Sing God a simple song . . . make it up as you go along.")

(Again, some students may need your help.)

(Maybe someone will—you'll never know if you don't ask. Use of a tape recorder might make your invitation more inviting.)

(Whichever it was.)

"If you have a piano or some instrument you can use, it would be a big help.

"If you can get the whole psalm, or even half of it, to music you will have done something very special and creative, like God the Creator. Anyone who gets this far should certainly get some extra credit for it, don't you think? . . . So, be sure to bring in your work if you finish this project on your own."

(Here's a chance for the quieter students to shine a little.)

DATE TRIED: **TIME:**   **REPEAT?:**

RESULTS:

MORE IDEAS:

1) If you are able to work instruments into this experiment, you might also discuss with students the traditional image of man as God's "instrument"—an instrument tuned just right so as to faithfully transmit His presence. Seals and Crofts sing about it:

> "Make me as a hollow reed,
> That I may play and plant Thy seed. . . ."
> *(Hollow Reed)*

Demonstrate—or let a student demonstrate—a chord on any stringed instrument properly tuned, transmitting the player's intention correctly, and the same chord with just one string out of whack. What, in each of us, corresponds to those strings? How are ours tuned? (Is your C-sharp flat?—oh no!)

2) Suggest to students that they begin song books of their own (illustrated?), with songs that speak to them of the presence of God. Their psalms could go in, along with other original compositions (poetry set to music, words and music composed from scratch). They could add to it from the church music they really like, and from music you or their former religion teachers may have used in class.

Many popular songs that aren't specifically religious are, of course, "holy" in the broadest sense of that word: songs about nature, about caring for people, about growing. Best of all for many students will be love songs that can be interpreted as though the soul were speaking to God (or vice versa). Sometimes a few deletions of words or minor changes are needed in these, but often they serve just as is (listen to Cat Stevens' beautiful *How Can I Tell You?* in this light, and also the old Beatles' song *In My Life,* to name two among many possibilities). Remember, too, that today's junior high students may never have heard the pop songs we used back in the late '60's . . . Simon and Garfunkel, et al. We can introduce them.

The criterion for a song going into someone's song book is that he or she is moved by it, moved in a spiritual way. After collecting a few songs, naturally the next step is to sing them ("Sing hymns and psalms to the Lord!"—Ephesians 5:19) just for one's self and, if possible, play them. This gives us another way of spiritual growth "on the hoof," i.e., a growth skill we can use while doing other things and in almost any place, at almost any time. Like Jim Croce, many of us may find we "have to say 'I love you' in a song. . . ."

3) Your students may be studying music appreciation somewhere along the line. You can hook in the work of any and all composers they may encounter with this experiment, pointing out the tremendous creative (therefore, God-like) genius given to the greatest composers. You might want to refer older students to the classic novel about the power of great music to move and inspire, Andre Gide's *Symphonie Pastorale* (1925).

4) It would be surprising if at least a few of your students weren't hooked by the Psalms after this. Why not suggest to them that they put together a small collection of their favorites, perhaps even divided up by subject—psalms for times of trouble, psalms for rejoicing, psalms about life-style? They could add their own or cut-out artwork. (The new translations are good, but many like the old Confraternity version best.) You won't interest many young people today with ideas of "saying an office" or reading the Breviary—as many lay people once did—but this idea could begin some on praying the Psalms.

REFERENCES:

Sources of sacred music (records, sheet music):

1) World Library Publications, Inc., 2145 Central Parkway, Cincinnati, Ohio 45214

   Publisher of Father Lucien Deiss' elegant, popular psalm settings and other compositions, available on records and in print. Much else, from traditional (*Latin High Mass for Nostalgic Catholics,* a record at $5.95) to selfy-helpy material for non-musical music leaders and singers (*Music Lessons for the Man in the Pew* by Omar Westendorf).

2) North American Liturgy Resources, 300 E. McMillan Street, Cincinnati, OH 45238

NALR is the publisher of Joe Wise, probably the finest natural talent on the American liturgical music scene. Here you can find his records with favorites like "Take Our Bread" and "Lord Give Me a Heart of Flesh," as well as booklets of words and music. Carey Landry's music is also from NALR.

3) Paulist Press, 545 Island Road, Ramsey, NJ 07446

A new translation of the Psalms has been set to the psalm tunes of Pere Gelineau, chantlike yet contemporary. Ask for: *The Psalms: A New Translation.*

4) F.E.L. Publications, Ltd., 1925 Pontius Avenue, Los Angeles, CA 90025

Publishers of a large collection of popular "folk Mass" composers on record and in print, including Clarence Rivers, Ray Repp, Paul Quinlan, others.

5) Weston Priory Publications, Inc., Weston, VT 05161

The Weston Monks' music is a cross between Joe Wise's and that of the Medical Mission Sisters; some of it is exceptionally beautiful. They have made five recordings.

6) Family Records and Tapes, Word, Inc., Box 1790, Waco, Texas 76703

A good source of popular Christian music, especially old hymns and country music, by performers like Pat Boone, Johnny Cash, Burl Ives, Ethel Waters and many others.

7) *Folk Mass and Modern Liturgy* (a magazine), P.O. Box 444, Saratoga, CA 95070

A well-done magazine with much of interest to religious educators, including new songs and ideas for paraliturgical celebrations that could be very helpful in the classroom.

Sources of simple instruments for non-musical teachers and students:

1) Local toy stores. Check here for children's zithers, ocarinas, kazoos, rhythm and percussion instruments, and the ever-popular harmonica (mouth harp, to the elite).

2) House of Musical Traditions, Berkeley Springs, West Virginia 25411.

A one-stop mail-order source of simple instruments (bamboo and snake-charmer flutes, pennywhistles, finger cymbals, Jew's harps), as well as finely crafted folk instruments from around the world (dulcimers and other psalteries, Near and Far Eastern instruments, lutes)—and the instruction books and records to go with them. Send for their catalog.

3) *Catalog of the Unusual,* Harold H. Hart, ed. (New York: Hart Publishing Co., 1973)

Available in bookstores; another mail-order source of varied instruments.

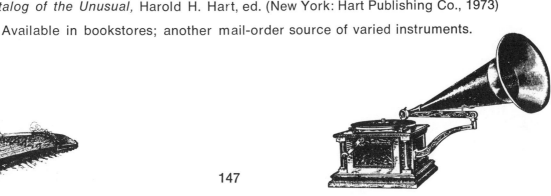

A Growth Game

EXPERIMENT NUMBER **18**

BACKGROUND:

A growth game is just that—a game that helps someone grow. (By that definition, even "Spin the Bottle" is a growth game!) As used in the jargon of education, however, growth games are those classroom activities that are gamelike in structure and, primarily, help participants expand affectively (heart), rather than cognitively (head). (This lets out learning games like "Baseball" and "Around the World.") Many of the experiments in this book are growth games; they aren't competitive; there is no winner.

A growth game is its own justification; if the "theology of play" spoken of earlier is a valid concept, then having fun and churning our creative juices (as well as getting to know ourselves and others better) is as much a path to God as lectures and questions and answers about Him. Maybe more so. Here is an easy growth game, using both non-verbal techniques (NVT's in educationese) and talking to others in a small group. It also serves as a vehicle for reacquainting students with another of those lost subjects—the angels—but this cognitive or head goal is not its primary point.

MATERIALS:

None, unless you have some angel pictures to post.

CURRICULUM TIE-IN:

Joy, fun, the angels.

"Today we have a game to play together. It's very simple, and I hope you'll enjoy it. First, how about forming groups of three? . . .

(If this isn't easily managed, you can divide the class up.)

"Our game is about angels. The Church has always taught that each of us has a guardian angel, and there are angels scattered throughout the bible. Can you think of any examples? . . .

(Michael in Genesis, Gabriel and Mary, Raphael and Tobias, Christmas angels and many others winging it through biblical pages.)

"What are a few of the things we think of angels doing? . . .

(Flying, singing, helping humans, fighting battles, praising God, having fun.)

"Now, angels don't have bodies and wings, but artists have always pictured them in that way so we can imagine a little better what they're like. I'd like you to pretend, just for the course of this game, that you are an angel. You can be any sort of angel you'd like to be, look any way you like, wear whatever you like, do anything you like. Take a minute to think about what kind of angel you would be. . . .

(If you like, you might add that only in comparatively modern times did angels become Cupid-like babies; many think these cherubs lack angelic dignity. Did anyone ever see an old angel?)

"For the next few minutes, go around your group and each describe just one thing to the others: *How you would look* if you were an angel. . . .

(Watch the progress and give all time to speak; give groups that finish early another question to share: "Would your wings be white or colored—and if so, what color?")

"OK, we've finished step one of this game. The next is a non-talking step. For this you have to be quiet. Take a minute to think of *one thing you would do* if you were an angel—it can be anything at all. Then go around your group, and act out that one thing without talking at all. Let the other members of your group try to guess what it is you're doing, just as in charades. Tell them when they guess it. . . .

(Watch and enjoy along with the rest.)

"While you were doing your angelic things, I was watching, and I really think the whole class ought to have the chance to see ——— as an angel. Would you like to repeat your non-talking act for us? . . .

(There's bound to be one or two students who were too good for the rest to miss.)

"Just so you know, we did this for a couple of reasons. What do you think they were? . . .

(To develop imagination and creativity, to have fun together, an experience which—in a religious setting — builds Christian (or other) community; finally, and secondarily, to raise consciousness about angels.)

"You could draw a picture of yourself as an angel, if you'd like to."

DATE TRIED: **TIME:** **REPEAT?:**

RESULTS:

MORE IDEAS:

1) Make up your own growth games after looking at some of the references below. You need to consider three ingredients:

   a) *Your Purpose:* What sort of human growth do you hope to effect? Some possibilities:

   - developing creativity and imagination
   - clarifying values
   - setting goals, life-planning
   - decision-making, problem-solving
   - awareness of feelings
   - body and sensory awareness
   - forming self-concept
   - assessment of strengths, affirmation of strengths
   - moral reasoning
   - increasing self-reliance
   - better communication skills
   - community formation

   b) *The Format* or type of strategy best suited to your purpose. Some possibilities:

   - values clarification strategies (voting, rank orders, continuums, questionnaires, etc.)
   - nonverbal games
   - simulation games
   - imagination games and fantasy trips
   - art exercises
   - music, dance or movement activities
   - role-playing, other dramatics-type activities
   - sensory awareness activities
   - writing (poems, journals, song lyrics, etc.)
   - storytelling (fact or fiction)

- happenings (often multi-media)
- variations on "party games" (often silly, used as icebreakers or warm-ups)

c) How to Divide the Class: Should the game be played
- by each person alone
- in pairs (dyads)
- in small groups
- in large groups
- by the entire class as one group?

Group strategies add an extra ingredient: the building of community.

Growth games come to us largely from the encounter group movement. Although we use games freely, that doesn't automatically imply a blanket endorsement of their parent movement and many of its excesses and failings (which have been likened by one critic to a "psychic strip tease"). (See *The Sensitivity Phenomenon,* by Joseph J. Reidy. St. Meinrad, IN: Abbey Press, 1973).

A couple of cautions may be in order: the temptation, at first, with using classroom games of this sort is to scotch-tape them in all over the place because they're such an improvement over discussions that never get off the ground or other classroom fizzles. It's all too easy to forget that they, just like audiovisual tools, must be designed and used with a definite goal in mind. Also, it's very easy to push people around with games—push them to participate, push them to come up with answers and ideas, push them to make religious connections that seem perfectly clear to you. We should really have a healthy sense of personal freedom before embarking on game-type activities in any classroom. Discretion is called for. Fortunately, the cream of encounter ideas seems to be rising, and the foolish/dangerous things filtering out—at least as far as education is concerned.

2) Can you collect and put up angel pictures? "Angelology" seems to have fallen on hard times in the past dozen or so years, and yet is a colorful and consoling branch of Church teaching. Angels are, in fact, a symbol of "man expanded," man at his best, even though they are not human. Their wings stand for spirit as well as swiftness and power.

Honestly, if you asked your students about their guardian angels would you get blank stares? laughter? sophisticated sneers? Would you feel foolish even mentioning guardian angels these days? Well, try it anyway—the alternative: Young people growing up never having tapped into this source of help. (In *An Angel in My House,* Tobias Palmer writes about his ongoing life with the angels, with the childlike simplicity that's really what it's all about, Ave Maria Press, Notre Dame, 1975).

Relatedly, the ancient Christian use of the bird as a symbol for the soul deserves more than a J. L. Seagull revival, along with the old hymns about rising and flying ("Rise, my soul, and stretch thy wings.") See Psalms 54 and 123.

REFERENCES:

Gaming: The Fine Art of Creating Simulation/Learning Games for Religious Education, Dennis Benson (Nashville: Parthenon Press, 1971).

151

One of the first—and still one of the best—treatments of games for religious education. Dennis Benson's work is unique, because of his imagination and his sure handle on how people learn. Religion teachers should see this book if only to familiarize themselves with one of the landmarks in their field. Includes two records; the simulation games (and that's a "let's pretend" game, just one of the many types of growth games) include *Ralph* and *Flight 108.*

Using Games in Religion Class, Jeffrey Schrank (Paramus, NJ: Paulist Press, 1973).

A pamphlet, and a very good introduction to gaming, with practical tips from a trustworthy author on how to do it—and background on why. The number one piece of advice is "don't expect miracles from games." Tips for designing your own games and notes on simulation games that can be purchased.

● Religion texts which include growth games:

Serendipity (Word, Inc., Waco, TX). See Experiment No. 12.

Experiencing Growth in Faith, Mary Cunningham and Charles Koop (Argus Communications, Niles, IL). Useful for teacher training or student groups.

Face to Face, Jackie M. Smith (John Knox Press, Richmond, VA). For adults, but adaptable to teens. A manual that goes with it: *Leading Groups in Personal Growth.*

Textbooks from many publishers, especially those from Winston Press, Minneapolis.

● Collections of (non-churchy) growth games, which you can adapt:

A Handbook of Personal Growth Activities for Classroom Use, Robert and Isabel Hawley (Educational Research Associates, Box 767, Amherst, MA, 01002. 1972). A basic book, very good.

Clarifying Values Through Subject Matter: Applications for the Classroom, Merrill Harmin, Howard Kirschenbaum, Sidney Simon (Minneapolis: Winston Press, Inc., 1973). The values clarification games with directions for applying them to any subject.

Growth Games, Howard R. Lewis and Harold S. Streitfeld (New York: Bantam Books, 1972). 200 growth games, arranged according to purpose (e.g., "Games for building warmth and trust").

Reality Games: Games People Ought to Play, Saville Sax and Sandra Hollander (New York: Popular Library, 1972). Theory built in; longer games.

Fantasy Encounter Games, Herbert A. Otto (New York: Harper and Row, 1974). Pick and choose; your class may be ready for fantasy trips.

A Dictionary of Angels, Including the Fallen Angels, Gustav Davidson (New York: The Free Press, 1967)

For angel enthusiasts, this is a delightful book with appropriate illustrations, detailing information about every angel we ever heard of and a lot we never knew existed. The sources: the bible, Jewish mystical literature, the ancient Greeks, many Eastern sources. There's even a "spell for the manufacture and use of a magic carpet," should you be planning any flying. . . . The angels invoked, of course, help keep one aloft (or high).

Time in a Bottle

BACKGROUND:

Here's an experiment to get students thinking about time, one of the most universal and compelling of all our human experiences. We're after an awareness of the difference between clock time (or chronological or linear or objective time) and non-clock (or psychological or subjective) time. (Jim Croce sang about the latter and his wish to experience more of it in his *Time in a Bottle,* hence our title.) The important end result, we hope, will be students' realization that non-clock time is the same as eternal time, God's time. This helps us use all the minutes and hours we have more creatively.

MATERIALS:

A clock with a second hand (if possible), or—even better—an hourglass-shaped timer for one, two or three minutes.

CURRICULUM TIE-IN:

Eternity, other people.

"Today we're going to conduct a short experiment. First, would you please get settled comfortably in your seats? . . . Then, would you please look carefully at the clock I have here? I'd like you to watch the clock silently and carefully from the time I say 'go' until the time I say 'stop'. . . .

(Or timer.)
(Start when the second hand is on the hour. Stop after two minutes—or three if you have a three-minute timer.)

"Now, the second part of the experiment is this: Will you please find a partner? . . .

(Or divide up the class yourself.)

"Between the time I say 'go' and the time I say 'stop,' I'd like you and your partner to carry on a two-way conversation about your favorite time of the day (and why). Tell each other what you do at that time. Then try to remember what your favorite times were when you were younger, and why—and share that.

"Go. . . .

(Call time when an amount of time equal to that above has elapsed.)

"OK, now if you'll stop your conversations and think for a moment, we can go on with the experiment. How much time went by when you were staring at the clock? . . .

"How much time went by when you were chatting? . . .

"Both time spans were the same: two minutes.

"Why is it that two minutes can seem so long and, then again, so short? . . .

"Tell me of some experiences you've had when time just seemed to drag, when you thought something would never end. . . .

"How about examples from your life when time seemed to fly by? . . .

"In both kinds of time, is the clock moving along at the same rate of speed? . . . Is a minute always 60 seconds? . . .

"This helps us understand that our experience of time is relative, even when the clock ticks at the same pace.

"So, there are two ways we can experience time in our lives. Clock time is one, when two minutes seem like two minutes. And 'psychological time' is another, when two minutes can seem like 15 minutes or just a second. What in the world has all this got to do with religion and spiritual growing? . . .

"Well, it certainly is helpful to be aware of clock time. If we ignored it and just went by our own inner clocks, what would happen to our lives? . . .

(Most will probably say the second time span seemed much shorter.)

(Or whatever it was.)

(When we're doing something pleasant, time seems to pass more quickly.)
(Waiting to open Christmas presents, some embarrassing moment when everyone stared, an endless class where all you could do was watch the clock, etc.)

(Good parties, "magic moments" with Someone Special where you lost track of time, etc.)

(Sure.)

(A timely question.)

(We'd be late for class! late for dinner! miss favorite TV programs!)

154

"On the other hand, lots and lots of people are so clock-conscious that they never break away at all from clock time. Their whole lives are ruled by clock-watching and scheduling, like what famous animal character in what famous children's book? . . .

(The white rabbit in Alice in Wonderland, *who may be familiar only through his song, "I'm late; I'm late, for a very important date.")*

"When we begin to stretch our souls and grow spiritually, one of the first things that happen is that we find a freedom from the clock. We experience more psychological time than before and less clock time. We can still be on time and plan, but we also become more tolerant of interruptions and unexpected demands on our time.

"For instance, did you ever have the experience of having your day or an afternoon nicely planned—when someone suddenly popped up with something that they wanted you to take care of? . . .

(Any examples?)

"What is a typical reaction most of us would have to that? . . .

"The person who is beginning to pull away from being ruled by the clock is also the person who is more likely to see an interruption as an opportunity rather than as a distraction.

"How is this a more enlightened way of living? . . .

(Henri Nouwen talks about tyros, opportunity, *as contrasted with* chronos.)*
(Chances to serve God and encounter Christ are seldom programmed; we have to be open to the possibility of them "just happening.")

"If we live more in the present—or the here and now, as they say—we not only flow better with whatever happens (and often get more done), but enjoy life more than if we're pressured by the clock. It's a more creative way of looking at our time.

"How about God and time? . . . Is He a clock-watcher? . . .

(Not if He's eternal—which really means timeless.)

155

"Well, if we grow more and more away from rigid living by the clock, we become more and more like Him. We can begin to see our own lives as timeless and eternal too. What do you think about all this? . . ."

DATE TRIED: **TIME:**   **REPEAT?:**

RESULTS:

MORE IDEAS:

1) This thinking about our time can be expanded by an art/growth activity. Ask students to paint or draw their whole lives as viewed from the present moment; their drawings will somehow show past, present and future and may be realistic or abstract or symbolic. In some way the three "time zones" each of us experiences must be viewed as a whole, and this gives each artist a new sense of his or her lifeline. (Suggested by Janie Rhyne and Miles A. Vich in *Readings in Humanistic Psychology,* Anthony J. Sutich and Miles A. Vich, ed. New York: The Free Press, 1969.)

2) If the time ideas have caught on, make the most of this theme by asking students to think of and/or bring in examples of time as a subject in art, fiction, on TV or in movies, in songs, etc. Have a few examples at hand yourself to start things off—and be sure they're examples with youth appeal (e.g., not Proust or *Last Year at Marienbad,* but Woody Allen's *Sleeper* and the popular story *A Wrinkle in Time,* and C.S. Lewis' *Narnia,* the world of Christian allegory where there is only eternal time). There are dozens of time songs too, the most famous perhaps being *Turn, Turn, Turn,* based on Ecclesiastes 3:1-8 ("To everything there is a season").

3) You may feel it's (spiritually) helpful to share some ideas on time management and "lifework planning." The subject can, however, make mincemeat out of the more scrupulous among us who can get very hung up on efficiency. Investigate on your own the popular ideas of Alan Lakein in *How to Get Control of Your Time and Your Life* (New York: Peter H. Wyden, Inc., 1973) and Gay Gaer Luce's research as described in *Body Time* (New York: Pantheon Books, Inc., 1971)

and her other work. Lakein's work, especially, helps us establish life goals, finish unfinished business and decide what's not worth doing. It helps us answer St. Augustine's question: "Where are you going? To what bleak places?" A good resource to work into this sort of discussion would be Joe Wise's fine song, "Time to Die."

REFERENCES:

Man and Time, J. B. Priestley (London: Aldus Books Ltd., 1964)

A personal and historical exploration of time by a theorist and playwright, presented in a handsome volume with beautiful artwork and photographs. We explored two types of time in this experiment; Priestley postulates three and illustrates his time theories with examples from many ages and cultures.

Time Being, John and Mary Harrell (Berkeley: John and Mary Harrell, 1970)

A kit for celebrating time in our lives, with its religious dimension. Like the Harrells' other happenings/celebrations, this one is marked by respect for each person's growth process and a backing-off from anything hinting of manipulation.

Getting There Without Drugs, Buryl Payne (New York: Ballantine Books, Inc., 1973)

Getting where? Well—there: that state of expansion where the kingdom of heaven within each of us becomes experienced rather than just acknowledged. A tall order, and Dr. Payne's collection of ways of consciousness expansion is a good one. A quarter of the book deals with "Breaking the Shackles of Time," and includes theory as well as practical experiments for doing so. He is a teacher.

On the Experience of Time, Robert E. Ornstein (Baltimore: Penguin Books, Inc., 1970)

Consciousness-researcher Ornstein's attention to time began with his study of Einstein on the subject. He traces the history of research on time and adds his investigative reports. For those who enjoy psychological research and data; technical presentation.

The Celebrating Life

EXPERIMENT NUMBER 20

BACKGROUND:

A second experiment about time in our lives—specifically, patterns of clock time. We start here with the calendar of the liturgical year, add our own special times for celebrating, and end up with a tool to help us get a sense of ebb and flow of the days and years we live. This enables us to be aware of our time creatively. The old spiritual books called it "redeeming the time."

MATERIALS:

Pencils and paper (journals?).

CURRICULUM TIE-IN:

Eternity, liturgical year, feast days.

"Today I'd like you each to make a calendar for yourself.

(Pass out paper and pencils if students have none.)

"Would you start by marking off a space of about one inch across the bottom of your papers? . . . Then, divide the rest of your papers into six equal blocks of space. . . .

"Now, at the top of each block, please put the name of one of the seasons of the Church calendar, or as it's sometimes called, 'the liturgical year.' What are those six seasons? . . .

(Straight A's for anyone who knows them in order: Advent, Christmas, Epiphany, Lent, Easter, Pentecost. Better write them on the board.)

"For reference, here are dates for each Church season, although some vary from year to year, as you know. You can put these under your titles:

(These can go on the board too.)

Advent: 1st Sunday of December to December 24
Christmas: December 25 to January 5
Epiphany: January 6 to middle or end of February
Lent: Ash Wednesday to Holy Saturday (end of March to mid-April)
Easter: Easter Sunday to eve of Pentecost (towards end of May)
Pentecost: Pentecost Sunday to end of November

158

"Look that over for a minute and then write in each box any religious holiday or feast day you celebrate each year during that season. . . .

"Next, let's add some of the special days we personally celebrate each year: our birthdays, other birthdays and anniversaries in our families, nonreligious holidays. See if you can put them in the right areas of your calendar, or as near as possible when you have approximate dates (as is true of the Easter season). . . .

"Can you think of other times that occur each year that are good times to remember? . . . How about deaths of people you've been close to? . . . How about birthdays of famous people you admire? . . . How about the beginning of each of the four seasons? . . . These are all good times to celebrate. . . .

"Anything else? . . . anniversaries of days important to you (the day you met Mr. Right, perhaps?) . . .

"How about your baptismal day? . . . or the day of your First Communion? . . . other sacraments? . . .

"Do you have any idea of your patron saints' feast days? (That's plural if you have a couple of saints' names). . . .

"When you get home, why not try to fill in any blanks that you're not sure of right now? . . .

"Now, there's a big difference between living a life that just goes by—and living a life that has pattern to it, a pattern of ups and downs and highs and lows, looking like a map of the ocean floor or the graph drawn by a lie detector. People who live creatively find that being aware of the patterns in their days and weeks and months and years makes their lives much more fun—and richer too.

"So, in the empty space at the bottom of your paper, see if you could draw a graph line that shows your year and how it goes up and down. You could start it with the first box, the pre-Christmas season, and work your way through the year until you have all the mountains and valleys in.

(Some of these things would have to be added after students could check them out.)

(Or, for younger children, something more suitable: "the day you got your cat," for instance.)

(A song to tie in: Graham Nash sings about "living from day to day" in Man in the Mirror.*)*

159

"Here's a sample of how someone's year might look:

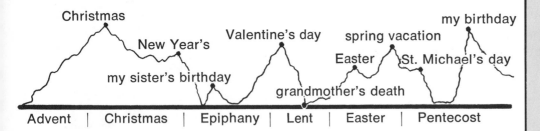

Christmas

New Year's

my sister's birthday

Valentine's day

grandmother's death

spring vacation

Easter   St. Michael's day

my birthday

Advent | Christmas | Epiphany | Lent | Easter | Pentecost

"Can you see a rhythm to your year? Are there times of new starts and getting ready, and then times that are very busy, followed by times of rest? . . .

"Now, a couple of final things. It's one thing to make these little charts. But making them won't help us live our lives any more creatively. What can we do about these patterns we've charted to get them operating in our lives? . . .

"How about celebrating the peaks on our charts? I assume you're already celebrating Christmas and your birthday. . . . But how about the smaller peaks? . . . What ideas do you have for celebrating them, either with your family or by yourself? . . .

"If all this appeals to you, you might want to go home and finish your charts, and then post your graph lines where you'll see them regularly. Check them often and celebrate the mini-peaks in some small way. Do try *not* to plan ways of celebrating that get too complicated, or they can drive you nuts—and then you'll just give up.

"If you could try to live as much in touch as possible with time patterns in your life for the next month or so, you might find it's a real means of growth for you. At the end of that time, we can talk about this again and see if it's been helpful to us in our 'soul-making.' "

(You can do this on the board; why not use your own special dates to celebrate, thereby sharing a little more of your story with students?)

(As on a farm.)

(Weave class ideas in with what comes next.)

(There are dozens of possibilities: a lit candle on the dinner table, doing something you especially enjoy on that day, etc.)

(Like the mothers who've vowed elaborate cakes for all possible occasions and end up hating every one of them because they're such a hassle.)

(Don't forget.)
(John Keats's expression.)

160

DATE TRIED: TIME: REPEAT?:

RESULTS:

MORE IDEAS:

1) You may already keep track of class birthdays and have some special way of celebrating these. How about baptismal days instead or in addition? Or patron saints' days (which may be easier to come by)?

2) By now, you may be wondering why you've seen no mention of the Mass in this book. Then again, you may not be wondering! At any rate, the omission—to this point—is deliberate. Many religion teachers, when searching for something to do with their students, end up with "Let's have a Mass." Not that that's not a good idea, but it's only a good idea if it can be a meaningful experience (to coin a phrase) for the students.

The Mass is, among other things, a celebration, and students just coming together at the beginning of the school year often have no shared experience to celebrate jointly. If we run them through the same paces they are run through by their parents each weekend, we're not doing a thing to increase their understanding of the Mass as prayer or celebration or anything else. This is especially true of students who may belong to a parish where the liturgy is still celebrated in a non-celebrating way.

Strong suggestion: save "having a Mass" until you reach a point with a group where there is a reason to do this, until you have a strong sense of being bonded together (and with some groups, of course, this never comes). Then, explain the celebrative aspects of the Mass and let the students help plan the liturgy, with the emphasis on shared rejoicing and the location (if possible) *not* in a church or chapel but some place more intimate.

Until you reach that point, build up to it with simpler things (celebrating feast days, etc.). If you have bible vigils and other paraliturgical ceremonies in a classroom, please look them over carefully to make sure they're really interesting—is reading a set of prayers from a book really celebrating? Does it really interest you? Your students? If not, each time we run our students through such little routines, we etch deeper in their minds the concept of church worship as boring . . . better to do nothing. Concentrate instead on helping students really get to know Jesus (Chapter Five); then they will want to know more about worshiping in the way He left us.

(A good chapter on the Mass is in the sensible high school religion text *Meeting the Living God* by William J. O'Malley, S.J. Paramus, NJ.: Paulist Press, 1973.)

3) You may want to point out to students the symbolism of the Church year as representative of the life of Jesus, as follows:

Advent—the time of getting ready for His birth, including the Old Testament time of preparation
Christmas—His birth and infancy
Epiphany—His growing-up years
Lent—His teaching years and His death
Easter—His coming back to life and the time He spent on earth after the Resurrection
Pentecost—His living on in the Church

In the same sense, each year can be a representation of the life of each of us.

And/or, you might want to pick up on *the day* as symbolic of a life (with its "death" (or sleep) at night—and "rebirth" the next morning); how does night work affect this natural rhythm? Do students feel their days have shape? How many have ever heard of a morning offering? You could also chart the pattern of *the week* and its symbolic associations, with each Sunday being a "little Easter," the day of rebirth and new beginnings; Fridays would, in this scheme, take on their traditional color as days of penance and dying (to selfishness), and the rest of the days would reflect the spirit of the same day in Holy Week (Monday, Tuesday and Wednesday of each week as days of preparation; Thursday as a day of thanksgiving, and of wrapping things up, as at the Last Supper; Saturday as a day of waiting for the Sabbath).

Older spiritual books, like the popular writings of Father Pius Parsch on the liturgical year, suggest many ways of sanctifying our time. Which would appeal to your students?

4) Another way of adding the ingredient of celebration to everyday life is the idea of "mini-vacations." A mini-vacation is any small thing one likes to do (go somewhere pleasant, eat something enjoyable, take a coffee break, take time to really listen to a good record, read something relaxing, watch a favorite TV program, plan a future trip, have a smoke, etc.) *deliberately* programmed into a day. All of us—kids too—get so plugged in to our particular rat race that we may not make time for these little pleasures. When that happens, our (religious, in the best sense of that word) rhythm gets out of whack: Instead of fast followed by feast, we have all fast, and instead of work followed by play, we have all work.

But by being aware of the need for mini-vacations, or mini-celebrations, we put balance back into our lives. Can we help our students see these breaks in their schedules as chances to "redeem the time"? Whenever they make an effort to stop for some small pleasure, can they learn to also make it a time of prayer and thanks?

162

If each of your students were asked to make a list of things that would be mini-vacations for him or her, what would go on it?

REFERENCES:

On the liturgical year:

In print, perhaps the best for our purposes is *Children of the Church* by the Sisters of the Servants of the Immaculate Heart of Mary, Monroe, Michigan (Collegeville, MN: The Liturgical Press, 1960). Two of the best books are out of print, but you may be able to find them:

The Year and Our Children, Mary Reed Newland (New York: P. J. Kenedy and Sons, 1956)

Around the Year with the Trapp Family, Maria Trapp (New York: Pantheon Books, Inc., 1955)

Resources for celebrating (liturgical, paraliturgical, or much more homely occasions) *in the classroom:*

—Three from Ave Maria Press with liturgies for young people on many themes:

How Green Is Green? by Rev. Etienne LeBlanc and Sr. Mary Rose (1973)

On Cloud Nine, by Rev. David B. Gamm (1976)

Touching God, by Rev. W. Thomas Faucher and Ione C. Nieland (1975)

—A trio of down-to-earth and very helpful books of celebrations on both church and non-church topics, by James Haas (with his wife, Lynne), from Morehouse-Barlow:

Shout Hooray (1972), *Make a Joyful Noise* (1973), and *Praise the Lord* (1974)

—Kits of creative liturgical happenings and celebrations from John and Mary Harrell (P.O. Box 9006, Berkeley, CA 94709) that have valuable background food for thought.

—Abbey Press, *Christian Family Catalog* (St. Meinrad, IN 47577), a gathering between two covers of visual material for religious celebrating. Even if you don't buy, you'll get lots of ideas here.

—Not least, certainly, Dennis Benson's great *Recycle Catalog* (Nashville: Abingdon Press, 1975), a collection of ideas from all his network of people. Religious educators have sent Dennis their ideas (that work) on everything from gaming to ministering, and many of the ideas are about celebrating. Format is fun.

A Very Special Place

EXPERIMENT NUMBER 21

BACKGROUND:

This is a very simple experiment to help students become conscious of the space(s) in their lives, and the effects of these environments on their spiritual growing. Each of us can find or create some small special place of our own, if we don't already have one, to reinforce our other attempts at re-creation. The experiment can trigger it.

MATERIALS:

If you can find them, how about pictures of special places (as per the experiment)? You might have very personal rooms, outdoor places that invite one to stop, church interiors, car interiors, castle towers, tree houses, walled gardens, etc.

CURRICULUM TIE-IN:

Prayer, solitude.

"Today, I'd like to do something very easy with you. Think for a moment whether you have—or ever had—some place that was your very special place. Perhaps you go there (or used to) to be alone, or to hide, or to think, or to daydream. Sometimes little children have a spot under a table with a long tablecloth over it down to the floor, or under a big bush that spreads to the ground.

"Let's go around the room and each, who would like to, tell us a little about your place. It can be a past or present place. It can be indoors or out. . . .

(Can you tell them about a place of your own? As students respond, try to help them give details that make their place more vivid, such as "Your place is in an empty car that's parked next door—tell us what it looks like inside.")

"These are all good places. Does anyone want to know any more details about anyone else's spot? . . .

"How about special spots of anyone else you know? . . .

(Dad's favorite chair? a window with a view that Grandma loves? a senior citizen's favorite park bench or church pew? a pet's corner or hole dug in the yard?)

"Have you ever heard of any famous special places—real or in stories or songs or movies—that other people have had and used well? . . .

"It's not too hard to guess that people who have such a spot find it a very good place to collect themselves and, also, to pray. Jesus talked about going into our rooms and closing the door when we pray, but He would also approve of getting into the shower (if that's your spot) or finding a special place outdoors.

"Let's take just a minute to talk about how often we use our spots, and what we do there. . . .

"Here's an assignment for this week. Make a point of thinking about your spot and looking it over; see if you can make it an even better place for you to go to and get collected. What could you do to improve it? . . .

"Then, try very hard to make use of it this week. Go to it, spend some time in it thinking or praying or just sitting. Those of you who have no spot, or who aren't too well satisfied with yours, perhaps you'll use this week to get a very special place of your own. Try out different ones, either in your home or outside it—anywhere you like, actually. Next week, we'll compare notes again.

"This is a way of re-creating yourself."

DATE TRIED: **TIME:**   **REPEAT?:**

RESULTS:

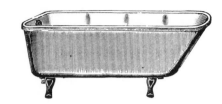

MORE IDEAS:

1) Can you make some sort of special place in your classroom, a spot set aside from the traffic flow where students can pause to cool down and bend themselves back into shape during their busy days? It could be a corner, perhaps with a comfortable chair with its back to the rest of the room. You could add posters, greenery, a bookcase divider—anything to make it an island apart. Younger children like boxes and playhouses and domes to go off into. One creative elementary teacher even imported an old claw-foot bathtub and cushioned it—why not? If you do this, you will have created an oasis in your room, a place where students can come to refresh and re-create themselves.

How can a home be the same sort of oasis? Or is it just a "machine to live in," as the famous architect Le Corbusier said? Or, best, is it "sacred space," a temporal resting place for God-bearers? How many students' homes have ever been blessed, just as new churches are consecrated?

How about animals and their sense of territory? Do humans have the same need? Is it for material space? Or, rather, psychological space?

2) You might want to take a look with your students at holy places: the very special places that were specifically designed as religious environments. Your examples can include pictures of the interiors of churches and temples and mosques (What ingredients have their architects used to create the feel of the sacred? Which work best for you as sacred space? In your own hometown, which religious buildings most appeal to you? Why?), with special attention to the focal point of such houses of worship—their sanctuaries or tabernacles or holy of holies (What is done to emphasize the specialness of this area? Have students ever seen the iconostases or screens in Eastern rite and Orthodox churches? How many have ever noted windows in the "eye of the dome" over church altars? These, like smoke holes in primitive houses of worship which let the smoke of burned sacrifices escape, symbolize a breakthrough from plane to plane and communication with the transcendent).

Go on to less familiar sacralized spaces: monastic cells; ancient labyrinths which hid a shrine; outdoor sacred spaces (often circular) like the holy ground around Moses' burning bush and those on ancient Greek hills which marked the home of a god and were an asylum for anyone in danger; prayer rugs of nomadic Moslems, sacred gardens (like Paradise) that they carry with them and spread out whenever in need of a holy place; Japanese gardens. Which are holy places students feel would help them? Why? Can they re-create any such place in their lives?

(One secret of a successful "place with presence" is that the space inside it is dynamic, not static; the emptiness is full—with light, with shadows and shapes that change and are alive. Churches with mosaics inside seem, especially, to have this flickering, mysterious quality of presence—God's presence. Can you find a picture of the best of all, the interior of the famous sixth-century Church of San Vitale in Ravenna, Italy?)

166

3) Discuss with students the effect space(s) has on people's behavior. Three families in one tiny apartment will act differently from three families in homes where everyone has a private room. Certain rooms—in homes, in schools, in public buildings—produce positive feelings, others produce negative feelings, both with resulting differences in behavior. Libraries are supposed to make us feel like getting into books; some do this, others defeat their purpose. Playgrounds are supposed to encourage children to play; not all do. Churches are supposed to help people worship; some do and some don't.

Behavior is especially affected by the idea that space we move in is sacred space, whether that be inside a church or a home or a grove of trees or on a subway platform. A person who moves in what he or she sees as sacred space is going to believe that his movements, his actions, and his life have sacred meaning. Some of your more mature students may want to chew this over and see what meaning and applications it has for their spiritual growth.

REFERENCES:

A Room of One's Own, Virginia Woolf (New York: Harcourt, Brace & World, Inc., 1929)

In a poignant statement of her need for her own spot, the novelist says it for each of us. We may not be able to come up with rooms of our own; a corner or chair or mental room may have to do.

Farallones Scrapbook (Point Reyes Station, CA: Farallones Designs, 1971)

This is a book about changing space in classrooms, a book about environments. Whether you hope to create spots in schools or homes or anywhere, this is a good catalyst that will start you on the path.

The Sacred and the Profane: The Nature of Religion, Mircea Eliade (New York: Harcourt, Brace and World, Inc., 1957)

A famous historian of religion from the University of Chicago describes two modes of being in this world: sacred and profane. In relation to this, he defines "sacred space" (and also, "sacred time"). The space we move in, he says, re-creates our view of the cosmos. Very readable.

A Sense of Place, Alan Gussow (New York: Saturday Review Press, 1972)

Landscapes by American artists that illustrate beautifully the "special place" ideas in this experiment.

Experiments in Prayer, Betsy Caprio (Notre Dame, IN: Ave Maria Press, 1973)

The companion volume to this book has an "Escape Meditation" designed to help us create an imaginary place of our own. The experiment takes students through all the ingredients: location, appearance, use of it, etc.

Handmade Secret Hiding Places, Nonny Hogrogian (Woodstock, NY: The Overlook Press, 1975)

A book for the kids, with drawings of small fry in easy-to-make special spots. There are directions for making a Between the Chairs Hideout, a Four-Poster Arabian Tent, a Behind the Stairs Hideout and other such places.

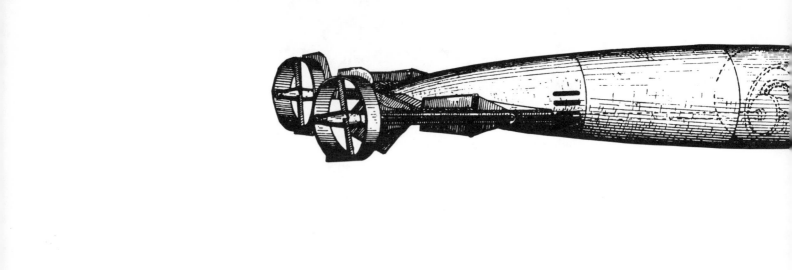

chapter 7
PRAYER

The most obvious means of spiritual growth, for believers of all faiths, is prayer. Note that the word used here is "prayer," not "prayers"—they may mean the same thing, but the second word often stands for a much more limited type of communication with one's God. Let's think of prayer, at least for the duration of this chapter, as a general sort of being in touch with God. It can be through actually stopping and talking to Him, it might be through an off-and-on awareness that He's with us, or it might be through a frequent sensing of His presence in the people, the natural world and the symbolic world around us.

Kids often feel self-conscious about praying in a classroom; some of the things that can be done to make this sticky scene more natural are described in *Experiments in Prayer,* which is the companion book to this volume and goes into much detail about how to help prayer happen. For the moment, let's just recall the good advice of experienced prayer leaders to work up to classroom praying gradually and to not attempt to pray until we have the complete attention of our students. Praying well—or even halfway decently—with a class is one of the hardest things religion teachers try to do, so we shouldn't get discouraged if it takes time and patience to get there. Regular prayer times help; perhaps every other or every third growth session could be a growing-through-prayer session.

This chapter starts with two experiments that give us very easy ways to pray at all times. It goes on with two more experiments that link our prayer to other people (people who are nice and people who are not so nice), and ends with a fancy experiment to music that may or may not be possible for you to try in a classroom, depending upon the amount of peace and quiet you have (Oh, for a sharp knife to take care of the intercom wires). Even if you don't have a good setting for this last musical prayer experiment, do try it at home on your own and see what happens. There are many other ways to pray, of course: an endless variety of memorized prayers and readings, prayers based on scripture, audio-visual-triggered prayers, pencil and paper activities that can lead to praying, meditations and fantasy trips and guided daydreams, many others, all described in detail in the book mentioned above. These are all good introductory methods

for getting prayer off the ground and for getting students interested in prayer, whereas the five experiments which follow teach prayer styles to practice and then live with for a lifetime.

If you're lucky enough to find yourself with a bunch of good pray-ers, any of the experiments in this book can be expanded to include a final "Would anyone like to thank God for what we've learned about Him and ourselves?" or "Let's take a moment to silently reflect on what we've just done and talk to God about it in our hearts." And some of the other experiments here are, as you may have noticed, also prayer experiments (e.g., Experiment No. 7, "Pain and Healing").

Well-loved Father Bernard Basset reminds us, rightly, that results in the prayer department depend on God's action, not ours. He says it's a "curious type of Pelagianism" to think we can do all our growing just by our own personal efforts (see *Let's Start Praying Again.* New York: Herder and Herder, 1972). Indeed, even the initiative to help ourselves grow is surely a response to His grace. As noted elsewhere, nothing in this book is meant to indicate that human development automatically equals spiritual growth, or that human potential exercises are the source of sanctification. But, on the other hand, we *can* lay foundations for God's work and open doors for Him so that He can "crown His own gifts." Not to use the knowledge we have of man's workings is yet another heresy, a modern sort of Quietism.

170

The Presence of God

EXPERIMENT NUMBER 22

BACKGROUND:

We all know about this ancient sort of praying. Nothing could be simpler to do, and no prayer could be more effective. Why, then, do so few of us do it? A good question, and perhaps the answer lies somewhere in the realm of our thinking that something is good only in proportion to its difficulty. What we're aiming at here is the experiential awareness of the presence of God, as well as the intellectual assent to that presence. We can't make it happen, but we can open ourselves up.

MATERIALS:

None.

CURRICULUM TIE-IN:

Prayer, God's presence.

"Praying—that is, communicating in some way with God—helps us to grow. There are lots of ways to pray. What are some that you know? . . .

(Only an unusual group will go beyond formal prayers.)

"Today, we're going to try a very simple sort of prayer together. In fact, it's probably the most simple and the easiest way to pray that there is. Before we begin, how about sharing some ideas on group prayer—what do you think we can do to help any praying we do in a classroom work out well? . . .

(Take it seriously; be still, etc.)

"That's good. If you'll sit comfortably now and try to tune out any distractions around you by closing your eyes or by concentrating on something on your desk in front of you, see if you can follow along with me for a minute.

"We've been taught that God is always with us. That means He's with each of us right now, here, in this room. See how still your mind and whole self can become. . . . Stop time right here. . . . Try to get in touch with Him. . . . See if you can almost soak in His presence the way a sponge soaks up water. . . .

(Pause for at least half a minute—or more?)

"That's the end of this simple prayer. Would anyone be willing to tell us how easy or difficult you found this? . . .

(Just a simple question, which may not be answered—no thumbscrews.)

"Where can a person do this kind of praying? . . .

(Anywhere.)

"And when can a person pray like this? . . .

(Any time, all times.)

"Do you think many people pray like this much of their lives? . . .

(Probably not.)

"If you like this kind of praying, which is called 'practicing the presence of God' or 'stilling the heart,' what could you do to help yourself remember to do it? . . .

(Remember the old cues? —passing a church, seeing a clock, walking up stairs. How about some visual reminder of God in a prominent spot that is a signal for this prayer?)

"If there was only one thing I could ask you to try to do in order to help your soul grow, this easy tuning in to God's presence would be that thing. People-watchers over the centuries tell us that this is the essential ingredient of spiritual growing, and that people who pray in this style seem to bubble over with deep joy, almost as though they had a very special secret inside them. Those of us who can learn to pray like this will never be alone again."

DATE TRIED: **TIME:**   **REPEAT?:**

RESULTS:

MORE IDEAS:

Because this experiment is about such a basic and essential ingredient of spiritual growth, if you get even a faint flicker of acceptance from your class you might want to try for a regular putting-ourselves-in-God's-presence time (perhaps to music). And, in the manner suggested by so many of the great spiritual masters of the past, this prayer could also preface any or all of the other growth experiments or classroom praying.

REFERENCES:

The Practice of the Presence of God, Brother Lawrence of the Resurrection (Mount Vernon, NY: Peter Pauper Press, 1974)

Many, many good books give background on being one with the Lord, but this is the 17-century classic, now reissued. It's a very brief collection of letters from and interviews with a discalced Carmelite kitchen brother of pre-revolutionary France. It could have been written yesterday, so immediate is the tone of Brother Lawrence's consciousness of "the divine indwelling."

Let's Start Praying Again, Bernard Basset, S.J. (New York: Herder and Herder, 1972)

A favorite author of our time sums up his 50 years of experience in prayer. He writes about work being prayer (or is it?), his special spot (as in Experiment No. 21), bodywork in prayer (as in Chapter 4), the use of the imagination in prayer and influences from the East. Much else. One of those "if you had to choose ten books for a year on a desert island" books.

Desert Call (quarterly magazine, published by the Spiritual Life Institute of America, Star Route One, Sedona, Arizona 86336. $4/yr.)

The journal of Father William McNamara's contemporary contemplative centers (Nada Ranch in Arizona and Nova Nada in Nova Scotia). The work of these centers is to foster, for all people, the contemplative spirit in our nutsy world. Many have loved Fr. McNamara's popular *The Art of Being Human,* and are finding even more help in his latest book, *The Human Adventure.*

A Seal upon the Heart

EXPERIMENT NUMBER 28

BACKGROUND:

This prayer/growth experiment is related to and just slightly more involved than the previous one. Students may want to weave both into their lives—or maybe just one will do. Its title comes from the beautiful line in the Song of Songs, "Put Me as a seal upon your heart." That's a great idea—but how do we do this? A lot has been written lately about the "Jesus Prayer" (which has Desert Father and Eastern Church roots); this experiment elaborates a little on the Jesus Prayer which, in its simplest form, is just the constant repetition of the Holy Name (put, as a seal, upon the heart). Note how the rosary is an evolution of this simpler form of prayer.

MATERIALS NEEDED:

None.

CURRICULUM TIE-IN:

Prayer, God's presence.

"In the Old Testament, God tells His people to 'put Me as a seal upon your heart.' That's a good thing to do and, today, I'd like to explore with you some ways to do it.

"Let's see if we can each choose some holy name or word or short phrase of a prayerful nature that we would like to 'engrave' upon our hearts. What are some possibilities? . . . Let's list them on the board—you might want to copy them for future reference. . . .

"We could start with the word 'God' or 'my God.' Then we could use the name 'Jesus' . . . or 'Jesus is Lord' . . . or 'Come, Lord Jesus.' Many people like these best because they have the name of God in them. What are some other words or phrases that use His name? . . .

"There's 'Come Holy Spirit,' or just the word 'Lord,' or 'God is love' or 'Lord, have mercy' . . . and there's 'Praise the Lord,' and 'Glory be to God.' Any others using His name? . . .

(Use the kids' ideas first, then go on to the suggestions here.)

"Well, what other possibilities are there? . . . How about some phrases from the bible or from the book we use in class that would make good seals upon our hearts? . . .

(Other possibilities: "peace," "I am with you," "I thirst," "Amen" or even "keep the faith.")

"Some people use words in foreign languages, like 'hosanna' or 'alleluia,' or even words from ancient root languages like Sanskrit. And how about song titles that would make good 'seals'? . . .

("My Sweet Lord," "Let It Be," "I Believe," many others.)

"What about short phrases from hymns or other pieces you've heard sung in church? . . . These could be musical seals. . . .

(Think ahead for possible answers from your parish musical life; ten syllables is about tops. How about short psalm antiphons, like "All the earth proclaim the Lord"?)

"OK, we have a good list now. Any other additions? . . . Now, will you each pick *one* of these words or phrases that seems to be right for you, one that you like best and that seems to slip onto whatever wavelength you're on these days. If it's a musical phrase, you can think of it to its tune. Or if you like, make up a tune for your words. . . .

(Are you old enough to remember when these used to be called ejaculations?)

"Do you all have your word or phrase chosen, something that will be a good seal for your heart? . . .

(It takes at least 30 seconds to get this, and a minute is better.)

"Fine. Now I'm going to suggest a few different things to do. Just follow the directions. First, just sit quietly where you are, doing nothing at all but allowing your special word or words to run through your mind calmly. See if you can begin to make them part of you, moving them from your head to your heart. Maybe they'll even fit with your breathing. . . .

(Again, a good pause.)

"All right. The next thing to do is this: Look at something on your desk and pick it up or fiddle with it, or take something from your pocket or purse and handle it, or tie your shoes over, all without talking. And at the same time, keep your word or words running through you. . . .

"Very good. Next step: Get up and move around the room, but don't talk to anyone else. See if you can find something to do in the room—look out the window, or write on the board, or pick up something from the floor, or straighten out the chairs and desks. And what do you think you'll try to do at the same time? . . .

"Now, please come back to your seats. . . .

"Finally, turn to the person next to you and just chat about some unimportant thing like the weather or what TV show you watched last night. If there are three or four of you that make a small group, chat together. All the time you're talking and listening, what else will you be doing? . . .

"Now, let's see what sort of results you had with this experiment. How many were pretty successful at thinking their word or words while just sitting quietly or while fooling around with something on the desk or in their pockets? . . .

"How many were able to keep things moving, mentally, while they were walking around the room? . . .

"How many had any success at keeping their word or phrase going while talking to someone else? . . .

"Well now, let's carry this over and see what it could mean to us in terms of spiritual growing. Would you call this a prayer? . . .

"Is it a prayer that anyone could pray? . . .

"Where could you do it? . . .

"When could you do it? . . .

176

(Right, continue going over your word or phrase.)

(Keeping your "seal" running through you.)

(Even the smallest success deserves praise—this isn't so easy to do at first crack.)

(Yes.)

(Yes.)

(Anywhere.)

(Any time.)

"How could you remember to do it? . . .

(Harder! How about posting one's word or words where they'd be seen regularly?)

"Why would you want to do this? . . .

(Constant prayer is a direct route to soul growth.)

"All we've done today is learn a technique, a way to pray. Those of you who like it will have to practice it on your own to make it work well. Would it help you remember to try this way of praying if I nagged you a little and reminded you about it the next few times we're together? . . .

(Make a note to do this.)

"Let me give you a suggestion to help you get started. Why not try to let your word or words run through your mind every time you hear a bell for the rest of this day? . . .

(Or whatever reminder seems appropriate to you.)

"Then, you can pray like this while you're going back and forth to school—even on a bus, surrounded by and talking to other people. You can do it in the shower, or while you're eating. What are some other times? . . .

(Upon waking and while falling asleep, the many times we have to wait, times when people are just yapping about nothing—but in math class, maybe we'd better not practice this mental prayer.)

"After a while, praying like this becomes second nature, and you can always have this prayer in the back of your mind while you're doing other things—just like you can drive a car or ride a bike and also think about something else. How many of you listen to music when you do your homework? . . .

"You don't have to think about the *meaning* of your word or words, although there may be times when you will want to; the prayer just becomes a background for whatever else you do.

"A final thought: You may find in time that some other word or phrase fits you better. The right choice has to do with the effects or vibrations in the body of different sounds. Experiment a little with different words and phrases, but then try to hit on one that seems best for you and stick with it. That way, the sound becomes part of you and has a chance to sink in and work its way into you.

"This is a way of praying always or praying without ceasing, which is the good advice of St. Paul."

(1 Thessalonians 5:17. Be sure to ask and nag about how students are doing with this technique. Practice leads to one-pointedness, single-mindedness.)

DATE TRIED: **TIME:**   **REPEAT?:**

RESULTS:

MORE IDEAS:

1) The physiological aspects of repetitive prayer are interesting. There are the effects of the repetition on the breathing rate, which in turn affects the heart beat, which in turn affects the oxygenation of the blood and the brain-wave patterns and the body vibrations, which in turn affect the whole physical, emotional and mental (thence, spiritual) functioning of the person. Most of the research on the effects of repetitive sounds on the body comes to us from yoga, the repeated sound being called a "mantra" (more correctly, a "mantram"). A good book tying together yoga and Christianity, with much material on both Eastern mantras and the Jesus Prayer, is *Yoga East and West* by Joann Sherwood and Robert Johnson (Belmont, MA: The Ashram, 1974).

2) Speaking of the East, many young Americans have been attracted to Eastern religions in recent years, seemingly finding in them what their Christian and Jewish teaching bypassed—the element of mystery, perhaps, or even that of rigid

discipline. (Converts to the Sikh branch of the Hindu faith, for instance, spend as much as two hours a morning in meditation. Imagine if any of their American parents had suggested something similar!)

Why not share with students some prayers from other religions of the world, looking for what is universal in all faiths. A Sikh (pronounced "seek") morning prayer, for instance, is

"I bow before the infinite God.

I bow before His transparent wisdom."

Students can hunt up other examples, the goal being to come full circle and find equally appealing/engaging/unique prayers from their own heritage. We head-centered Westerners have such a rich mystical tradition, but few of our students are ever exposed to it. Father Raimundo Panikkar is a transcultural theologian whose work points out meeting grounds between East and West. Look for his research in the heavier theological journals.

REFERENCES:

The Way of a Pilgrim, translated from the Russian by R. M. French (New York: The Seabury Press, 1965)

An anonymous 19th-century Russian tells his story, which includes his struggle to pray all the time. He arrives at the Jesus Prayer, and Jesus becomes the only reality in his life (no need to worry that we'll get *that* tuned out—if the idea should disturb anyone).

The Cloud of Unknowing, translated by Clifton Wolters (Baltimore, MD: Penguin Books, 1961)

Another anonymous classic from the past, this time the work of a 14th-century English parson. The theme is love, and the author suggests that we "dwell on a monosyllable"—in other words, a "seal" for our hearts. Most students are short on the historical roots of their faith, and dipping into writings from other times and places that are as timeless as these two (and the reference in the previous experiment) helps them gain a sense of the span of church history.

Prayer Ideas for Religion Teachers, Betsy Caprio (Notre Dame, IN: Ave Maria Press, 1974)

This cassette has both Experiments 22 and 23 on it, as if done in a typical religion classroom. Teachers can hear and practice them on themselves before trying them out in class. (Three other demonstrated prayers from *Experiments in Prayer* are also on the cassette.)

Shared Prayer

EXPERIMENT NUMBER 24

BACKGROUND:

Some of the best religion teachers have brought their students to the point where they easily have "shared prayer" or Quaker-type prayer sessions as a regular part of their classes. Others have attempted spontaneous all-pitch-in prayer sessions, only to back off when teacher turned out to be the only one pitching. Still other teachers struggle along with occasional shared prayer times, hoping that in spite of giggles and blank stares something good will happen. This one-on-one experiment is designed to help teachers who haven't tried shared prayer—or haven't been successful with it. Its options make it fairly easy and nonthreatening to students and with perseverance you *may* arrive at that flowing, uninhibited community prayer that is the ideal (or, maybe you won't—but it's worth a try).

MATERIALS:
None.

CURRICULUM TIE-IN:
Prayer, community, friendship, Christ in others.

"All through the bible we read of people coming together to pray. There seems to be a lot said about the special value of praying with others, as well as praying alone. Can you think of any particular examples from the bible of people coming together to pray? . . .

(Lots: Israelites in the wilderness with Moses, Jews in the synagogues and temples, the Last Supper.)

"Why do you think both the Old Testament and the New Testament, the Jewish and the Christian sacred writings, stress group prayer as well as praying by yourself? . . .

(Matthew 18:20)

"Off and on in this class we talk about prayer, and usually we mean praying alone. But, you probably remember that Jesus said: 'Where two or three are gathered together in my name, there am I in their midst.' Let's go on with that idea today and try some praying as a group.

(If they can't guess, you can surely tell 'em.)

"First, here's a question: What do you think are some of the problems in trying to get people in a class like ours to feel comfortable about praying together? Many teachers won't try anything in the classroom other than silent prayer or prayers everyone recites together. Why not? . . .

"Maybe we can overcome some of those problems if we start with a mini-person-to-person prayer instead of just expecting everyone to speak out and pray in front of the whole class. To begin with, I'd like to ask each of you who is willing to try this experiment to find a partner. If anyone doesn't want to try this, he or she can sit and observe and take down a few notes so I'll have some opinions on how our experiment worked. Will you find a prayer partner? . . .

(Usually it's neater to pair students off yourself, but here's one time when friends can work more effectively together. An unmatched person can be your partner.)

"OK. Now, with your partner, would you take a couple of minutes to explore your feelings about praying with other people? You might each ask yourself a couple of questions and share the answers:

(Before trying to pray together we talk about praying.)

1) What usually happens in a group that's supposed to be praying together—in church, or in the family? Do I find these are usually times when I communicate with God? . . .

2) Is my idea of group prayer more like winter snow or a summer breeze? . . . Why? . . .

(Either answer is right, of course. The point is to get everyone thinking about what prayer is like for himself/herself.)

"Next step: Now that you and your partner have talked, see if you can do one more thing together. You'll have to be serious for it to work. Can you think of some comfortable way to communicate with each other *without talking,* some way of saying to each other, 'yes, I understand what you told me and I feel that I know you a little better'? Before we do this, how about some suggestions on possible ways of communicating without speaking. Any ideas? . . .

(Look at each other; shake hands; hold hands; write notes.)

"That's a hard question. One other thing you might do is pick up something belonging to the other person and hold on to it. Try to get the feel of being its owner. Or, you might just close your eyes and try to imagine that you're inside your partner's skin. What does it feel like to be there? . . . These are two other, slightly different, ways of communicating. Choose your way and then do it. I'll give you about one minute. . . .

"Now, we've talked and we've communicated without speaking. Here's a prayer step. As Christians, we believe that Jesus lives in each of us—and that includes our partners. Can you, sitting very quietly with your partner, tune in to the presence of Jesus in that person? . . . This will have to be done in a very mysterious way, but see if you can pick up His presence on your antennae. Let's take about half a minute to try to do this. . . .

(Indwelling references, should you want them: 1 Corinthians 3:16, John 17:21-23.)

"Let's add another prayer step. Would you each tell your partner of one person or group of people you are concerned about? . . .

"Now, can we each quietly pray for our partner's person (or persons)? . . . Just make up a prayer inside yourself. . . .

(Half a minute's fine.)

"Now, let's see what we can make of this experiment. Will anyone tell us how successful he or she was in sensing the presence of God in a partner? . . .

(Maybe no one will.)

"When we come in touch with God anywhere—when we're alone, or enjoying the outdoors, or with another person—is that prayer? . . .

(Don't be surprised if many don't think of this as praying.)

"Observers, can you give us some feedback on what you saw here? . . . Did you see or feel anything prayerful happening? . . .

(Maybe not; be prepared for multi-shrugs.)

"This experiment can lead to a couple of things for our lives. One might be a clue it gives us on how to improve our praying. Any ideas? . . .

(E.g., praying with others may help us pray better because they carry the Lord in them.)

"Another thing we can learn from what we did today is that there might be a new way we could look at some of the people we live with or see a lot. If each of us went around able to find Christ in our friends and parents and brothers and sisters (and, naturally, our teachers), couldn't that make a big difference in our lives? . . .

"Where could you practice looking at people like this and trying to come in touch with God in them? . . .

(Anywhere: at the dinner table, when shopping, in the classroom.)

"Would the other people have to know that you were doing this? . . .  *(No.)*

"Today we've just made a start on praying with other people. It would be nice if we could get to the point where we could have a real shared prayer session where we all join in. What are some of the ingredients we could include in that sort of prayer time? . . .

(Music, readings from scripture and other sources, spontaneous prayer—especially for special intentions, stories about God in our lives, etc.)

"Do you think we're ready for a shared prayer time like that? . . .

(If so, see below; if not, why not try this experiment again with the same partners?)

DATE TRIED: **TIME:**   **REPEAT?:**

RESULTS:

MORE IDEAS:

1) As suggested in the experiment, a possible goal might be a regular shared prayer time, and the younger the students' ages, the better. Teachers who arrive at this unanimously endorse the value of such sessions to their students. Along with the ingredients mentioned above can go formal prayers, comments on the readings, periods of silence and trappings like incense, candles and even "prayer rugs" (compliments of the local carpet company?). Chairs close together help.

You can build on the theme of your lesson, and start slowly. (Five minutes is ample.) Beginners may need a reminder that shared prayer time isn't the time for just conversation or chatting with each other, but for talking to the Lord. They may (undoubtedly will) need time to become able to speak out and pray without embarrassment, depending upon their age and your particular church tradition. Have a few leads ready, such as, "Let's stop and think about what's

keeping us from loving and growing. Maybe you'll want to pray about it to yourself and ask the Lord for His help," or think of some current news story or school situation and build on it.

You may be the only one praying at first—Bonnie may be giggling and Clyde may be muttering "how queer," but hang in. Always be sure students feel free to sit out. Overlook a lot. Most of all, ask for students' intentions in various categories (those who are sick, those who live in oppressed countries, etc.). Someday someone is going to have a real need and may bring it to the prayer session, and things may very well jell from that point on. Be patient. Good luck!

2) If you have any organized prayer groups in your community, be sure to visit them for ideas and to help yourself be completely comfortable with spontaneous prayer. Perhaps students will do the same. Some of these may be charismatic prayer groups; some may be old garden variety prayer groups; all will be worth checking out. If students visit, ask them which features of the group's approach would work or would not work with your own class. Why? Why not?

REFERENCES:

I and Thou, Martin Buber (New York: Scribner's, 1970)

A third reference to this famous description of encounters with God. One of the "dialogic spheres" is the sphere of communion with another—and with God in the other. The other person is, Buber writes, "seamless; he is You and fills the firmament."

Friendship in the Lord, Paul Hinnebusch, O.P. (Notre Dame, IN: Ave Maria Press, 1973)

The story of a cluster of friends, whose friendship helped them grow closer to God as they found Him in one another. The logical next step to our simple introduction.

The Workbook of Living Prayer, Maxie Dunnam (Nashville: The Upper Room, 1974)

A real find for prayer leaders, teachers and anyone working on better praying. Exercises and readings for each day of six weeks and dozens of ideas for small group get-togethers at the end of each week that focus on each member's growth and community prayer. This will really help. (Write to The Upper Room at 1908 Grand Avenue, Nashville, TN 37203.)

Crabby People

EXPERIMENT NUMBER 25

BACKGROUND:

Prayer and crises go together. We can train ourselves to meet crises with prayer (and some degree of calm), and come through in one piece. Here's an experiment to help us cope with one of life's very real crises: being on the receiving end of verbal abuse. This is the flip side of Experiment No. 7, "Pain and Healing," which dealt with the "victim" and his damage. Here we have some aids to help keep the damage from being so great in the first place.

One of the chief sources of psychological harm (and therefore of stunted emotional and spiritual growth) is abuse, mainly verbal but sometimes physical, we receive from others. Children, especially, are often on the receiving end of others' frustrations. Please don't think that

a) this is too rare to bother with (it's not) or

b) this experiment undermines the authority of any parent or teacher who is using kids as his or her dumping ground. (They undermine themselves; what we have here is a survival technique for the "dumpee.")

MATERIALS:

None, unless you want students to copy down the steps.

CURRICULUM TIE-IN:

Prayer, crises, Jesus, forgiveness.

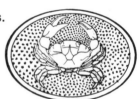

"A lot of people who rarely pray still find themselves praying when there's trouble or pain in their lives, don't they? Did you ever find yourself doing that? . . .

"Prayer and crisis times go hand in hand. If we prepare ourselves for crises before they happen and figure out in advance how the prayer part fits in, we find we can handle the bad times better when they come along. What sort of crises are you prepared to handle right now because you've practiced what to do in advance, with or without prayer as an aid? . . .

(Home and school fire drills will have prepared many people for fires; first-aid and lifesaving courses for other sorts of emergencies; kung fu and judo classes for still another sort of crisis.)

"Today, let's talk about one special sort of crisis time, one that almost everyone bumps into sooner or later. It's those times when our lives are made unhappy by mean things other people say. Can you give us some examples of 'mouth attacks' you've known? (One caution: no names or clues as to who the people you're copying might be. . .)

(As someone starts to describe a situation, why not have him act it out, using the person next to him as victim?)

"Now, who'd like to come up front and act out a little longer situation, one involving a really crabby person who's telling someone else off in full force? . . . What would be a good example to act out? . . .

(Or, if no ideas: a girl ripping her boyfriend to shreds, a nasty big brother bullying a younger one, a parent off on a verbal bender.)

"Let's see how it sounds. . . .

(Sometimes kids have trouble ending spontaneous role playing like this. Don't be afraid to step in with "Thanks—that was fine.")

"Now, maybe most of you have no one in your life right now—or never did—who makes you unhappy by the things he or she says. That's great! But many of us do have this problem and if you don't have it now, you may have it later. What I'd like to do today is work out with you some steps we can all remember the next time we're on the receiving end of a blast or a verbal beating or any other such 'sins of the mouth.'

(Is it true that "Words can never hurt me"?)

"Let's list some steps. I guess we have to start with: 1) Is there any truth in what the person is saying?

(Mothers who flip their bonnets at messy bedrooms or food under couch cushions; fathers raging over bashed fenders; teachers exploding when classes pass the patience point.)

"This is really important, isn't it? What are some examples of people who are blasting away with good reason? . . .

"Sometimes what we call 'verbal abuse' is just the result of our own actions, isn't it? Have you any suggestions about what we can do in such cases to remove the unpleasant words from our lives? . . .

(Reform! Apologize! Shape up!)

"So, step one involves a judgment about whether or not our 'abuser' is correct. Sometimes we learn a lot about ourselves this way. Next step: 2) If we decide that another person's words are *not* fair—or, if they're much stronger than we deserve—we have a different situation. Why do you think people give others the sort of grief we acted out when there's not much reason to do so? . . .

(The kids know as well as we do: the scapegoat needs of others which are almost never created by the victim.)

"Step two, then, has to do with recognizing the fact that the problem may lie with the other person and not with ourselves.

(Students may have some good steps of their own to insert.)

"Now, what can we do next? . . . Well, Christians usually turn to Jesus as their model of how to act. Did He ever have people hurt Him with things they said? . . . Who? . . .

(Establishment types who ridiculed both His teaching and His teaching methods, mockers— especially during the Passion, Peter in denying Him, Judas in lying.)

"Do you think it really hurt Him when these things happened, the way we would feel hurt by such treatment? . . . Or, because He was God, did these things just roll off Him? . . .

(An important point: the first answer is correct, of course, and the second— which will be chosen by some—has all sorts of unfortunate implications about the humanity of Jesus and, at its extremity, is the old heresy of Docetism.)

"How did Jesus handle the abuse dished out to Him? . . .

(He pitied, forgave and prayed for the abusers. He turned the other cheek and then tried to help them.)

"And that's very, very hard to do, isn't it? . . .

"Now, on to step three:
3) Try to picture yourself in some situation where you're being hurt by another's words. Any example will do—a real one or an imaginary one. . . . Try to pick up your feelings as they would be in real life. . . . And now, try to imagine yourself acting as Jesus acted in such situations. Can you picture yourself feeling sorry for the other person and forgiving him even as he's yapping away, and then, finally, praying a healing prayer for him? . . .

"This is so hard to do, isn't it? Let's add one more step to our list of suggestions that may make it easier:
4) Sometimes it helps to *picture* ideas, to try to put things we can't see into some sort of shape we can see. That way we can get a handle on them.

"Let me stop here and tell you a story. Did anyone ever read the old fairy tale *Diamonds and Toads*? . . .

"It's about two sisters who are enchanted by a good witch. One is a sweet sister who is kind and gentle, and whenever she speaks diamonds and other jewels fall from her mouth. Now the other sister is mean, and guess what happens to her when she opens her mouth? . . .

"Now, back to step four, combining it with step three. If you saw yourself being yelled at or put down by someone else, what could you add to your mental picture? . . .

(Any mini- or maxistruggles of your own that you could share here?)

(This is a good place to stop and share reactions.)

(A tale found in the folklore of more than 20 widespread peoples.)

(Yes, toads and snakes and other creatures fall out. Very inconvenient, unless you happen to be a builder of terrariums.)

(Assorted amphibia and reptilia coming from the mouthy person's mouth.)

"Does that make the person who's saying the words seem different? . . . Does it make it clear that it's the other person and not you who has the problem? . . . Can you feel at all sorry for him or for her? . . .

(Crabbiness: a symptom of unenlightenment and "non-evolvement" spiritually. Sympathy and help called for.)

"Once you feel sorry for the other person, can you find it in your heart to forgive him for his words? . . . Can you pray for him to be healed of his crabbiness? . . .

(Note where the attention has been refocused. It's no longer on "poor little me," the victim who has the poor choice of either striking back or curling up with self-pity and/or self-hatred. The attention is now on the attacker; there's a measure of detachment.)

"Let's act out our original scene again, with the same actors. This time, Victim, will you please try to use the mental picture of the miserable words turning into toads and froggies and so forth. . . .

(Run through skit as before.)

"Victim, will you tell us if you were able to imagine the animal life? . . . Did it make a difference in the way you were affected by the words? . . . What do the rest of you think? . . .

(Fairy tales often give us leads—we tried the kiss-a-frog approach.)
(Hear theirs first.)

"Now, maybe some other mental picture would suit you better than having a bunch of creeping or hopping things dropping out of your speaker's mouth. That is sort of messy. What other ideas could we use? . . . Can you make up some other mental pictures? . . .

"Well, you might picture yourself as having word-proof skin, like Superman has bullet-proof skin. Then, words would bounce right off you. See them there all over the floor? . . . Or maybe you have word-proof feathers like a duck has waterproof feathers, in which case words would roll off instead of bounce. . . .

"Here's another picture to try: People who hurt others unjustly—whether with their mouths or any other way—are usually not very happy people inside, even when they think they are. Maybe you could picture them wearing T-shirts that say I AM UNHAPPY or I HAVE A PROBLEM. How would that work for you? . . .

"Well, we've listed four steps to use when we get into situations of verbal attack. Let's go over them again:
1) Decide whether or not the attack is justified and, if it is, do something about it.
2) If the attack is not justified, recognize the fact that the other person may have a problem.
3) See if you can imitate Jesus by forgiving this person and praying for him or her.
4) If that's impossible, add a mental picture to the situation that helps you view things more clearly.

"Let's add one more:
5) Ask yourself, 'What can I do to help this person be happier and more settled, so that his unhappiness won't overflow onto other people?'

"Maybe that's asking too much. Remember though, Jesus said, 'My power is strongest when you are weak.'

"I hope you don't have to put these steps into practice very often, but if you run through them now and again when you're *not* on the firing line then you'll have a crisis technique ready in case of emergency (just as we practice in fire drills)—and, maybe, save yourself a lot of pain.

"Can you make up other crisis techniques for different sorts of troublesome times? What other crises do we meet in life that tend to throw us? . . .

"For each, you could figure out some way to handle it that involved evaluation, the example of Our Lord, prayer and, if necessary, the mental picture and/or a physical practice.

"Finally, just one more thing. When you speak, what comes out of your mouth? . . . Is it diamonds. . . . Or is it toads? . . ."

(Matthew 5:44 tells us to pray for those who persecute us; the Lord's Prayer that we be forgiven as we forgive.)

(Are the causes of crabbiness identifiable?— health, aches, pains, lack of sleep? overwork or pressure? Is the crabby one another's scapegoat? Can he be helped? Often, no.)

(2 Corinthians 12:9.)

(Getting angry, being so tired we can't see straight, meeting deadlines, etc.)

(Oh moment of truth, what if they asked us the same question?!)

DATE TRIED: **TIME:**   **REPEAT?:**

RESULTS:

MORE IDEAS:

1) How about a detailed list of the ways we do damage with our mouths, creating problems like the ones acted out in this experiment? Most of us never realize all the ways in which the gift of speech can be misused or the reconciliation missed out on because of our words. You could draw a big pair of lips on the board and have the following words coming out of them. (If you can, make the words look froggy or snaky, or toady. . .):

criticizing/nagging/correcting/fault-finding/putting down/blaming/accusing/lecturing/analyzing/tongue-lashing/griping/complaining/whining/grumbling/muttering/arguing/quibbling/mocking /making fun of/picking on/name-calling/bullying/ridiculing/teasing/gossiping/detraction/slander/insinuations/telling tales/lying/betraying confidences/twisting others' words/butting in/minding others' business/embarrassing/rudeness/sharp words/sarcasm/patronizing/language that offends (varies from place to place!)/shrieking/howling/yelling (when inappropriate) and silence . . . in some situations. (Looks a lot like the old checklists we used to use, doesn't it? See the similar lists in the book of Sirach [Ecclesiasticus.])

2) The end of the experiment suggests making up "crisis techniques" for the differing troublesome times in our lives. Why not work this out in more detail with students, especially if they've shown an interest in the coping-with-crabby-people ideas? Can you all draw a grid, with spaces across the top to list whatever emotional and physical mini-crises each has to deal with most regularly, and spaces down the side for:

● the prayer style that works best in the situation. (E.g., if one such mini-crisis is "I lose my temper," a possible prayer at those times would be "Pray to be calm" and another would be "Pray to be able to put myself in the other person's shoes." Which works best would vary from student to student.)

● some saying or bible verse that is a good reminder in the situation. (E.g., for getting angry, again, how about "Anyone who is angry with his brother will answer for it" (Matthew 5:22), or something like "You can tell how big a person is

191

by the things that make him angry.'')

● a mental picture that helps dissolve the mini-crisis. (E.g., for anger, imagine what one's face looks like when in a rage.)

● some physical practice that seems to help also. (E.g., for almost anything, one of the simplest is pausing to take a few deep and slow breaths.)

These ideas would have to be worked over by each student on his own, until the best combinations clicked into place. By thinking about mini-crises before they happen, however, we really do handle them better in reality. Prayer is a very real factor in this handling.

REFERENCES:

You Are Not the Target, Laura A. Huxley (New York: Farrar, Straus and Co., 1968)
    Many mini-crisis techniques for coping with life's little (and big) annoyances are in this book by Aldous Huxley's widow. The title exercise gives a good way to handle crabby people, by converting the energy aroused by them to positive use. Down to earth.

What Do You Say After You Say Hello? Eric Berne (New York: Grove Press, 1972)

    A sequel to the author's best-selling *Games People Play,* which is the source of the T-shirt idea above. Controversial, but fun to read. (See reference in Experiment No. 29.)

Heavenly Music

EXPERIMENT NUMBER 20

BACKGROUND:

Music listening can facilitate spiritual encounters, if we provide settings and the freedom to allow students to really get into the music. This experiment is based directly on the pioneering work on music and human consciousness being done by the Institute for Consciousness and Music in Baltimore. If there's any possibility of trying this prayer approach in some spot where students can really be comfortable, by all means grab it. At best, perhaps the office can silence an ever-squawking intercom long enough for you to play the music. If Mr. X in the next room is a screamer-teacher or has 'em rolling in the aisles with laughter, maybe you could ask him for a small chunk of quiet time.

MATERIALS:

Pencil and paper, tape or record of musical selection. (See suggestions below.)

CURRICULUM TIE-IN:

Prayer.

"We're going to experiment with something a little different today. I'm going to ask you to take a musical trip, and I have absolutely no idea where it will lead. This is really just a trial run for a way of praying that you might want to practice on your own at home, where you have more privacy and quiet. Today you can test whether or not you might like to explore it further. Are there any of you who have ever used music as a means to help you pray? . . .

"Let me describe the steps of this approach to praying, and then we'll do it. We're going to listen to a piece of music, music that probably isn't too familiar to you, and have the intention of letting that music somehow unite us with God or with the divine or with the Spirit. (There are many ways we could say this, and just what happens or how we express it isn't really the point.)

"In order to help us make this connection between ourselves and God, using the music to smooth the way, it helps if we plant an idea—any spiritual thought—in our minds before we begin listening. Any suggestion on some good 'seed' ideas? . . .

(The best we can do, sometimes, is teach a technique, hoping students will make it theirs on their own time.)
(Students may have discovered this approach on their own—or invented others.)

(See what the kids come up with; then you might add the following:)

193

"One might be the idea that God is here with each of us right now. Another might be the image of God calling each of us to Him—remember the story of Jesus walking on the water and saying 'Come'? Choose any such idea you like. . . .

"Perhaps it will help if you picture the thought you choose. How about seeing yourself 'putting your hand in the hand,' etc. . . .

"Now, I realize that this isn't a very easy place to get completely relaxed in, but will you get as loose as you can? See how comfortable you can get. If you don't mind sitting in a corner on the floor, go right ahead! Remember, if you were doing this on your own, you'd find some really relaxing spot. . . .

"Are you pretty well settled? . . . OK, now let's add one other step: Think about your breathing for a minute. Can you slow it down just the slightest bit? . . . See if you can . . . and close your eyes if you like. . . .

"Now, recall what 'seed' idea you want to plant inside yourself during this experiment. I'll give you a few more seconds to do that . . . and perhaps you want to add a picture to go with your thought. . . .

"Now, I'll turn on the music. It will last about _____ minutes. See if you can just let yourself flow with it. Don't try to concentrate on the idea you planted—it's there. Let the music help the seed grow in its own way. If you let the sound wash over you and take you along with it, that's all that's necessary. . . .

"And now the music is over. Try to come back to our room slowly, letting yourself linger a bit with whatever might have been happening, and then we'll see how things went. . . .

"We can talk about this if you like. . . .

(Matthew 14:29.)

(If this experiment already seems too heavy for your setting, see Experiments in Prayer for a simpler version, a "Pick-a-Thought Prayer.")

("Seeding the mind" is an ancient, transcultural meditative technique.)

(Don't give the name of the piece, especially if it has some suggestive title, like "The Holy City.")
(Start tape or record. You might keep an eye on the door to ward off interruptions.)

(Did anyone fall asleep? Wake him gently!)
(Don't rush.)

(What sort of reaction does this bring?)

194

"Or, perhaps it would be better to write down a few sentences about anything that may have taken place inside of you. Would you rather do that? . . .

"I really encourage you to try this again on your own, choosing whatever sort of music seems to work for you. Researchers find that music you can sing along to and fill in words for isn't as effective as wordless music. You'll note that you didn't really *listen* to the music I played, as you would if you were trying to understand how the composer put it together; the music was more of a catalyst.

"A whole book has been written on experiments like this with music, and people have reported with astonishment on how deeply they could go inside themselves and, also, of the beautiful experiences of God they've had."

(One way or another, try to debrief your students so they can think about all of this enough to decide whether or not to keep experimenting on their own.)

(Perhaps you'll want to mention that music deliberately listened to with a seed idea, for the purpose of prayer, is quite a different thing from just flicking on the radio and relaxing, as so many of us do.)

(See below.)

DATE TRIED: **TIME:**   **REPEAT?:**

RESULTS:

MORE IDEAS:

Experiment Number 23 in this book features the use of sound, and suggests another sort of musical praying; Experiment Number 17 deals specifically with music making; Experiment Number 14, with sacred music. These three experiments plus this one on "Heavenly Music" comprise a quartet of techniques which could become a whole spiritual road map for anyone who is a music lover. Have you one student, or more, who would volunteer to spend some extra time on these four ways of

growth? That person could report back to the entire class at regular intervals as proof that we can, indeed, help ourselves grow if we are given the skills and use them.

SOME MUSICAL SUGGESTIONS

Here's a list of musical selections which the author has found most helpful as "prayer starters," both on her own and with students. You'll see that it consists of short instrumental classical selections that are mostly slow in tempo, with a bitter-sweet and often a minor or modal flavor. Folk-type themes run through this listing, half of which was composed during the 20th century. (The selections are arranged in chronological order.) Note the near-absence of religious music, even of organ music. Using music of that sort seems somewhat like stacking the deck in an introduction to musical praying. ("Doesn't that just make you feel like you're in church? . . .")

This is a rather lengthy list, much of which is chosen from the standard repertory in hopes that readers will be able to put their hands on several of the works mentioned; if not, look up other works by these composers, and symphonies and concerti of the Classical and Romantic periods (1700's and 1800's) in general. (Experiment with the slow movements of these—often the second movement—usually labeled "andante" or "adagio" or "largo.")

COMPOSER	SELECTION	APPROXIMATE TIME
Pachelbel	*Canon in D Major*	7 minutes
Vivaldi	*Concerto in D Major for Lute,* second movement	2½ minutes
Vivaldi	"The Spring" from *The Four Seasons,* largo	3 minutes
J. S. Bach	"Air on a G String" from *Suite No. 3 in D Major*	4 minutes
Mozart	*Concerto for Flute and Harp,* second movement	9 minutes
Mozart	*Concerto #21 for Piano,* second movement	7½ minutes
Beethoven	*Symphony #6,* second movement	first 4½ minutes
Beethoven	*Concerto #5 for Piano,* second movement	7½ minutes
Mendelssohn	*A Midsummer Night's Dream,* "Nocturne"	6 minutes
Mendelssohn	*Symphony #3,* third movement	7½ minutes

Liszt	*Concert Etude #3 in D-flat* (for piano)	6 minutes
Berlioz	*L'Enfance du Christ:* Overture to Part II ("The Flight Into Egypt")	5 minutes
	Trio for Two Flutes and Harp (last scene, midpoint)	7 minutes
Brahms	*Concerto for Violin,* second movement	9 minutes
Brahms	*Symphony #2,* second movement	9 minutes
Brahms	*Quintet for Clarinet and Strings,* third movement	5½ minutes
Richard Strauss	*Ein Heldenleben (A Hero's Life)* Part III: "The Hero's Helpmate" Part VI: "The Hero Escapes From the World"	7 minutes 9 minutes
Debussy	"Nuages" ("Clouds") from *Nocturnes,* orchestral version	7 minutes
Ravel	*Pavane for a Dead Princess,* orchestral version	6 minutes
Ravel	*String Quartet in F Major,* first movement	8 minutes
Ravel	"Pavane of the Sleeping Beauty" and "Hop O' My Thumb" from *Ma Mere L'Oye (Mother Goose)*	5 minutes
Mahler	*Symphony #5,* fourth movement	9 minutes
Sibelius	*Concerto for Violin,* second movement	8 minutes
Sibelius	*Symphony #5,* second movement	10 minutes
Vaughn Williams	*Fantasia on a Theme by Thomas Tallis*	first 4 minutes
Vaughn Williams	*A London Symphony,* second movement	9 minutes
Holst	"Neptune" from *The Planets*	8 minutes
Respighi	"The Dove" from *The Birds*	5 minutes
Respighi	"Campanae Parisienses and Aria" from *Ancient Airs and Dances, Suite #2*	7 minutes
Villa-Lobos	"Prelude" ("Modinha") from *Bachianas Brasileiras #1*	7½ minutes
Prokofiev	*Romeo and Juliet,* pas de deux (beginning of Act III)	6 minutes

Prokofiev	*Cinderella,* pas de deux (near end of Act II) (or, in the Stokowski concert suite version, "Cinderella and the Prince" and "Apotheosis-Finale")	4½ minutes
Poulenc	*Aubade,* conclusion	4 minutes
Hovhaness	*The Holy City*	8½ minutes
Hovhaness	*Mysterious Mountain,* first movement	7 minutes

Finally, here are five selections which are quite a bit longer than those above, and therefore less suitable for a classroom. They are, however, among the most magical of works and so usable for the sort of musical tripping we've been describing that you may want to try them on your own. None of these pieces can be chopped up without doing violence to its flowing musical shape. Written by masters of "the long line," they really should be used whole.

Brahms	*Concerto #2 for Piano,* third movement	13 minutes
Mahler	*Symphony #3,* sixth movement	22 minutes
Mahler	*Symphony #6,* third movement	14 minutes
Mahler	*Symphony #9,* fourth movement	22 minutes
Sibelius	*Symphony #7* (all of it)	20 minutes

You may find that some other style of music appeals to you more than the somewhat dreamy, lyrical pieces listed above. By all means, experiment until you find the type of music which works best for you and your students—note, that's not necessarily what you *like* best, but what *works* best as a facilitator of prayer. Here are some other categories:

- Plainchant
  (not because it's churchy, but because it moves us)
- Classical:

  bubbly instrumental (typical Mozart, Rossini, etc.)

dramatic instrumental (typical Beethoven, Schubert, etc.)
super-shlurp instrumental (typical Wagner, Tchaikovsky and the other Slavic composers)
atonal instrumental (Schoenberg, Ives, others)
electronic music
vocal (cantatas, Masses, oratorios, choral symphonies, songs)

● Ethnic:
   instrumental (native American Indian, east Indian ragas, etc., Japanese koto and bamboo flute music, Appalachian fiddle tunes, African, etc.)
   vocal (folk songs from all over the world—choose languages which can't be understood)

● Pop:
   instrumental jazz (try Chick Corea, Miles Davis)
   instrumental rock/folk rock (try Moody Blues)
   "mood music" (i.e., Mantovani et al. A caution: If listeners can fill in the words of a song mentally, they will probably do so—defeating the purpose of this experiment. So, if using this sort of music, pick *unfamiliar* pieces)

● Not very useful:
   golden oldies, hum/sing-along favorites, including some classical pieces like *The Nutcracker Suite,* top ten tunes and all-time banjo hits from Nashville (or anywhere else) that make toes tap and feet dance

REFERENCES:

(First four references below are available from the Institute for Consciousness and Music, Room 104, 31 Allegheny Avenue, Towson, MD 21204, along with tapes of music for different sorts of listening, such as Death/Rebirth.)

Music and Your Mind: Listening With a New Consciousness, Helen L. Bonny and Louis M. Savary, S.J. (New York: Harper and Row, 1973)

Methods for using music to open doors to inner space for "pilgrims of the mind," both in groups and alone. An exciting book, with excellent background material on consciousness research and two chapters on music and religious experience, including ten experiments with seed ideas and suggested music. Experiments are in more detail than the one in this book.

Creativity in Children, Louis M. Savary, S.J. (Baltimore: ICM Books, 1974)

Father Savary's expertise includes understanding of the very young. Any teacher or parent could use these musical ideas—and the background matter—with joyful results.

Opening the Bible, Volume 1 (Baltimore, ICM Books, 1975)

Music and imagination experiences based on the stories of the books of Genesis and Exodus, on a record for adults and children. Similar to the *Creative Listening* records described below.

Creative Listening: Music and Imagination Experiences for Children (Baltimore: ICM Books, 1973)

Records, two of them, with fantasy trips narrated by Father Savary and appropriate musical selections to help young people take the trip. A Bach Cantata, for instance, serves as a vehicle for "Spacemen's Message." No religious trips, in the strict sense of the word "religious," but models for teachers of all subjects. Make up your own.

Psychosynthesis, Roberto Assagioli. (See Experiment No. 28.)

Chapter VII treats music listening as a negative and positive factor in our lives. The late Dr. Assagioli, primarily interested in music therapy, gives historic examples of the therapeutic and healing uses of music.

chapter 8
STORIES AND SYMBOLS

Stories and symbols, you'd agree, go hand in hand with the language of all world religions, even though most of our students may not be up on this aspect of their religious heritage. From primitive explanations of the universe's turnings—remember the sun supposedly rising and setting because the god Apollo rode his chariot across the sky?—to Jesus' very special sort of tales, to the sophisticated riddles of Zen Buddhism and the stories of the Moslem Sufis, the world's religions have always made use of story and symbol.

In this chapter we have a collection of ideas for reintroducing young people to the vocabulary of story and symbol for the purpose of spiritual growth. Some of the stories and symbols are from the traditional heritage of Christianity (believers of other faiths can substitute from their own lore) and some are what we would call psychological symbols common to all people in all times and places. All have as their purpose helping us get in touch with our "insides": that which makes us one with humans of cultures past and present. Erich Fromm calls symbolic language the one universal language man has ever had. He would like to see the language of symbols taught in schools like any other foreign language. (See *The Forgotten Language: An Introduction to the Understanding of Dreams, Fairytales and Myths.* New York: Holt, Rinehart and Winston, 1951.)

These last five experiments need a little more time to do with a class—some are in parts which can be spread over more than one session—and they also need time for the symbolic language to sink in. It's a slower way of speaking and its pace should be unhurried. Most teachers will probably use only one or two from this group of experiments because of their length and because of the need in most religion classes to give maximum time (of which there's never enough) to topics more easily seen as "religious." Indeed, their greatest value may very well be to the teacher who is working on his or her own spiritual growing at home. Several other experiments in this book have symbolic angles. (See Nos. 3, 10, 11, 15, 16, 17 and 20.) A final note collecting the sometimes-confusing suggestions for using stories and symbols for growth is to be found after the last experiment.

A couple of cautions apply to each experiment in this book, but particularly to the experiments in this chapter. The first is the necessity for the teacher working

with this material to bend over backwards to avoid manipulating students into coming up with "easy answers." It's so tempting to say something like ". . . OK kids, here are these neat little symbols, and you can see—of course—that they stand for this and that. Now you each have 60 seconds to apply these symbols and what they stand for to *your life* and tell us What You Have Learned About the Real You. Ready? Go. . . ." This quickie introspection technique isn't uncommon, unfortunately, and is a 180° distortion of the ideas of learning what your soul is like and of trying to help yourself grow spiritually. The facile approach may get by in the do-it-yourself psychology column of the Sunday supplement, but used in our context it certainly breeds contempt among our students. Even the littlest ones know that the shallow answers evoked in this way really haven't much to do with their growing and have a lot to do with keeping a techniquey, method-happy teacher off their backs. The experimenters should never feel that they're just being put through their paces or being asked to jump through our (ever-so-helpful) hoops.

Another tone to avoid is the equally foolish Searching-For-Deep-Meanings approach! Sure, the kids are important and beautiful and when you stop and think about the implications of what it means to teach religion/help nourish souls, yes, that can be very heavy. But the students we have that lovely feel for think of themselves as "just kids," and any attempts to make a continuing soap opera out of the stuff of their lives won't set too well with them. Working with symbols can lend itself to that abuse.

We might also note here that teachers, not unreasonably, tend to like tidily packaged lessons with beginnings, middles and ends—and effects that can be tested and measured. The whole point, however, of working with symbolic ideas (and all the spiritual growth techniques, for that matter) is to plant seeds that may need months and years to take root. Then, they may or may not sprout. Much, much later they may even bear fruit—but we won't be around to see or taste or evaluate it, and that's OK too. Can we be satisfied with just being sowers and planters rather than harvesters and consumers and judges? With the experiments in this chapter, we must be.

With these cautions we find ourselves right back to the touchstone of what it means to help someone else grow and be: awe and respect at the wonder each person is (even on those days when classes aren't so wonder-full). This respect keeps our role as the chief experimenter a suggestive, tentative and thoughtful one rather than that of

dictator

or answer man

or animal trainer

or puppet master.

Sacred Symbols

EXPERIMENT NUMBER 27

BACKGROUND:

The logical place to start, if we're thinking about symbols, is with the many traditional symbols of Christianity. Not too long ago, these were part of the sight vocabulary of all Christians—today's students are fortunate if they can identify a dozen symbols of their religious heritage. We can keep this language alive. Here's one way, an art project.

MATERIALS:

Slips of paper, one for each symbol you want to cover. (Can you do most of those in the first section of the list at the end of this experiment?) Each paper should have two words on it: the symbol and what it stands for. Unlined paper for drawing; if possible, reference books on Christian symbols.

CURRICULUM TIE-IN:

The Trinity, saints, the Church, sacraments, symbolism.

PART I:

"Our growth experiment today is wrapped around the many old and beautiful Christian symbols which have come down to us since the beginning of the Church. What religious symbols can you think of off-hand? . . .

(Hope springs eternal—surely you'll get one answer.)

"We should make a distinction between a sign and a symbol. What is the difference? . . .

(One way of saying it: A sign copies the way something looks or gives us a direction; a symbol stands in place of something else.)

"In religious art, we make another distinction if we want to be very precise. Some things we call symbols are more properly called 'attributes' or 'emblems'—they go with certain saints, for instance, rather than stand for them. Can you think of the attribute or emblem of any saint you know? . . . Think of saints holding things in stained glass windows. . . .

(Surely someone will remember Joseph's lily. You hope.)

"All the symbols and attributes have reasons behind them which are very interesting. We won't take the time to go into them today, but if anyone would like to study these on his own for extra credit, just let me know.

"I have a lot of slips of paper here. Each has two words on it. The first word is the person or thing in our faith which a symbol stands for, and the second is the name of the symbol itself. For instance, a paper might have on it 'Jesus' and 'shepherd,' because the shepherd is an ancient symbol for Our Lord. Why? . . .

(The Good Shepherd reference is John 10:11-16.) (Each student will probably get a few.)

"I'll give these papers out, and as you get yours think of how you'd make some very simple sketch of each of the symbols. We're going to put these on the board, a category at a time. Religious art is often very simple and childlike, so even stick figures for shepherds and other people will be fine—this isn't an art contest!

(Give out papers, which you will have prepared earlier.)

"Now before we draw on the board, there's one other ingredient to this experiment. I'm also going to give everyone a sheet of blank paper. As the different symbols are drawn on the board, watch to see which ones really 'click' with you, which ones really seem to say something to you. You might end up with five or six out of all of the symbols drawn that just seem to be special. When you see one like this, a symbol you really respond to, sketch it on your paper and label it. Keep all the sketches on one side of your paper.

"All right, let's start with symbols for the Trinity. Will everyone who has one of these come up and draw a quick picture of it on the board? . . .

(And identify it.)

"Good. Take a good look at these symbols for the Holy Trinity. Does any one of them really appeal to you? If so, copy it down and write 'Trinity' under it. . . .

"Next, let's draw symbols for God the Father. Who has any of these? . . .

(And so on, drawing, copying, labeling, moving on to the next category and reminding students with each to draw the ones they find speaking to them.)

"Now, we've got a lot of symbols before us, haven't we? The ones on your paper are the ones you felt had a special meaning for you. Probably no two papers in the class are alike, because a symbol that is uninteresting to one person might be filled with feeling for someone else. How about putting these papers away until our next class or, better still, taking them home and putting them up where you can look at them from time to time. . . ."

PART II:

"If you'll take out the papers with your special symbols on them, the ones that seemed to ring a bell with you, we'll do something with them. . . .

"On the other side of the paper, will you see what you can come up with in the way of a design or sketch using all the special symbols you chose earlier? Try to weave them together somehow, so that you end up with a personal statement about the aspects of your faith that mean something to you.

"If you'd like to add other symbols, symbols of your patron saints, put your hand up and I'll come around with the reference books I have. We'll see if we can help you find a symbol for a patron of your family's original country, or for the saint 'in charge' of the sort of work you'd like to do someday or the kind of hobby you have now. We may be able to find a symbol or attribute for the saint you're named for. You can add these emblems to your total drawing.

"Let's see what we come up with. The idea of all of this work is to help us get a handle on some of our feelings about our faith. . . .

"Would anyone like to share his design with the rest of us? . . .

(Or, if your kids are hopeless at keeping things, you had better collect the papers and save them.)
(You needn't stop here, but this is a long activity —and, also, there's a value in allowing a sinking-in period when working with symbols.)

(Some are going to need a fresh sheet of paper.)

(A vague direction, just so kids have freedom to create.)

(Or they can use the books in small groups.)
(Unless you included the saints in your original drawings.)

(Encourage non-artists as you go around.)

(If some seem especially good, ask permission to show them so the uninspired can get a few more ideas.)

"Here's a suggestion. Would you keep this drawing where you'll see it often? It could go inside your notebook or it could be put at home where you do your homework. Think about it a little whenever you see it. Ask yourself from time to time if you would change it or add anything to it or take anything away or rearrange its parts. Your new ideas can tell you something about your growth in faith.

(Here's where we get out of our heads and into our hearts; the head/thinking/research part was fine, and now if students begin to live with the symbols and associate them with themselves, they are growing in an affective way as well.)

"If anyone makes a major change in what he or she has done today, we could all learn by hearing about it, if that change was something you are willing to share."

DATE TRIED: **TIME:** **REPEAT?:**

RESULTS:

MORE IDEAS:

If this experiment has been at all successful, keep using the symbols in other ways, such as

1) If you have time and talent to invest, each student could make himself a "Me Box"—a box of any size whose six sides each show a symbol chosen from the special group. This visual reminder is likely to be kept and looked at and thought about longer than just a drawing on paper. The inside of such a box might have other symbols—not necessarily sacred—or a collage showing special things about the person: his interests, his hopes and dreams, his family background, his favorite things.

2) Symbols can be cut out of cardboard and decorated to make hangings for a Christmas tree or a mobile. Symbols of patron saints of family members make nice Christmas gifts and personalize a family tree, making it sort of a modern Jesse tree.

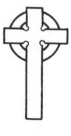

3) For celebrations in the classroom (liturgical or otherwise) banners and drawings of symbols have all sorts of possibilities, many of which you've probably already tackled. Can you get your students' artwork into the church for worship purposes?

4) For a class that is symbol-prone, you can design several projects based on finding sacred symbols in the world around us. For instance,

—We live with many of the traditional religious symbols described in the experiment (circles, candles, keys, fish, etc.). How many can students spot in their daily comings and goings? How conscious are they of these things as reminders of their faith?

—Shapes of traditional symbols pop up in funny places, like cloud formations and kaleidoscopes, in the embers of dying fires and in phosphenes (the colored shapes we see when our eyelids are closed). Let students hunt for some of the symbols you've worked with in this experiment in these and other places.

—Can students make up new meanings for things that don't seem symbolic at first glance? Corita Kent started us off with a new look at names like "Wonder Bread" and "Grand Union." How about students looking around their homes for good Religious/religious mottoes and symbols. Perhaps one of them, for example, has at home an old clock (or, for that matter, a new clock). He could use it as a reminder of the passing of time—certainly a spiritual thought—practicing that invested association until it is as automatic as the response of Christians to the cross as a reminder of Jesus. Or does the vacuum cleaner a student uses to help out at home have the name "Fail-Proof" written across it? How could this be used as a spiritual reminder?

SOME OF THE MOST COMMON CHRISTIAN SYMBOLS

The Trinity:
   triangle, shamrock, three interlocking circles
God the Father:
   hand (usually coming from cloud), eye, six-pointed star, sun
Jesus Christ:
   fish, shepherd, lamb, pelican, phoenix, lion, candle, star, sun, unicorn, various crosses and disguised crosses (anchor, etc.), monograms (XP, IC, IHS, etc.)
The Holy Spirit:
   dove, seven tongues of fire, seven-branched candlestick, tree with twelve fruits
The Church:
   ark with rainbow, ship, rock, beehive, pomegranate
Christians:
   stag (see Psalm 41), hare (hastening to God), squirrel (laying up treasure, planning ahead), bird (rising/getting high?), caterpillar-butterfly ("dies" and is reborn)

The Sacraments:
   Baptism—font, streams of water (swimming with fish), shell with water

Eucharist—wheat and grapes, loaves and fishes, stag and fountain, birds and grapes

Penance—keys

Confirmation—dove, seven tongues of fire

Matrimony—two interlocking rings, joined hands

Holy Orders—chalice and host, stole, book, keys

Anointing of the Sick—lighted candles, dove with olive branch

PATRON SAINTS OF COUNTRIES

Most countries have several patrons and most of these saints have more than one symbol or emblem. Here is a cross section for those nations which are most likely to have family ties for students.

Canada: St. Anne (nest of birds)

China: St. Joseph (lily)

England: St. George (slain dragon)

France: St. Joan of Arc (stake with flames)

Germany: St. Boniface (fox)

Ireland: St. Patrick (shamrock)

Italy: St. Francis of Assisi (birds)

Japan: St. Peter Baptist (cross)

Mexico: Our Lady of Guadalupe (roses)

Philippines: Sacred Heart of Mary (heart)

Poland: St. Casimir (scroll with music)

Portugal: St. Francis Borgia (musical notes)

Russia: St. Nicholas (three bags of coins)

Scotland: St. Andrew ("X" cross)

South America: St. Rose of Lima (crown of roses and thorns)

Spain: St. James the Great (scallop shell)

West Indies: St. Gertrude (mice and rats)

Cuba: The Virgin of Charity (crescent moon and 12 stars)

PATRON SAINTS OF WORK AND PLAY

Actors: St. Genesius (masks)

Altar boys: St. John Berchmans (cross)

Animals: St. Anthony, Abbot (pig)

Athletes: St. Sebastian (arrows)

Artists: St. Luke (winged ox)

Architects: St. Thomas the Apostle (ax)

Astronomers: St. Dominic (dog holding torch in mouth)

Boy Scouts: St. George (slain dragon)

Candlemakers: St. Ambrose (bees)

Carpenters: St. Joseph (carpenter's square)

Comedians: St. Vitus (dog)

Cooks: St. Martha (broom)

Dentists: St. Apollonia (pincers and tooth)

Doctors: St. Raphael (fish)

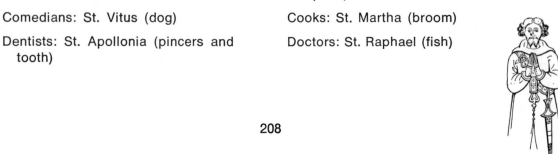

Druggists: Ss. Cosmas and Damian (phials and jars)

Farmers: St. Isidore (plow)

Gardeners & Florists: St. Dorothy (flowers and fruit)

Hunters: St. Hubert (white stag)

Librarians: St. Jerome (lion)

Mothers: St. Monica (tears)

Nurses: St. Catherine of Siena (wedding ring)

Postal Employees: St. Gabriel (lily)

Priests: St. Jean Vianney (devil)

Seamen: St. Nicholas of Tolentino (ship)

Scientists: St. Albert the Great (book)

Singers: St. Gregory (scroll with music)

Skiers: St. Bernard of Menthon (big dog)

Students: St. Thomas Aquinas (sun with eye in middle)

Teachers: St. Jean Baptiste de la Salle (pen)

TV workers: St. Clare (monstrance)

Writers: St. Francis de Sales (flaming heart)

Engineers: St. Ferdinand (crown)

Firemen: St. Florian (flames)

Homemakers: St. Anne (door)

Lawyers: St. Thomas More (book)

Missionaries: St. Therese of Lisieux (roses and crucifix)

Musicians: St. Cecelia (organ)

Policemen: St. Michael (flaming sword)

Pilots: St. Joseph of Cupertino (airplane)

Radio workers: St. Gabriel (lily)

Secretaries: St. Genesius (mask)

Shopkeepers: St. Francis of Assisi (birds)

Skaters: St. Lidwina (skates)

Soldiers: St. George (slain dragon)

Sweethearts: St. Valentine (heart)

Travelers: St. Christopher (lantern)

Women in armed forces: St. Genevieve (flock of sheep)

REFERENCES:

The Catholic Almanac, Felician A. Foy, O.F.M., ed. (Huntington, IN: Our Sunday Visitor, Inc., 1975)

If you have the current—or even an ancient—copy of this annual in the classroom while doing this experiment, you'll have a ready source of symbols of many of the saints.

Christian Symbols, Ancient and Modern, Heather Child and Dorothy Colles (New York: Charles Scribner's Sons, 1972)

Try reference rooms of libraries for this expensive and extensive and comprehensive volume that tells you all you want to know about symbols—and then

some. Books of symbols are often in art sections of libraries (700's) or the religion section (200's).

The Book of Symbols, Jana Garai (New York: Simon and Schuster, 1973)

A handsome paperback covering symbols (mostly from the world of nature) such as "Creatures of Mud and Water," "Earth and Her Gifts" and others. The author juxtaposes the Christian meaning of the symbols with their meaning in other cultures and/or religions. This is particularly interesting in light of the early Church's facility for "baptizing" pagan customs and signs (like the Christmas tree).

My Nameday—Come For Dessert, Helen McLoughlin (Collegeville, MN: The Liturgical Press, 1962)

An old favorite that tells *who* is the patron saint of just about everyone, from Tammies (St. Thomas) to Tracys (St. Teresa) to Sean (St. John). Emblems too, and fancy desserts if you would like to celebrate.

My Tree

BACKGROUND:

Instead of using a slew of symbols, this experiment concentrates on just one very evocative symbol—the tree, one of the most commonly recurring images in the history of spiritual systems. By using the idea of the tree in this way, we are hooking up with the religious traditions of both the Old Testament and the New Testament, as well as the traditions of many other peoples. If your school has trees nearby, could you combine the two parts of this experiment and do it outside? (Experiment No. 6, "Natural Highs," is a similar, but nonsymbolic nature experiment.)

MATERIALS:

Pencils and unlined paper. If you go in for classroom decorations to stress a theme, then anything having to do with trees could be on hand: pictures of them, branches from them, leaves, drawings and so forth.

CURRICULUM TIE-IN:

Scripture, Genesis, the cross, prayer.

PART I:

"Today we're going to try a way of growing that uses nature to help us out. First, let me ask you a couple of questions. What do you think of when you hear the word 'tree'? . . .

(Make a list on the board of the many possible word associations.)

"If I asked you to name some famous trees, which ones would you think of? . . .

(G. Washington's cherry tree, the Garden of Eden trees in Genesis, California redwoods, many others.)

"Trees have been thought of as special for a long time. They were among man's earliest living 'companions' and in a world of dinosaurs and caveman violence they were friendly beings. Some people even believed them sacred and worshiped them. Do you know of any examples? . . .

(Ancient Egyptians, Chinese, American Indians, primitive Arabs today, others.)

"Trees were often thought of as sacred because they united earth to heaven, matter to spirit. What is there about a tree that could lead people to this conclusion? . . .

(The branches reach up to the heavens and the roots down into the earth.)

211

"Next question: What famous piece of wood—something made from a tree—do we find in the life of Jesus? . . .

(The cross. The old legend is that St. Michael told Eve to plant a branch of the Tree of Knowledge on Adam's grave. This became a tree, which Solomon moved to the Temple garden, and which eventually became the cross.)

"Right. And did you ever hear the cross referred to as 'the Tree?' . . .

(If you're really doing this up, you might read the Reproaches from the Good Friday liturgy, or play Joe Wise's version of it, "My People," which sings ". . . and you have raised me upon this tree.")

"Like other trees, the cross mediates—or goes between—earth and heaven.

"Today, to help us get more of a feeling for trees and what they symbolize, I'd like to ask you to draw a picture of a tree that could be you! If you were a tree, what sort of tree would you be? . . . Would you be an evergreen or would you shed your leaves? . . . Would you be short or tall. . . . Bushy or thin . . . stiff or bending? . . .

(The Serendipity "Sampler" book has a draw-your-family-tree exercise that is helpful too.)

"Psalm One, in the Old Testament, compares the good man to an unfading, fruit-bearing tree. Do you have fruit to nourish others? . . . Do your branches give shade? . . .

(Cf. Jesus cursing the non-fruiting fig tree, Matthew 21:18-21.)

"Sort of follow your sixth sense on this, and after I pass out paper take three or four minutes to draw a tree that stands for you. . . .

(If you have time, it would be very good for all to have a chance to share their drawings and ideas, either with the class or a partner or small group.)

212

"Why don't you each take your drawing home, and put it up somewhere where you can see it? Think about it. Add to it. Keep going back to it and learning from it.

"Now, here's an assignment for our next class. It has three steps, so you might want to write them down.

1) Find a tree anywhere in your part of town—or near the school— that somehow seems special to you. Look for one that seems to have a real "tree personality."

(If you live where there just aren't any trees, you can substitute shrubs or settle for pictures of trees. Better still, rework this entire experiment with some other nature symbol you do have plenty of, like stars and constellations, or flowers, or pebbles and rocks, which lead to the idea of us as "living stones"—I Peter 2:4.)

2) Next, try to get a real feel for *that particular* tree, first by standing next to it quietly and listening to the noises it makes, feeling the trunk, leaning on it, examining its leaves, and then by looking at it from a distance and asking questions like:

(Other authors mentioned in this book also have tree thoughts—Buber, Experiment No. 6, and Sherwood and Johnson, Experiment No. 23.)

—What makes this tree special and different from all others?
—What would it be like to have roots and branches, to go between the heavens and the earth?
—What must it be like to stand in one place through many seasons and years, in all weather, to be blown by wind and coated with ice?
—How would it feel to keep producing and losing leaves or needles? to have birds sit in you and raise families there?
—Can kids climb in your tree? What would that feel like?
—What pictures do the branches of the tree make? Are there pictures in the bark?
—What must it look like inside the tree? Who lives there?
—How deep do you think the tree's roots go? What's down there with the roots?

(Is this a lot of time to spend on a-religious matter? Perhaps, but without it, the prayer/religious part of the experiment is far less effective.)

"Take time for this, until you really feel that you know the tree you've chosen. Then, finally, see if your tree works as a prayer spot for you. Stand under it or near it—or climb it—and think of its symbolic meaning as a mediator or go-between between heaven and earth. See if you can talk to God about yourself in this spot. Are you a mediator? . . . Does your life unite heaven and earth in any way? . . ."

PART II:

"Today I'd like to ask you to share with each other some of your experiences with your tree. First, how many found a special tree? . . . How many chose evergreens? . . . How many chose non-ever-greens? . . . (And who can remember what you call non-ever-greens?) . . .

(Music that could be worked into this experiment: Cat Stevens' good song to a special tree, "The King of Trees," in his Buddha and the Chocolate Box album; the old Girl Scout song "The Growing Up Tree," which echoes Rilke's poem about "the tree inside me grows.")
(Deciduous trees.)

"How many chose big trees? . . . small trees? . . . stiff trees? . . . bending trees? . . . old trees? . . . young trees? . . .

(Young children may be open enough to be their tree, showing its shape with their arms and bodies.)

"Who would share with us some of the things about his or her tree? . . . What is it like and why do you think you chose it? . . .

(A quote you might want to throw in: "Christ is the Tree of Life," St. Ambrose.)

"Did any of you find that after getting to know your tree and thinking about how it symbolizes the union of earth and heaven (or matter and spirit), it was a good place to pray? . . . Will anyone tell us about what sort of praying seems good next to a tree? . . . What works for you? . . .

"I'd like to suggest that you keep experimenting with your special prayer spot near the tree, or in the tree. See if going there again helps trigger you into a special awareness of the presence of God.

(Another experiment dealing with "my special place" is No. 21.)

"Maybe you'll even be lucky enough to find a sacred grove of trees someday like the ancient Druids and Assyrians used for worship. And if anyone wants to report back to me or to the whole class on what's happening, that would be great. You can tell us, or write an anonymous story, or draw a picture and leave it on my desk. See how it goes, OK?"

(How about the teacher? Do you have a tree? What happens with it? Did you have a tree when you were growing up? Can you share this with the kids? In New England, we learn not to fall in love with elm trees.)

DATE TRIED: **TIME:**   **REPEAT?:**

RESULTS:

MORE IDEAS:

1) Older students might be interested in researching the sacred tree theme, taken up by all cults and religions of both East and West. Sacred trees include the oaks and ashes of the cold north and the cedars and palms of the Middle East, Egyptian sycamores and Oriental cassia trees. Here are some leads on both sacred trees and scriptural trees, chosen from a vast number of possibilities:

—From the Old Testament, there are the two trees in the garden: the Tree of Life and the Tree of Knowledge of Good and Evil (Genesis 2:9, 17 and 3:24); the "Jesse tree" idea, which foretells Jesus as the offspring of the "stem of Jesse" (Isaiah 11:1); Psalm 1, mentioned in the experiment; Psalm 91, where we hear that "the just man shall flourish like the palm tree" and grow like "a cedar of Lebanon." In the Canticles, there are apple trees and fig trees, cypresses and cedars, palms too, all with quasisymbolic meaning.

—From the New Testament, the Tree of Life reappears in Revelation 22:2, where it bears fruit once every month. Jesus uses the fruit tree to say, "By their fruits ye shall know them" in Matthew 7: 16-20 and Luke 6: 43-45; He curses the fig tree (Matthew 21:18-21) that wasn't productive. Paul tells the Romans about salvation by describing the olive tree that stands for the Jewish roots of Christianity (Romans 11:16-24).

215

—In ancient Greece, trees were oracles to be consulted about the future. Zeus's voice could be heard among the rustling leaves in the sacred oak groves.

—The Norsemen had Yggdrasil, with the stars hung in its branches. This gigantic ash symbolized the universe.

—From the life of Buddha there is the sacred sal tree and the bo tree, the sacred wild fig or Tree of Enlightenment of India. The leaf of the wild fig is a fertility motif and we see it today in the many paisley designs to be found in fabrics and rugs.

—In Tantric mythology the Tree of Life is pictured between the sun and the moon, symbolizing the reconciliation of opposites into the essential oneness of the universe.

—Many primitive Arabs today think that trees are the homes of angels and gods and departed souls. Some live in trunk hollows like hermits (as did St. Simon Stock) to be near these spirits.

—Finally, there are the beautiful Persian prayer rugs that depict the Celestial Tree of Islam complete with garden. (See Experiment No. 21.)

2) If you should have a great hit with trees, how about devising your own similar experiments with other nature symbols? You might start with the four ancient elements: earth, water, fire and air, with all their biblical and religious associations. Other so-called "transformation symbols" (like mountains) used by the authors below seem to have particular value in helping us bring to life and formulate our own feelings and experiences—about ourselves and about God. We have an ever-present source of symbols in the changing weather. Snow, wind, rain, breeze and sun all carry their own associations (as do the garden/farm images: seed, plants, etc.) *if* we can train ourselves to be responsive to them.

How can we do this? One way is to put up a picture of, say, the sun as a reminder that we want (as the hymn has it) to "be like the sun and shine on everyone," giving warmth and light (see Matthew 13:43). Then, when we're outside, soaking up some of the real sun's life-giving warmth and light, the symbolic meaning of its shining (and, therefore, of our doing the same) will be more easily remembered—and put into practice.

For obvious reasons, the sun has been a symbol of Jesus, of God the Father, of Mary and of more than one saint, and in many non-Christian societies, a symbol of man's indefinable religious experience. What, really, is a halo?

Castaneda's Don Juan speaks of "reaffirmation from the outside world" among his people, as when the sun breaks through clouds just as a wedding starts. We also use nature terms to describe people: "like a fresh breeze," "a ray of sunlight," "you're like a rainbow coming around the bend," "like a thundercloud." Why not have special classes—Air Day, Earth Day, Sun Day, Tree Day, Water Day—to help students tune (or re-tune) in to God's world and see it as His mirror?

3) Another point to research, also important: Has nature always been seen as a facilitator of spirituality? Try texts of ascetic theology from the misty past (i.e., pre-1965); keep going back through the centuries. In *The Devils of Loudun,* Aldous Huxley has many interesting asides on the Church's view of nature in the 1600's: It was seen as "a dangerous distraction from the proper study of man," which was, of course, God (but not His world). The common folk had to be protected from a pantheistic approach to God which saw Him as identical with His universe (a danger avoided when nature is approached symbolically, as in "My Tree" or "panentheistically" as in Experiment No. 6). John Calvin called for aggressive mastery over nature, another view.

But the natural world was not always so suspect. How about the medieval attitude? What is it like to be in a Gothic cathedral (not unlike a grove with over-spreading branches)? Check out the ornamentation from the animal and vegetable kingdom found in and on these great buildings. Franciscan spirituality is certainly big on the unity of all created things, and Benedictine on the importance of natural setting—and the wise cultivation of it—to spiritual growth. (See Rene Dubos' *A God Within;* New York: Charles Scribner's Sons, 1972.)

How about Jesus' relationship to and teaching use of nature (lilies, birds of the air)? What are the implications of each of these varying approaches for today's nature children?

REFERENCES:

The Tree of Life, Roger Cook (New York: Avon Books, 1974)

One of the beautiful books in the paperback "Art and Cosmos" series, dealing with art whose imagery has a symbolic, often religious, function. Fascinating pictures and explanations of the tree as a religious image in many times and places.

Symbols of Transformation, Carl Jung (Princeton, NJ: Bollingen Paperbacks, 1956)

Not easy reading, but the source book for this experiment. Jung saw the tree as a symbol of the self in the process of growth. See also the work of Jung disciple, Ira Progoff.

Psychosynthesis, Roberto Assagioli (New York: The Viking Press, 1965)

One of the important books on the humanistic psychology bookshelf. Specific exercises with some of the transformation symbols (see "More Ideas" #2 above) that resonate deep within men and lead to "enlarged and healing perspectives." The journal *Synthesis* is published by the Assagioli followers, and has a very large workbook section built in, full of growth games and exercises (The Synthesis Press, 150 Doherty Way, Redwood City, California 94061).

What's My Plot?

BACKGROUND:

Stories are universally told and loved, but few students would think of them as means of growing closer to God (unless they had been raised on a steady diet of bible tales, unusual these days). This experiment helps the experimenters to pull together their long experience with all sorts of stories, religious and non-religious, and put it to work for soul growth. We must be careful not to restrict our selection of stories to "good literature"—all sorts of stories (fact and fiction) count here. This experiment, and the two sandwiching it, are based on Carl Jung's theory of archetypes ("ch" pronounced like "k"). An archetype, described simply, is more than a symbol. It's an unconscious impulse common to men of all times and places, and represented by similar plots or story themes, or images of people, places or things (like the sacred tree) that recur over and over. When we identify archetypes and their images that are especially meaningful to us and explore them and live with them and let them work in us, we grow.

MATERIALS:

Pencil and paper (journals?). Teachers who like to decorate can probably come up with pictures from well-known stories.

CURRICULUM TIE-IN:

Bible stories and themes.

"Today we're going to talk about stories, your favorite stories. If you'd each get out a pencil and paper and make a narrow column on the left-hand side of the paper, we'll begin.

"Let's see how many *categories* of stories we can come up with. As we mention each one, write the category in the left-hand column. You can skip a line between them so you'll have more room.

"Well, what kinds of stories are there? . . .

(See what you can get from the class before adding from this list.)

"Here are some I know about:

    fairy tales
    myths and legends
    series of books for young people (like the Hardy Boys and
       the Bobbsey Twins)
    tales of adventure (explorations, hunts for buried treasure,
       etc.)
    bible stories, both Old and New Testaments
    sports stories
    ghost stories
    animal stories
    fantasy tales (like *Alice in Wonderland*)

"How about movie and TV stories? Can we break these down into different categories? . . .

    comedies
    mysteries
    private eye shows
    cartoons
    tearjerkers and soap operas
    science fiction/space stories
    Westerns

"Any others? . . .
"Now, here's the thinking part of this experiment. Go down your list of categories, and in the right-hand column write down favorite stories of yours in each category. There may be some categories where you have nothing and some that have lots of stories in them. Be specific; put down names of stories—or major characters if that's how you remember the story.

"Think back to stories you loved when you were little. Did you go to story hour at the library? . . . Did anyone in the family ever read to you? . . . Did anyone ever write a story about you? . . .

219

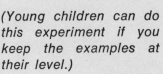

(Young children can do this experiment if you keep the examples at their level.)

(This part will take time; you do it, too.)

"Now, let's look at our lists. We want to find out what they can tell us about ourselves, and the way we can do that is to look at the stories we've chosen for things they have in common. For instance, here in my list I have the *Nancy Drew* stories under 'series,' and under TV shows, I've put down *Columbo,* and under movies, my favorites of all time are the *Sherlock Holmes* movies. It's easy to see what these have in common, isn't it? . . .

"OK, now look at your list of favorites. Are there any common threads that run through it? . . . plots that are really very similar even though they're in different categories? . . . You might find two or three groups like this.

"Look for themes, too, like bravery or patriotism or love of nature or homelife. . . .

"Who can give us an example of something he or she has found? . . .

"Now, here's the next step in our thinking. This is harder, so why don't you write down the two questions I'm going to ask:

1) If you've found at least one plot or theme or type of story that is especially 'yours,' *why* do you think it appeals to you?
2) How does this plot or theme happen in your life? . . . Or does it?

"Now, these might be very tough questions. Does anyone have any ideas about himself and his plots that he would like to share with us? . . .

"Someone who had the detective stories for favorites and asked himself our two questions would have to do some good thinking, wouldn't he? . . . Perhaps the detective fiction fan is one who really wants to fight the good fight. Perhaps he feels he *doesn't* do enough to combat wrongs. Any other ideas? . . .

(Use whatever examples are true for you, or refer to these examples as things "someone might have written.")

(Obviously, all are detective stories—and enthusiasts make a sharp distinction between these and plain old mystery stories.)

(Maybe some help is needed.)

(Strictly voluntary.)

220

"Are you wondering what on earth all this has to do with religion? Let's talk about that for a minute: What *does* this have to do with religion? . . .

(Someone may suggest that knowing yourself better helps you have a better thing going with God, one of the basic themes of this book.)

"Being in touch with yourself humanly is certainly an aid to spiritual growth. We can even go beyond that. Many of the plots that keep popping up in stories over and over again are echoes of the greatest story of all—the story of God and His people and what happens between them. Take a look at our example again, the detective stories: What is it about detective stories of all types that you might say is a reflection of God and His action in the lives of His people? . . . There are probably several answers to that question. . . .

(Or, perhaps your favorites are stories where all live happily ever after. Cf. the promise of heaven, and note that fairy tale/romance characters usually achieve this bliss only after being tested, which is true for us too.)

(If no bright ideas materialize): "Well, for one thing, who usually wins in a detective story? . . . Sure, Nancy Drew always catches the crook, and so does Columbo, and so does Sherlock. The good guys come out on top—so this is an echo of the universal theme of. . . .

(Good defeating evil.)

"Can you think of particular bible stories that tell about good winning over evil? . . .

(Lots of examples: God vs. Satan, Joseph in the Old Testament coming out on top of his rotten brothers, Jesus "winning" over the "bad guys" who had Him killed, and the "final victory" of eternity over death.)

"Here's another hookup with religious themes for the whodunit fan: In a typical detective story, the sleuth pieces together all sorts of little tidbits of information, doesn't he? None of the things seem to fit together at first, but then, at the end, he shows us how everything is really part of some grand plan or pattern. What idea with God-dimensions does this suggest to you? . . .

(The wish we all have to sense order in the universe, so that it—and our lives—not be meaningless chaos, but a reflection of divine order.)

221

"Now, how about your plots? . . . If you've found one or two themes and perhaps see their connection to your life, can you take them one more step? What basic religious story, a story about God and man, is in these plots? . . .

(This can be question 3 to write down.)

"Well, this is a very difficult experiment, really. We've just made a beginning in working with plots and stories in our lives. What might be a good idea now is for each of us to keep our list handy. How about putting it up somewhere at home where you'll see it?

(Another example, in case you're afloat: Star Trek *fans will recognize both Kirk and Spock as authentic heroes. Does the unique self-transcending friendship between the two—a rare, living "thing" which is one of the show's most appealing plots—reflect our wished-for love relationships with others? with God? How? And how about the* Enterprise *herself, made up of people representing a head, a heart, the will, etc.: is it an archetype of the Christian community? of the Mystical Body?)*

"You'll find that you think of new stories and even new categories of stories. Look for one or two or three plots or themes that seem especially to appeal to you; these may not be the same plots that someone else finds appealing. Think about the following three questions (things to look for):

(A tough experiment, therefore a review at the end.)

1) *Why* do you think these plots are important to you?
2) *What* do they mean in terms of your life? (Are they happening? How? Do you want them to?)
3) What grander, bigger 'model plans' do your favorite plots reflect? How do they echo the story of God and all men?

"Now that's a lot to think about!"

222

MORE IDEAS:

1) Throughout the year you might slip in references to other universal or archetypal plots with obvious religious connections. Here are a few of many possible examples; can you work them into some appropriate place in your curriculum? (After each plot, there's both a nonreligious and a religious example.)
   Creation:
      (*Frankenstein,* artists' stories/Genesis)
   Man's need for land of his own:
      (many Westerns/ Adam in Eden)
   The dispossessed, searching for a new home:
      (the *Little House* series/Abraham's search for the Promised Land)
   Sibling rivalry:
      (*King Lear*/Cain and Abel, Joseph and his brothers)
   The struggle of a royal or superior person in everyday dress—or animal form—who must be accepted as is before his royalty/superiority can be revealed:
      (*Beauty and the Beast, The Frog Prince, Cinderella*/Jesus—remember the people of Nazareth? Judas? Others?)
   The dead (or seemingly dead) are given transfiguring new life through the perfect love of a royal person:
      (*Sleeping Beauty, Snow White*/Lazarus, all men)
   Man struggling to keep his identity and his soul:
      (zombie and vampire tales, *1984*/Jews in exile, believers of all times)
   Tests to prove someone worthy:
      (*Bluebeard*/Adam and Eve and the forbidden fruit)
   "Movin' on," hitting the road:
      (*Easy Rider*/the Jews and Moses in the desert)
   The lowly are exalted and the proud humbled:
      (anyone's wicked stepsisters and stepmothers/"He who humbles himself. . .")

2) If these ideas really click with a group, why not have them write parable-allegory-fable-type tales to illustrate whatever Scriptural concept you're studying, in the mode of Jesus the Storyteller? We've spent this experiment doing a few things with archetypal plots; how about investigating archetypal people and finding

223

examples of them in scripture? There's the Villain, the Joker or Trickster, the Best Friend, the Ruler, the Wise Old Man or Woman and, in the next experiment, the Hero, among others. (In *Four Archetypes,* Jung explores in detail the archetypes of Mother, Rebirth, Spirit and Trickster; Princeton: Princeton University Press, 1969.)

3) Start a collection of archetypal pictures, for the classroom or for your own use. Put them up, one at a time, where they'll catch eyes, changing them when they've had time to sink in and generate their energy in viewers. Some will have a powerful attraction for some students, others much less—and different pictures will appeal to different onlookers.

You might find pictures of people (a typical wise old man, a typical mother, a typical farmer or gardener, etc.), pictures of striking places (the jungle, a walled garden, ancient ruins, a cathedral, an island, etc.), pictures of oft-recurring basic plots or themes or human activities (shoot-out on Main Street in the old West, war, parents bringing home a new baby, love, flying, the *Star Trek* idea of exploring new worlds, etc.), pictures of universal things (the "transformation symbols" of the last experiment, a door or a gate, a tower, a road, etc.)—all of these, things that recur over and over in real life and in stories.

Such pictures are everywhere: in books and magazines, on record album covers, in movie ads, on postcards, as art reproductions. (Or, if you're artistic, draw your own.) Watch for used book sales or visit stores selling secondhand books and magazines. Inexpensive finds can be cut up to give several pictures (or you can prop them open if you don't like to cut up books). Two especially good sources of archetypal pictures are:

Children's books of fairy tales and myths of the early 1900's, which often have beautiful, evocative illustrations (a color collection of 40 of these by different artists is *The Fantastic Kingdom,* David Larkin, ed., New York: Ballantine Books, 1974.)

Reproductions of paintings by "primitive" artists, who were listening to the child within them, and by artists who have painted story and/or dream subjects. Try almost any period of art up through the Middle Ages (especially illuminated manuscripts and books of hours), followed by the Italians of the 14th century (Duccio, Giovanni di Paolo, the Lorenzettis, Giotto, Simone Martini) and their later Northern counterparts in the storytelling mode (Bosch, Brueghel, *some* of the early German and Flemish artists)—most of of this will be Christian art. Closer to our own lives is the primitive painting of Hicks and Rousseau, Nolde and even Grandma Moses, and the dreamworlds of di Chirico, Tanguy, Klee, Magritte, Redon, Chagall and Hopper. Try also Blake, Ryder, Munch. Also rich with universal themes are the miniatures of Persia and India, much oriental art, the art of primitive peoples of all times, and folk art of all cultures.

You can tell students that these pictures will keep changing and suggest that they wait for one that really catches them. They can then ask the questions about that picture that we asked about plots in the experiment: Why does it have a pull for me? Does it happen to me? and so on. Ask them to look for the religious parallels. (There are many.) Suggest that they tune in to the pictures at the feelings level, not by analyzing them or thinking about them. See what happens—to them, to you.

REFERENCES:

Man and His Symbols, Carl G. Jung (Garden City: Doubleday and Co., Inc. 1964)

A special book introducing the layman to Jung's major work, including the archetype work. Beautiful illustrations in the hardcover edition; also available in paperback. If Maslow is the father of humanistic psychology, Jung is the grandfather—and important reading for growth people.

An Introduction to the Interpretation of Fairy Tales, Marie-Louise von Franz (Zurich: Spring Publications, 1973)

Analyst von Franz, one of Carl Jung's closest colleagues and a personable writer, sees fairy tales as the purest depositories of all the archetypes. They depict the most general human state. She translates the tales into the language of psychology, with humor and with freedom from the pretentiousness that is the curse of some of the best writers in this field. Interesting background on the history and study of fairy tales, and parallels to religious climates of different times.

What Do You Say After You Say Hello?, Eric Berne (New York: Grove Press, 1972)

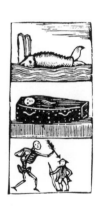

Another T.A. book, about being "scripty." A good catalyst for teachers (not kids) who want to chew over the why of plots and their appeal. Berne leaves himself open to potshots with his dogmatic statements about people who are living "Cinderella" or "Little Miss Muffet," but his works are important and good reading.

Scripts People Live, Claude Steiner (New York: Grove Press, 1974)

The follow-up book to Berne's by a fellow T.A. therapist. Very sane and thorough, but recommended only for those with the strength of character *not* to read and say, "Ha—there's my husband" or "That fits my mother-in-law to a T" and the like. One of the most sensible authors around, with especially on-target ideas for dealings with children.

Wonder and Worship, James Carroll (Paramus, NJ: Newman Press, 1970)

A collection of fairy tales that bridge over into worship, with titles like "Piercing of Spiderland" and "Heaven?" Four of James Carroll's stories are also on filmstrip as *Tales of Wonder* and *Dragons and Other Scary Things,* from the Paulist Press.

Collections . . .

Collections of fairy tales, myths and legends (like the Opies' *The Classic Fairy Tales* with commentary,) and modern-day parable-type tales along the lines of *The Little Prince* and C. S. Lewis' Christian allegories, the Chronicles of Narnia *(The Lion, The Witch and The Wardrobe* and six others).

FINIS

St. George and the Dragon

EXPERIMENT NUMBER 30

BACKGROUND:

The myths and legends of Christianity, from the earliest apocryphal ones to the saint stories of the Middle Ages, are a heritage of which many students know nothing. Their connection with the magical land of fairy tales (the broader, more general category) makes them naturals for leading story-lovers to a deeper appreciation of their faith. The St. George story is a Christianization (not necessarily deliberate) of the old Greek legend of Perseus and Andromeda and other monster-slaying tales like *Jack and the Beanstalk.* We have here both an archetypal plot of good vs. evil, and an archetypal Hero and Villain. (See Experiment No. 13 for another sort of hero.) Young students will enjoy the audience participation in this experiment; with junior and senior high ages, you have the choice of omitting the sound effects or, more fun, doing the story with mock seriousness, tongue-in-cheek.

MATERIALS:

Can you put your hands on a copy of any of the many famous paintings of this legend? Try books of Russian (or other) icons. St. George, as protector of peasants and guardian of herds, has been especially popular in Russian art. There is also the famous painting of St. George and a reluctant maiden-led dragon by Paolo Uccello, and a beautiful Raphael and a Memling on the same subject.

CURRICULUM TIE-IN:

Saints, victory over sin, Christian mythology.

"Today I'd like you to help me tell a story, a famous story from the days of knights and fair ladies. Do you know the story of St. George and the dragon? . . .

"Here's how you can help me tell it. There are four main characters in this story. When each one is mentioned, you can provide a sound effect for that character. For instance, there's a faithful horse, a beautiful milk-white steed. What would be a good sound effect for him? . . .

"Then there's St. George, the brave knight in shining armor. How about a sound for him? . . .

"How about the fair maiden in distress, the princess? What shall we have for her? . . .

(Galloping hoofs? Let the class decide.)

(Applause?)

(Sad sighs?)

226

"And, finally, there's the nasty dragon, breathing fire and smoke from his snout. . . .

(Hissing sounds? Snorts?)

"Now, as I read the story, you can fill in the appropriate sound effects whenever a character is mentioned. But listen carefully, please, so that you don't miss the story. There'll be other places, too, where you can add something.

(You could also divide the class into four groups for sound effects. The brackets are reminders of pauses for sound effects. How about four actors to pantomime as you read?) (Traditionally, this happened in Libya, just in case you were wondering.)

"Once upon a time, there was a town, and near the town there was a pond, and in the pond there was a terrible dragon (———).

"The dragon (———) terrorized the people of the town. What are some of the things you think he did to them? . . .

(The younger your students, the more gory the details they'll offer.)

"Finally, the people decided that they would have to offer a daily sacrifice to the dragon (———) so that he would leave them alone. They fed the dragon (———) all their sheep and all their cows until none were left. They decided then that they would have to offer a person a day to the dragon (———) and that the only fair way to choose a victim would be to draw lots.

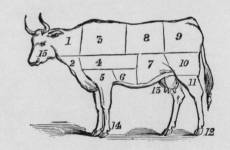

"One day, the beautiful princess (———) was drawn by lot. Her father, the king, was horrified. What do you think he said? . . .

(A chance to call on someone who's usually quiet—such an easy question.)

"It was no use. The beautiful princess (———) had to go to the dragon (———). Her father kissed her good-bye with tears streaming down his face, and off she went to the lake where the dragon (———) lived. She was not happy.

(In the old stories, the princess even has a name: Cleodolinda.)

227

"Just about this time, quite by accident, a handsome and brave young knight in shining armor (———), named George, was riding by on his trusty horse (———). He saw the beautiful princess (———) dripping tears into the lake, and he saw columns of fire and smoke rising up from the lake. St. George (———)—yes, he was a saint, even then—said to the beautiful princess (———). . . Well, what do you think he said? . . .

(We trust your students won't offer any less-than-saintly opening lines from George to an as-yet un-introduced princess.)

"The beautiful princess (———) told St. George (———) her story and he said to her, 'Be of good courage' and then he prayed, 'Lord Jesus, I ask you for the strength to defend this beautiful maiden (———).' His trusty horse (———) pawed the ground in agreement.

"Just then, with a terrible roar, the dragon (———) rose from the lake. He was very happy, for he saw a chance for three dinners instead of just one: the princess (———), the knight (———), and the trusty horse (———).

(Again, blood and guts all over your nice, neat classroom.)

"But St. George (———) made the Sign of the Cross, and went forward boldly to meet the dragon (———). There was a terrible fight. What do you think happened? . . .

"Well, the dragon (———) wasn't quite dead. St. George's (———) horse (———) reared up on its back hoofs, and St. George (———) said to the princess (———), 'Take off your yellow hair ribbon, Princess (———) and make a leash out of it and put it around the neck of the dragon (———).

(If someone doesn't bark after all this, you've got a very shy class.)

"She did this, even though she didn't like to touch the icky neck of the dragon (———). St. George (———) rode his trusty horse (———) to the town, and the princess (———) walked beside him leading the dragon (———) like a dog.

"All the people saw them coming and ran to tell the king. The dragon (———) was conquered, in the name of God, and he lay down at the town gates to guard them for ever after. What do you think happened to St. George (———) and the princess (———)?

(Since this is folk legend and we're the folk, we can add our own variation.)

"Well, that's the end of our story. St. George was a real person who lived in the early 300's, and he's the patron of soldiers. His legend is very popular (even though it was once banned by a pope), and it encouraged men to try to be saints in ways of life other than that of the hermit or the monk.

"Now, here are a few questions to ask yourself about this little story and you. Just think about them in your mind, OK? . . .

"Can you get inside this story? Which character are you most like: The hero? . . . The victim? . . . The persecutor? . . . The helper and companion? (That's the horse.) . . .

"Is the story in any way a parable of any situation in your life? . . . If you're not the dragon, is there anything in you the dragon might stand for? . . . What needs 'taming' and 'leashing' in your life? . . .

"Are you strong enough to do this taming? . . . Do you have any help? . . . What kind of help did St. George have in getting rid of dragons? . . . How did he tap into that help? . . . How can you do the same thing? . . .

"Just in passing, let me ask if this story reminds you of any other where the reptile is the villain and a shining knight appears. . . .

"In the next few days, you might think some more about all these questions. If you know or can find other myths of Christianity, try getting into those tales too. You might even work up a story for the class, complete with sound effects and follow-up questions.

"See if this part of our tradition about people from long ago helps you tell any part of your story. See if St. George's tale and other such tales mirror you in any way. See if God in the legends is like God in your life. Christians have kept these stories alive for centuries because of these reasons. I'll always be glad to hear about your discoveries in this area, as in all others."

(494 A.D.)
(St. Paul had once talked about Christians as soldiers, fighting the good fight: Ephesians 6:11-17.)

(Cf. Experiment No. 12 where bible passages are treated similarly.)
(Or maybe their dragons are more like the Reluctant Dragon, who prefers poetry to war.)

(Don't rush.)

(Genesis: the serpent in the garden and St. Michael at the gate.)
(Do your students know the famous Christmas legends—the cherry tree, the robin's breast, the talking animals?)

(Open door policy.)

MORE IDEAS:

1) If you were able to find a good St. George picture, or could have one of the kids draw one, by all means leave it up as a reminder of our personal dragons. You might call attention to it every now and then. How about listing some of the "dragons" we do battle with next to it: lack of confidence, fear of taking risks, shyness, grudge-carrying, all the others.

2) Until the early 20th century, there were generally two approaches to legends such as St. George's story. You could accept them as correct reports of reality, or dismiss them as the childlike, prescientific literature of primitive peoples. Recent years have brought us a third alternative for understanding myths and legends: The emphasis (as in this experiment) is on their religious and psychological and philosophical meanings.

   This experiment could be a springboard for study and discussion of the fundamentalist view of scripture vs. the demythologizers, form criticism, and all the ins and outs of scripture scholarship, should your curriculum lend itself to that area of study—and if you're up on it yourself. (*Understanding the Bible* by Ronald J. Wilkins, a 1972 high school text from William Brown Company in Dubuque, is a good source of sound scripture background material.)

REFERENCES:

Christian Mythology, George Every (Middlesex, England: Hamlyn Publishing Group, 1970)

   One of a beautiful series on the mythologies of different cultures and religions. The creation story, the flood, the tower of Babel, figures of Christ, pseudogospels, lives of the saints and visions of the afterlife are all discussed. The author is an Anglican brother and student of comparative religion; reaction will vary with the degree of fundamentalism of your denomination.

Tales From Eternity: The World of Fairytales, Rosemary Haughton (New York: Seabury Press, 1973)

Christianity and fairy tales—how the latter mirror the former, and how the former answer the primordial questions of the latter. There are chapters on archetypes like the "Youngest Son," the "Real Princess," "Witches, Emperors and Ogres." Examples are from the folk literature of the entire world.

A Wreath of Christmas Legends, Phyllis McGinley (New York: Macmillan, 1974)

The Christmas legends from early and medieval times, beautifully told by this graceful and well-loved writer.

Myth, History and Faith: The Remythologizing of Christianity, Morton T. Kelsey (Paramus, NJ: Paulist Press, 1974)

Rev. Kelsey is both a theologian and Jungian psychologist. He sees religious myth as contributing to personal growth, and today's mythless religion—in the sense that it is almost totally cut off from its history to the point of being one-dimensional—as flat. Provocative food for thought.

The Hero with a Thousand Faces, Joseph Campbell (Princeton, NJ: Princeton University Press, 1968)

Professor Campbell, the best-known "myth-detective" of our time, traces the recurring figure of the Hero through many diverse cultures.

DRAGON

A Dream Collection

EXPERIMENT NUMBER 81

BACKGROUND:

The idea of asking students to keep in touch with their dreams may strike you as far removed from religious education. If your texts and classes already have plenty of material for putting one's self together at the human level (and dreams help us do that), then perhaps you don't need still more ways. Our students, however, seem to tune in far better to a God who wants them to be all they humanly can be than to a super-transcendent God remote from the daily bits and pieces of life. So, by this light—to repeat in this last experiment what has been written earlier—religion classes that aren't solely about Religion *can* be the most religious of all.

MATERIALS:

Students' journals, if there are such things, or a section of a few pages in students' notebooks.

CURRICULUM TIE-IN:

Dream stories in scripture, self-knowledge.

PART I:

"Today we're going to talk about dreams. What do you think of when you hear that word? . . .

(Forewarning: Stories of "what I dreamed last night" can chew up a whole class.)

"Think of the bible for a minute. Are any dreams or dreamers mentioned in it? . . . Here's a clue: think of people who got messages in their dreams. Does that help? . . .

(Maybe students will recall some before you mention those in the list.)

"Here are some:
Joseph, twice, about Mary and the Baby
The Magi, about going home the non-Herod route
Paul being called to Macedonia

(Matthew 1:20 and 2:13.)
(Matthew 2:12.)
(Acts 16:9.)

"How about biblical dreams that were prophecies? . . .
Here are some:
Jacob's ladder
Joseph (O.T.) and his dreams
Pharaoh's dreams

(Genesis 28:10-16.)
(Genesis 37:5-11.)
(Genesis 40, 41.)

232

Daniel and King Nebuchadnezzar
Pilate's wife

(Daniel 2-4.)
(Matthew 27:19—the kids may be more familiar with the Jesus Christ Superstar version, which gives Pilate the dream about the Galilean.)

"Obviously, the bible peoples and writers took their nighttime movies seriously, more seriously than we do. Dreams are picture stories of what we're thinking about while we sleep; they're sort of letters to ourselves.

(Tertullian wrote, "Almost the greater part of mankind derive their knowledge of God from dreams.")

"One word of caution: How many have ever seen 'dream books'? . . . Sometimes they have them in the supermarket with titles like *Your Dreams—the Secret to Your Inner Self.* What are they like? . . .

(Bad news. They usually give specific interpretations for places and actions and things in dreams, such as "a dream about teeth falling out is a sign of a relative's death.")

"Well, that sort of quickie dream analysis is exactly what we're *not* about in this experiment. We're not going to approach our dreams as secret messages which need decoding. There's a saying in the Talmud (What's that?) that 'The dream is its own interpretation.' That just means that by remembering our dreams and the feelings that go with them, we begin to find another way to listen to ourselves and our story, to get in touch with our own personal symbols.

(The book of Jewish civil and religious law.)

"So now, in your notebooks, would you please set aside a few pages with the title, 'A Dream Collection'? . . .

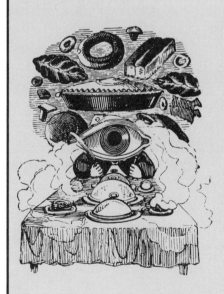

"See if you can remember any dreams you have had recently—last night, perhaps, or this week. Write down what you can remember of them, even if it's just fragments or only feelings. . . .

"Think back a bit: What dreams or snatches of dreams can you remember from the past? . . . Are there any that you keep dreaming? . . .

"Here's an assignment. For a week, see if you can remember your dreams. Write down as much of them as you can first thing in the morning. It will help if you do it the minute you wake up. Keep your book right beside your bed if you can, so you can capture a dream before it escapes.

(Those who can't recall their dreams may say they never have them. This isn't so; we dream several times each night.)

"Use the present tense when you write the dreams down. For example. . . .

("I am in a big house," rather than "I was. . .")

"And put down as many details as you can . . . and the mood (happy, sad, fearful) in each dream.

"Here's another tip: Before you fall asleep at night, you might remind yourself that you want to recall your dreams in the morning. Do you think this will be hard to do, or easy? . . ."

PART II:

"Well, what success did you have in keeping track of your dreams? . . .

"Now, in your dream collection section, would you write down these questions? They'll help you use the dreams to know yourself better:

1) What seems to happen over and over again in my dreams? Are there the same people, the same places or things or plots? Are there colors or sounds or tastes or smells that are repeated often? . . .

2) Even more important, what feelings do I keep having when I dream? Are my dreams happy, or sad, or scary? . . . Or very calm and peaceful? . . . Or a pretty even mixture? . . .

3) How do I see myself in my dreams? Am I strong, or weak? . . . Successful? . . . Rushed? . . . Witty? . . . In charge? . . . Out of control? . . .

4) How do others see me in my dreams, and how do they treat me? . . .

"You might try answering each of these questions briefly, now, with a few notes in your book. . . .

(If there's time to discuss results, you will be affirming the kids and telling them that their dreams can be of value.)

234

"What I'd like to suggest is that you keep on recording your dreams. (You'll probably find that remembering them gets easier if you do it regularly.) Ask the four questions; turn the dreams over in your mind, even give each dream a title. Over a month or a year or more, what you'll probably find is that a part of you you didn't know is becoming more familiar to you. It's as though we can round ourselves out, get a more complete picture of ourselves by doing this—even though it's 'through a glass, darkly' as the bible says. Does this ring true with you? . . . Does it seem to make sense? . . .

"And, a final question: Does all this dream work have anything at all to do with religion? . . .

"Yes, dreams were taken seriously by the people of the bible. Even more important to us is the fact that the more we know ourselves, the more whole we are—and the more of us there is to walk with God and do His work.

"If anyone would like to share any findings from dream collections in the future, of course I'll be interested."

(For those who just can't plug in to dreams, there should be freedom to abstain.)

(And, again, if you do the experiment and bring back some results off and on, even better.)

DATE TRIED: **TIME:** **REPEAT?:**

RESULTS:

MORE IDEAS:

1) In this experiment we have barely opened the door on a complex and multi-leveled topic. If a class, or one student, seems to take especially well to dream collecting, you can recommend the following step, a typical Gestalt method:

When recalling a dream, let each person or thing in the dream "speak"—that is, pretend to be, say, the ocean you have dreamed about. What does the ocean have to say to the other things or persons that were in the dream? Then be the beach, if there was one, or the seagull flying over the waves, if there was such a dream-bird. Does each thing or person in a dream represent, perhaps, a facet of the dreamer? Only months and years of such working with dreams will tell—and then, often, only at an intuitive level.

Look for puns and plays on words and acting out of idiomatic expressions in dreams too. For example, one dreamer kept dreaming of crawling around the floor with an electric light cord and plug in her hand. She decided she was looking for light in her life.

2) To go on, here are two more steps for proficient dreamers, based on the dream-work of the Senoi people of the Malay Peninsula (as westernized by Patricia Garfield in the work cited below):

—Students who keep logs will, in time, be able to single out a few characters or themes or activities or props which repeat themselves. Can they give that thing or scene or person or action waking form, i.e., can it be drawn or sculpted or made the basis of a story or acted out? (A famous dream image given day-time existence is the painting of the golden bird in Hesse's *Demian.)*

Could dreamers cut out magazine pictures of the recurring images in their dreams? These can be put up where they'll be seen and chewed over, mentally. They can be made the topic of prayer. These show parts of the dreamer that must be important for them to keep recurring.

Dreamers should note, especially, any changes in the recurring images over a period of time. How do they change? Does this suggest anything about change in the dreamer's life? Again, it's reasonable to assume that we can ask the Lord for help on this. Remember: Dreams tend to concentrate especially on the parts of ourself we are neglecting in waking life and that are therefore threatening the growth and development of one's personality.

—Dreamers should watch, too, for "dream gifts"—things given to the dreamer in a dream. These may be beautiful things (poems, songs, designs) or useful things (inventions, solutions to problems). These should be written down, and used in waking life if possible, say the dream experts. Encourage dream-loggers to write down even "unimportant dreams"; one dream, like one still of a movie, may seem trivial, but later when seen as part of a whole, may be very important.

3) Serious dream-followers make it a point to go over their dreams at fairly regular intervals, usually at the end of some segment of their life—perhaps when some project is being wrapped up, or when they are entering a new period of activity, or have gotten a fresh sense of self. They will write down what this time in their lives has been about and then try to understand it more fully in terms of the images and situations and emotions in their dreams. They will compare this reflection to the summing up of their previous dream cycle and reflect further on

the growth shown there. (For example, a dreamer may find that in his present cycle of dreams he has not had one instance of some image or place that was very prominent in the previous cycle. Apparently, the implications of that former image are no longer of such great importance to the dreamer—a fact he may not be aware of in his conscious mind, but which may be very helpful once he grasps it.)

Yes, this all takes time, but not as much as one might think. The skills come with practice, and the dream-listening becomes almost second nature after a year or so.

REFERENCES:

Creative Dreaming, Patricia Garfield (New York: Simon and Schuster, 1974)

A book of next steps: We can shape our dreams so that our waking life is benefited. An exciting book for both educators and therapists; the basic, sound thesis is that when conscious and unconscious work together, a person is more integrated and centered (the psychological parallel to the body centering of Experiment No. 9).

Myths, Dreams, and Religion, Joseph Campbell, ed. (New York: E. P. Dutton & Co., 1970)

A valuable collection of essays, including two good background chapters on myths and dreams in Hebrew and Christian scripture. Helps us to realize to what extent people of many cultures have agreed with Emerson that "a skillful man reads his dreams for his self-knowledge."

Dream Power, Ann Faraday (New York: Berkley Publishing Corp., 1973)

You'll like Dr. Faraday's warm and open story of dreams in her own life; she gives many suggestions for taking dream collecting beyond the simplest stage (which is all we have done in this experiment). There's a section on "Dream Power in the Churches."

The Dream Game, by the same author, is a sequel (New York: Harper and Row, 1974).

The New World of Dreams, Ralph L. Woods and Herbert B. Greenhouse (New York: Macmillan Publishing Co., 1974)

A big anthology with a section on dreams and religion, and reports from famous dream researchers Stanley Krippner, Calvin S. Hall, and others.

Dreams: Visions of the Night, David Coxhead and Susan Hiller (New York: Avon Books, 1976)

Another of the "Art and Cosmos" series, with beautiful artwork. This work describes how dreams were temporarily discredited by rationalism and are now being vindicated as a voice of inner truth.

A P.S. FOR ANYONE WORKING WITH STORIES AND SYMBOLS

The experiments in this chapter are the most drawn out and time consuming in *Experiments in Growth.* Increasing evidence shows, too, that they are among the most richly rewarding in terms of spiritual growth, well justifying the time spent with them. They can also be confusing!—just because there are different categories of symbols and stories (church symbols, archetypes, symbols we make up, dream symbols, etc.), because there are several ways of approaching them, and because their home is in man's non-conscious mind.

To make stories and symbols work a little easier to implement, here's a brief rundown that applies to all of it in general. Use it as a guide for the classroom for students who have taken off in symbolic directions, or for yourself. See if it helps make what you do more growthful.

1) *Hunt for stories/symbols that are meaningful to you.* This can be started off in any of the ways suggested in the experiments: by researching and copying symbols, by looking around the house or office or school for them, by creating new symbols (No. 27), by examining them and living with them (No. 28), by making lists of stories or symbols and choosing from them, or putting up pictures to choose from (No. 29), by retelling stories, acting them out, recreating both stories and symbols (No. 30), or by keeping logs of them (No. 31).

It's not at all by accident that children—and adults—like to make lists under headings like: "These are a few of my favorite things." Smoke your favorites out.

2) *Use these special symbols and stories to learn about yourself.*

This can be done in one or two or all of three ways:

—Stay with your *feelings* about the stories or symbols which seem to be powerful for you, recognizing, accepting and even praying about the feelings associated with each of them.

—Get into your head, *asking* yourself the questions scattered throughout this chapter: What particular meaning does an appealing picture or story or symbol have for me? Does it tell me something about myself, or about a pattern unfolding in my life? or about some place or thing or theme which is special to me?

Do some research on the symbols you've singled out: biblical and other references to them, reminiscing about past associations of them in your life, examples of them in music and art, etc. Don't rush, however, to try to figure out this inner world; just carry it with you and watch it.

—*Try to find groupings* or "image clusters" among your special symbols and signs. These show us paradigms or patterns with special meaning for our lives; "finding the paradigm" is a good way of growth. The connections between several favorite things or recurring images (if not forced) can lead to basic understandings about self.

3) *Keep working with the special symbols* (one at a time is most effective).

—Remind yourself of what you've learned. Put up drawings or some other visual images of an important symbol, start a folder for it for artwork (yours and others'), quotes and notes and memories about it.

—Make symbols in art form and/or sing songs that mention them.

—"Seed" your dreams with the special symbols; think about them before falling asleep.

This sinking-in, jelling phase is important.

As we become more in touch with the image-producing part of our cores (a part of us which is often bypassed or rejected as babyish on our way to the from-the-collar-up world of adulthood), we change. Interestingly, even if we can't fathom reasons *why* a symbol or tale is evocative for us, apparently just our serious attention to it, the turning over of it in our minds, and the listening to ourselves lead to good things. It seems that the image works in us and helps to pull the myriad pieces of self together.

Also, the world around us becomes a source of all kinds of associations and interconnections, and they are spiritual/religious ones. We're talking about a whole alternative way of living for the person who pursues these ideas.

239

chapter 9
DOING IT

If you've gotten this far, you may be saying, "OK, I'm already doing this and that. Next I'll do this and then I'll do that." You may be planting some of the seeds here with your students and/or yourself, probably have been for years.

On the other hand, you may find yourself at one of two ends of a pole when it comes to all these experiments. For instance, at one end is the person who is over-powered by all the ideas here, and even more overpowered by the thought of squeezing any of them into an already tight classroom format. Three suggestions, if this is where you find yourself:

1) Go back and read over the section just before Chapter One that's designed to make a little sense out of all the trees in this forest and help you work the material into your classes.

2) Encourage students to take over their own spiritual growing. You're right—there *isn't* enough time in the regular religion class for all or even much of this. (Can you get a separate course in spiritual growth started?) However, if students have access to this and other such books, and you've helped them realize their responsibility to themselves in the spiritual nourishment department, they can continue their self-gardening on their own. The three suggestions below, in fact, are designed for people who want to go beyond just "trying on" the experiments.

3) Do what you can with the kids, but—more important—use *Experiments in Growth* as a workbook for yourself. As you begin to expand and find things that help you stretch yourself, the mention of them and the fruits of them will flow over into your classes. Shiny people illuminate, and an old adage has that "you can only work on yourself." The three suggestions below are for the serious grow-yourself teacher as well.

Or, perhaps you're at the other end of the pole in your reactions to all these do-it thoughts. At the other end is the person who says, "Who needs all this?" And would rather be than do, and who has found that he can "be" without a whole lot of "doing." This person would say that none of us needs to go anywhere because we're already there, that the answers are within us, that "Experiments in Growth" are superfluous. There's a saying in Taoism: "The more you study, the farther you are from the way." The Christian parallel would be Jesus' teachings about childlikeness, about just living the gospel in as simple a way as possible. If you can do this as He did, then you really have no need of more spiritual growth ideas or books—just do it.

But those of us who aren't there yet need a little help to transform our everyday lives into that kind of thing of beauty. If you've been graced with this sureness, please be patient with the rest of us. When you tell us "just let it happen," you leave us in the dust.

— Getting Ideas Off the Pages of Books and Into People's Lives —

Reading books with ideas to improve your life is one thing, and getting them into your life is something quite different, as you know only too well. Don't you expect that the most famous of last words are probably, "Gee, what a good idea. . . I really ought to try that!"?

Most of us probably tend to apply good ideas about self-improvement in Band-Aid fashion: One fall we read a line from scripture each morning, then we let that drop; the next spring, we decide to jog daily—then that falls by the road (unless we do first). A TV commercial convinces us to improve our marriages by baking more cookies, and that's nice; after a while we've switched to improving those same marriages by joining a prayer group. All good ideas, but still so many of us have the feeling that we're just not organized and that our growth—on all levels—is hit or miss.

Here are three suggestions that may help anyone get a handle on the ideas in this book, at least, and ground them. (See the end of Chapter Eight, also, for specific suggestions on getting symbols and story-learning into effect.) They are for students who have shouldered the responsibility for their own spiritual growing; some of these students may also be called "Teacher" from time to time.

1) *Zero in on those spiritual growth ideas which seem especially attractive and/or useful to you.*

With a class of students, you might have been suggesting this all along, especially if your students have kept logs. At the end of a school year, you might ask students to try to isolate a couple of the growth ideas most appealing to them to practice during vacation.

If you own this book, make it a workbook by underlining and starring (one star, two stars, etc.) in bright red ideas which seem especially valuable to you—either entire experiments, or one little piece (only a phrase, maybe) of an experiment or supplementary idea that gives a growth clue.

Pay special attention to growth skills you can practice "on the hoof," that is, while doing something else. So many of our best-laid schemes fail because we haven't time or energy for even one more thing in our day, right? But there are many things we can do to help ourselves grow while we're walking, working, waiting, driving, or even talking to someone else. Pretty soon the transformed walking, working, and so forth become part of our path too.

You may find yourself drawn to rather trivial things rather than skills you would label "Important," but a strong subjective response to any idea indicates that it may have important value to you at this time. Carl Jung wrote about the "readiness of the psyche" to move in a certain direction, and Carl Rogers writes of the importance of following one's intuitive sense about what he or she needs at a particular time. He cites the ability to do this as a sign of maturity/self-actualization. So follow your hunches about what will help you best.

2) *Put up visual reminders of the things you want to do—especially the new things—and then look at them. Often.*

Perhaps you noticed that several of the experiments conclude with words like "Post a reminder to yourself. . ." or "Put up your picture where you can see it. . . ." or "Think about this off and on. . . ." These suggestions were made because getting most good ideas into our lives isn't too easy. We need a push, and usually no one will give it to us but ourselves. God doesn't often flatten people to make them start moving, does He? (That is known as the lightning-bolt school of religion.)

You can post visual reminders of the things you want to do. They can be notes to yourself, eye-grabbing pictures, posters, charts, symbols, and so forth. They can be spread around your house or room, or (better still) clustered in one spot where you practically trip over them off and on each day.

Whatever memory-jogging system you use—plain or fancy—try to plug into it at least in the morning and again in the evening (or more often, if possible). One day you might feel moved to think about one or two things, the next day about something else—or the same things as the day before.

If you are getting a feel for living in rhythm (Experiment No. 20) you'll find that there are regular times of new beginnings (every week, every month, maybe every season, or only once a year—on your birthday, New Year's Day, the start of the school year, the beginning of Advent) when you feel naturally drawn to revamp your visual reminder setup, take stock of how things are going and what you need most *right now,* what worked and what flopped . . . and then start over.

Whether or not you scribble charts or put up pictures, there's one other step you can take to improve all this growing. It's one recommended across the board by spiritual masters and people-growers of all times and places:

3) *Keep a journal.*

A journal (or psychological workbook, if you like) is for recording what's happening inside you. The reason for keeping a journal is that the act of writing helps us to formulate our thoughts, clarify what's going on, define problems, witness our own growth and let off steam, among other things.

You needn't write in a journal every day, but only as things seem to lead you to do so—and once you start, this will be more and more often. In it can go:

reports of events in your life that affect your spiritual growth
questions (and answers) about life, ideas, yourself, other people

dreams
drawings, doodles, diagrams
reports on how you're doing with any of the growth experiments
quotes you like and good lines from songs
experiences and feelings which come about as a result of seeing a movie,
    reading a book or a poem, looking at a picture
signs of growth—sproutings, branchings, new leaves!
anything else you like.

Try out different sizes and shapes of notebooks or binders or folders, until you hit on one that feels right. Put it where you can get at it to use easily. Keep a pen with it. (Do your children steal your pens?) Abbey Press has blank journals at reasonable prices with a wide variety of appealing covers. (Write for their catalog: Abbey Press, St. Meinrad, IN 47577.)

How about dedicating each new journal to (as an old white spiritual calls Him) "the Lord, who into His garden comes" with some sort of prayer telling Him where you're at and where you think you're going? When each volume is finished, take time to look it over and see what's happened. Star any especially significant entries—they might not have been significant when you wrote them, but future events can make them astonishingly so. Look for synchronicity: similar learnings/teachings/growings that occurred during one period. At the time they happened, you may not have seen any relatedness; later you can. Leave a page or two at the end of each journal to summarize this chapter of your pilgrimage.

A final caution, once again, about getting ideas off the pages of books and into our lives: We're prone, usually, to overload ourselves and blow a few fuses. Less is, usually, more. A particularly seductive variation of the overloading syndrome is experienced by the person who decides to put himself on a time schedule:

"At 7:00 I get up and say my morning prayers and at 7:10 I do ten push-ups and at 7:25 I read a line from my collection of holy books and. . . ."

That sort of horarium is, perhaps, suitable for some few people, but for most of us we could expect it to end in a short circuit with

". . . and at 10:03 I'm a terminal case from all the pressure. . . ."

At first you may want to time and schedule some things, flexibly. But then you discover that being "on the path" involves everything you do, and that the in-between times and cracks of time, and the coping with crabby people are as much a part of the path as the natural highs. The things you need to know and the people you need to teach you are there when you need them. How could it be other when "it is God Who . . . makes the plant grow" (1 Corinthians 3:7)?

Hang loose, unless you really can't get rid of that military discipline you learned in the Marines or the detention center. Pressure/deadlines/clock-watching and growing don't go together. Ask any flower.

RESOURCES FOR KEEPING UP

Gardeners of the spirit may feel that they are cut off from what's happening professionally in the field of religious/spiritual growth. Every day, old and new stretch-yourself ideas are being put into usable form by a network of leaders, teachers, authors and all sorts of people—but how can we hope to keep in touch with what's going on? Here are a few ideas, one or more of which may be helpful.

1) *Religious Publishers:*

Get your name on the mailing lists of the religious publishers who are helping people live the life we're talking about. They're doing a tremendous service. A card to any or all of these publishers, asking to be put on their mailing lists, will take care of it. Some of the best growth material comes from

Abingdon Press, Nashville, Tennessee 37202

Abbey Press, St. Meinrad, Indiana 47577

Alternatives in Religious Education, 3945 S. Oneida Street, Denver, Colorado 80237

Argus Communications, 7440 Natchez Avenue, Niles, Illinois 60648

Ave Maria Press, Notre Dame, Indiana 46556

Concordia Publishing House, 3558 S. Jefferson Avenue, St. Louis, Missouri 63118

David C. Cook Publishing Co., Elgin, Illinois 60120

John and Mary Harrell, Box 9006, Berkeley, California 94709

John Knox Press, 341 Ponce de Leon Avenue, N.E., Atlanta, Georgia 30308

Mark IV Presentations, La Salette Center, Attleboro, Massachusetts 02703

Paulist Press, 545 Island Road, Ramsey, NJ 07446

CEBCO Pflaum Publishing Co., 2285 Arbor Blvd., Dayton, OH 45439

Seabury Press, Inc., 815 Second Avenue, New York, New York 10017

Twenty-Third Publications, P.O. Box 180, North Mystic, Connecticut 06388

Winston Press, 25 Groveland Terrace, Minneapolis, Minnesota 55403

Word/Creative Resources Inc., 4800 Waco Drive, Waco, Texas 76710

Truly a cross-continental effort, isn't it?

If you can't spend much money for books or other resources, see what your library has (or will buy). Check the reference department of your library to see if interlibrary loan service is available. How are your local churches and temples and any regional church offices fixed as far as libraries and resources? Prowl in bookstores too. All these things help teachers keep their fingers on the pulse of the growth movement, even if we don't buy.

2) *Periodicals:*

The two old favorites are *Religion Teacher's Journal* and *Catechist.* There're also *Interaction* and *Church Teacher,* as well as (heavier) *The Living Light* and *Religious Education.* Jewish readers, especially, will find *Alternatives in Religious Education* helpful.

Dennis Benson collects the cream of the secular and church-produced teaching aids and tells us about them in *Scan* nine times a year. (He would probably agree that the apocalypse won't be stars and locusts and frogs raining down on us, but books and tapes and films smothering the earth.) Among the many good general religious publications, *Faith at Work* is outstanding for its recognition of the growth ideas and practical suggestions for integrating them into Christian life.

Look for these in church-related libraries, or get their addresses from your library and write to ask for sample copies.

On the nonreligious front, most helpful for our purposes seems to be the popular *Psychology Today,* which is very eclectic in orientation but filled with good nuggets that a creative teacher can translate into spiritual growth skills for students. It's available at bookstores and newsstands and is an excellent barometer of where people are at, even if you will want to read it with discernment. See the good education magazines too, like *Learning.*

3) *Growth Centers:*

Do a little checking to see whether or not there are growth/renewal centers in your area offering weekend (or shorter or longer) workshops. Religious growth centers are often seminaries whose administrators are trying to be responsive to the needs of the times. The names of a few of these, across the country:

Roslyn, Richmond, Virginia; Espousal Center, Waltham, Massachusetts; the Institute for Advanced Pastoral Studies, Bloomfield Hills, Michigan; the Center for Human Potential, St. Stephen's Church, New York City; the Mid-Atlantic Institute for Christian Education, Catonsville, Maryland; Rocky Mountain Workshops, Denver.

Non-church-affiliated growth centers have lots of things to offer too. The granddaddy of them all is Esalen in Big Sur, California, and you can subscribe to their fat and informative quarterly catalog for $2.00 a year.

4) *Your Community:*

Check diocesan newspapers for local church-sponsored workshops, especially those for religious educators. Find out who are the good private teachers in your town. (But watch out for the specie *guru-vy guru,* who's floating off somewhere in his own transcendental world—and is, occasionally, an outright fraud.)

Visit various houses of worship in your community to discover what's best in local liturgy and music and preaching—but be familiar with the least inspiring

245

as well, because of the effect it has on students. Young people tend to equate the one religious body they belong to with "the Church" as a whole, and if they don't care for that one congregation may wipe off "church" in general. If you have a broader spectrum in your head, perhaps you can share it with them. Talk to people who move to your area from out of town, too, and try to get a feel for where your area is religiously by comparison. Is it very conservative? changing? typical? avant-garde?

Most of all, take advantage of the people you meet to take the temperature of the climate in your area as far as your work is concerned. Chat with kids, with the lady next to you at the laundromat. (Go ahead! Run the risk of being called a masher! Live dangerously!) Talk with the parents of your students, with the mailman, the paperboy, your baby-sitter. Do it not only in the spirit of friendship but also to keep your feel for where the typical people in your town are at—and then ask yourself, is what I'm doing in religious education relevant? Will it fill the needs of people just like these? Are these people concerned about spiritual growing? If not, what could their churches have offered/offer them that would have made that difference? It's too easy to lose touch if we don't stay grounded like this.

5) *Professional Associations:*

There are religious education associations, either of one denomination or ecumenical. For our purposes, however, the major benefits coming from them are usually reported in the magazines listed above. More pertinent to the growth-oriented religious educator's needs might be The Association for Humanistic Psychology (325 Ninth Street, San Francisco, California 94103) and/or The Association for Transpersonal Psychology (P.O. Box 3049, Stanford, California 94305). The former has both an education network and a religion network, both suitable and helpful for church teachers. Membership in either association includes a subscription to their excellent non-jargony journals and to their newsletters.

You might also want to explore the references scattered throughout *Experiments in Growth* and other works by the same authors. If you haven't had a chance to do it yet, a little time (?) spent reading the basic books about learning through experience will be worthwhile. A good place to start is with the classic *Freedom to Learn* by Carl Rogers (Columbus, Ohio: Charles E. Merrill Publ. Co., 1969), and the work of his religious education counterparts: Pierre Babin, Ronald Goldman, Gabriel Moran, et al.

Now, maybe by the time we're all zipping around in our wheelchairs and are too ancient to see—or even think—we'll get all this done! Seriously, these suggestions sound like a lot for a part-time volunteer teacher to tackle, and no one can ever hope to keep up fully . . . but they can make the difference between crossing a line to where you're really on top of your teaching or remaining on the fringes of the work. It's amazing how much we can stretch ourselves, if we just begin to collect some of these resources and use them.

WHAT'S AHEAD?

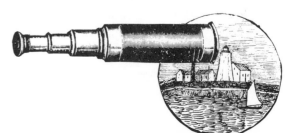

It's almost obligatory to end books like this with some sort of hope for the future, a look at the utopia that could be if only everyone did just what you told 'em to do! Actually, of course, people have been trying to improve themselves since the year 1, and ideas and techniques and skills like the ones in *Experiments in Growth* have been around for centuries.

As mentioned earlier (in Chapter One), this book draws on two main sources for its ideas. The first source is traditional religious asceticism (mainly Christian), the "science of the saints" which has been perfected, lived, and argued about for centuries. The second source of ideas is humanistic psychology: the study of human potential and growth, especially spiritual (or the psychological word, transpersonal) growth.

The 1960's and 70's have seen the synthesizing of these two fields of knowledge, this book being one small product of that merging. And, useful as the syntheses to date may be, they're just at the preliminary bits-and-pieces, patchwork stage that is the preface to a much more important work: the drawing of a total map (or maps) of growth based on both the traditional teachings and values of religion and the practical techniques and methods of psychology. Graham Greene wrote with anguish of the *Journey Without Maps,* which is just the sort of trip most of us are taking. We need (especially for the young) road maps, to use an ancient analogy. We need comprehensive guides just like those put out by Exxon and Shell that show us how to progress not to Massachusetts or Indiana, but to (pick your favorite term) holiness, self-actualization, individuation, expanded consciousness. (Not that these goals are ever really arrived at; they are processes.)

Ideally, a really complete "map" should meet these five qualifications:

1) It should give details of a path, complete with skills to master and checkpoints to mark one's progress along the way. High ideals and goals given to us are lovely, but hard to arrive at without some step-by-step road signs. Such models must be flexible enough to allow for the great variations among people as they participate in their own evolutionary process *consciously* (not by accident).

2) It must deal with all of man—not only his spirit but his mind and body as well— and not only with his "religious" or "churchy" life, but also with his mundane and worldly activities.

3) It must have as its aim the full flowering of a person, not just a settling for some cultural norm of "normal." (Read: "mediocrity.") That is, it must help each person aim for and maybe even arrive at his or her best possible self, not just the C+ self.

4) Behind the map there should be reasons for each segment of the path. Just handing someone a plan and saying, "This is good because it works" isn't enough. We need maps about which we can say, "This is good—it works, and here's why."

5) The ultimate goal of any map should be that it can be thrown away—or, better, tucked into the glove compartment.

247

You may say, reading this, "Well, I have my map—the gospel of Jesus Christ, and that's enough for me." Certainly, it's all there—and the closest road maps to our five points above are probably the monastic rules. (But how many of your students are following the Rule of St. Benedict or —— these days?) Yet, was it yesterday or the day before that you read the latest commentary on how unchristian Christians really are, with the usual litany of religious war in Ireland, tortures of the Inquisition and all the rest? Wasn't Chesterton right on target when he asked us not to say that Christianity hadn't worked when so few had really tried it? Maybe you're a beautiful person who lives the gospel message fully, but many of your fellow believers have a lot of problems harnessing the Good News and making it operative in their lives.

The classic story, perhaps, is of the woman who intellectually accepted all the virtues taught by Christianity, especially those having to do with forgiveness and peacemaking. She often told herself that, in God's name, she forgave her husband for his numerous grungy affairs with other women. Nightly, however, she dreamt of bashing in his head with an ax. The preaching and teaching approaches of her church and her own good will, by themselves, hadn't really enabled her to forgive. She didn't have the skills (point number one, above). Three skills that might have helped her forgive are in this book: Experiments No. 7, 15 and 25.

We've also noted (in Chapter Four) how often the religions of the West tend to bypass the body, our emotions and feelings, and all things physical (point number two). How many of your fellow believers can you count who practice bodily strengthening for the purpose of growing closer to God? How many of us really live (not just give lip service to) an incarnational theology, a view of God that recognizes and delights in Him both in us and in the everyday things of this earth?

Psychology alone doesn't provide the map. Until recently, it was primarily concerned with bringing man up to the state of "normality" from some deficiency level (point number three) and most psychiatrists and psychologists are still stuck in that therapeutic slot. For believers, the only thing that can fulfill point number four of our road map requirements is a view that includes God and His grace as the cause of both our being and our growth.

Our fond (some would say naive) hope is that, by the year 2000, we pilgrims will have these road maps. Some will be linear; some will be circular; others spiral, from the center out to some infinite goal, or from an outer spot to the peak of the "holy mountain." They'll contain the "what" and they'll give us the "how" as well. They will take us—by evolution more than by revolution—beyond the recipe book phase this volume represents to a stage where we can start children out from infancy with a chance at training and know-how to become all they can be. Futurists Aldous Huxley, in *Island,* and George Leonard, in *Education and Ecstasy,* envision this happening. The teacher's role becomes that of fellow pilgrim, one a little farther along.

An even fonder hope has to be that the Christian churches (and other religious bodies) won't abdicate their leadership in the formation of these maps. If they do, the maps will fall short in both historical roots and theological depth, and (far more important) in hope for eternity and in compassion and love: not the "everybody get

248

together, love one another" variety, but the love of God. A lot of good material for growing is coming to us from nonreligious sources, but much of it lacks the very things religion could give. One picks up a book with a title like *Ways of Growth* and is struck by the absence of a sense of purpose and of knowing what people are here for. It's two-dimensional, too existential. Input from the Eastern religions seems to have tempered, fortunately, another tone found in some of the earlier growth literature, the hedonistic gobble-all-the-goodies-you-can (for tomorrow we die) approach. Still, for believers who know that growth comes from a personal relationship with God, no maps will be complete without Him; for Christians, no map is complete without Jesus.

Many church leaders and nonleaders have been busy working for social change over the past couple of decades, but not as many of them have been working to effect individual change—as if there could be an enlightened social order without enlightened people. There are, fortunately, some shining exceptions: Christians who have been working to put together workable maps, maps containing Jesus Christ and the skills of growth psychology (many of these people are mentioned in the references in this book, and others are to be found in places like house churches and marriage encounters and seminaries and schools that are becoming growth centers) and members of other religions who are doing the same thing within their own settings.

The greening is happening. A "new age" spiritually oriented sort of person is more and more on the scene. This person, eventually, will be to today's average person as *he* is to medieval or even Neanderthal man. Our students see this change and want to be part of it. They're going to take that trip whether their churches and synagogues and temples go with them or not. Sadly, all too many of their religious leaders (local and world-wide) don't even seem aware that there is a trip to take or a place to go, much less want to lead it. Cat Stevens sings "Old world, goodbye," and for so many of the kids we teach, religion seems to be part of that old world.

The texts we use in our religion classes are full of maps, old maps of long-finished pilgrimages. There are Abraham's desert route, and Moses' lengthy trek. There are Paul's dotted lines criss-crossing the Mediterranean. Will our students look in vain for a map for their own journey in these guides offered them by their churches? They're searching for a map that spells out the human potential message that's in the air, a message that, lived, will enable them to say on their death-beds "I wasn't wasted." If we can use the network of religious education classes we have now, a network that touches over 40 million young people each year (!), as mini-growth-centers then the voice and message of organized religion will have a place in their maps. To do less is to say that the Good News is out of date—and that, surely, is not what we believe.

249

AN AFTERWORD FOR RUFFLED BELIEVERS:

A Theology of Growth

by Louis M. Savary, S.J.

Growth of Total Persons

Human growth is an integral part of spiritual growth. Growth in prayer is strongly influenced by personal maturity. The two are quite inseparable. This belief has a strong Christian tradition. Paul the Apostle encouraged believers in the early Church to grow daily and "stand *mature and fully assured* in all the will of God" (Col 4:12). Origen, Gregory of Nyssa and other Church Fathers reminded believers that prayer involves body, mind, and spirit, and that spiritual growth involves growth of the total person. (See Origen's *De principiis* III, 4, 3 (PG 2.323B) and Gregory of Nyssa's *De hominis opificio* (PG 44.24OD).)

In the Middle Ages, theologians like William of Saint-Thierry and Thomas Aquinas turned to thinkers of the East to enrich their awareness of human growth and to see how it influenced spiritual growth. (See William of Saint-Thierry, *Epistola ad Fratres de Monte Dei* (PL 184.307-354.) St. Thomas' dictum, "Grace builds upon nature," implies that humans cannot really become all God wants them to be until they become integral human beings. This means they need to set in order *body, mind* and *spirit*—not to destroy these three sources of growth in any way, but to harmonize them: nurturing the organic body, the thinking mind, and the feeling spirit (or heart) so that they grow to maturity together, so that they act in unity. Spiritual growth involves the total human person, not just the soul. Human and spiritual growth are inseparable. These themes were continually taught throughout the centuries, and today are stronger than ever. Vatican Council II solemnly affirmed: "It is the goal of this most sacred Council to intensify the *daily growth* of Catholics in Christian living." (*Constitution on the Sacred Liturgy,* art. 1).

Ruffled Christians

Sometimes it seems difficult to harmonize Christian living with human growth, especially in some of the ways it is presented in today's culture and society. Certain new or unusual pathways to human growth seem bewildering, even frightening, to many believers. They hear labels like atheistic humanists, Zen masters, Tibetan gurus, existentialist philosophers, charismatics, Freudian psychiatrists, and sensitivity trainers. No wonder believers feel ruffled.

When I first entered the seminary, we felt ruffled, too. Our way of resolving problems was to avoid them. Any book or writer who didn't profess philosophy or theology in complete harmony with the Roman Catholic Church was held suspect. Seminarians spoke of such thinkers as "opponents," "enemies," or "heretics," and reacted defensively to them. Sometimes we whispered about them, as if the mere mention of their names would invite the devil into our minds. Sometimes we scoffed at their teachings, or labeled them trivial or worthless, convinced that God had deposited the fulness of all truth in our own inexperienced heads. Sometimes we feared to look at their writings, afraid that we might catch some infectious heretical disease and thereby become contaminated.

We later found out that what we feared was what everyone always ultimately fears—*the unknown.* Seldom, if ever, did we actually study or discuss deeply what these "enemies" or "heretics" had to say. Later, those who did take the time to read such writings in depth were often surprised to discover their authors were loving, serious people, searching for answers to the same questions we were.

Totally Ecumenical

Mainly as a result of Vatican II's ecumenical spirit, the Church's conviction about the harmony of human and spiritual growth is again quite strong. Its *Document on the Church Today* encouraged Christians to face the difficulties in integrating human and spiritual growth, no matter how insurmountable these difficulties seemed. "These difficulties do not necessarily harm the life of faith. Indeed they can stimulate the mind to a more accurate and penetrating grasp of the faith. For recent studies and findings of science, history, and philosophy raise new questions which influence life and demand new theological investigations" (*The Church Today,* art. 62).

In a word, the Church no longer condemns outright the ideas of people outside the small circle of Christian belief. Instead, in a spirit of total ecumenism, it wishes to cooperate with everyone and utilize whatever ideas might prove fruitful. The Church does not wish in any way to suppress the rich variety of theological, scientific, and psychological insights emerging in our day. Instead, it encourages a spirit of open inquiry which integrates ideas from modern science and learning into spiritual development. This open spirit is recommended not only in universities but in religious seminaries as well (*The Church Today,* art. 62).

Religious Educators

Teachers of theology and religious education are encouraged "to collaborate with people well versed in other sciences" (*The Church Today,* art. 62, see also art. 67). Some believers, even some teachers, are still reluctant to examine insights of nonchristian thinkers. They may feel that such teachings—theological and otherwise—are just so much phony currency, worthless play money having no value in authentic Christian spiritual life. Such believers are like children who would throw away pieces of foreign currency, saying, without knowing any better, "This stuff is no good because it doesn't look like American money."

251

Some ruffled believers may see certain new ideas about human growth in much the same way that the unaware children viewed foreign money, saying, "This stuff is no good because it isn't the way I've always been taught about spirituality." Rather than allow children to throw away foreign money, a person who understood its value might take the child to a place where the foreign money could be exchanged for American money, which the child recognizes and knows how to use. In a similar way, Betsy Caprio in this book leads the ruffled believer to places where "foreign ideas" about spiritual growth are translated into experiences that are familiar to believers.

Experiments in Growth

The "experiments in growth" in this book are really exercises in prayer in the broadest sense of that word. They enrich the believer's approach to growing and praying by a happy combination of unsuspecting elements taken from many sources. Instead of negating, scoffing at, or avoiding sources such as psychology, humanism, pentecostalism, Eastern schools of thought, and the like, Betsy Caprio has utilized each of them in fresh and inspiring ways. She has discovered what they have to teach us about human growth and religious experience, and she has shared the results of her research in this book.

What she does in *Experiments in Growth* is eminently in line with the Christian spiritual tradition and with prayer experiences continually needed and called for by contemporary believers. Many of the most prominent theologians in the world today would agree with her approach to growth. With her, they would affirm that for Christians "nothing genuinely human fails to raise an echo in their hearts" (*The Church Today,* art. 1, see also art. 3). "In Christ," wrote Dietrich Bonhoeffer, "we are offered the possibility of partaking in the reality of God and in the reality of the world, but not in the one without the other" (*Christ the Center,* Harper & Row, 1966).

AN INVITATION

Dear Reader,

As you've seen, this book has been a collection of the good ideas of many people: teachers, students, theologians, psychologists, saints, parents, little kids, lots of people.

I'd like to invite you to share what you're doing too. It's very likely that what you're about may be just what someone else needs to know. Pooling our ideas can lead to better spiritual growth—a contribution to a "spiritual revolution," perhaps, in this time of celebrating our country's first revolution. Send us:

First-person accounts of how you and/or your students are making out with the spiritual growth ideas in this book—or any of the hundreds of similar ideas *not* in this book. Tell us your story (like Chapter Three urges). Let us know what happens in your life or your students' lives when you put the spiritual growth skills into action. Share with us the "continuing saga" (as they say on the soap operas) of how everyday people in a somewhat plastic world are stretching their wings and drawing closer to the Lord. If your story includes artwork, or photography, or music—share those, too.

Please concentrate on down-to-earth spiritual narratives. Not "my years with the Trappists" (we *know* that works), but "how I tune in the Lord while waiting in line at McDonald's." Not "I found God on a barefoot pilgrimage in the Himalayas" but "I found Him on Route 66 in my old Chevy wagon." A tennis player who is trying the meditation-in-sports ideas of Experiment No. 11 might write us about spacing out at the baseline, making the hookup to his spiritual life, and someone who's found a symbol that helps her expand in the spirit could tell us how that happens. Everything we do is part of our path, even "chopping wood and carrying water," as the Buddhist expression goes.

We may end up with a "casebook" about how people of all ages across the continent are coming closer to God. It could give hope—and ideas—for spiritual growth to those of our post-Watergate society who have none, who have given up and are ready to be stuffed and mounted. And your good ideas may find their way into print someday. You'll get credit for them, of course, if this happens. Let's make our sharing a two-way street. You've been kind enough to hear me out, and I'd like to have the chance to do the same with you. Perhaps the Spirit of '76 will be the Holy Spirit as people spread the love of God.

Live long and prosper,

Betsy Caprio
% Ave Maria Press
Notre Dame, Indiana 46556

253

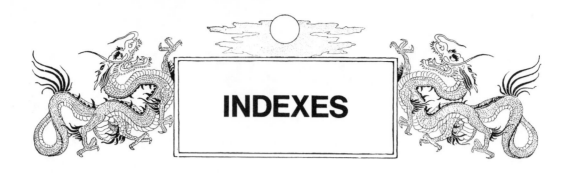

INDEXES

AN INDEX OF WAYS PEOPLE GROW SPIRITUALLY

Here are all the ways of spiritual growth mentioned in this book. Pick from them to collect stepping-stones for paths for your students and yourself; add other growth ideas you know of that aren't mentioned here. All paths lead to the same goal—Jesus' direction to "love God, love each other, love ourselves"—but each person's path will be a unique combination of growth means best suited to his or her own experiences and tastes and temperament and strengths and gaps.

I. THINGS TO DO

GROUP 1: These can be done while going about other matters. They are "on the hoof" skills.

Physical things:
balance yourself, 89
breathe:
- to energize, 83
- to meditate, 98 ff.
- to relax, 192

center yourself, 85 ff.
feel rhythms of life, 140
look at a concentration point, 92 ff.
meditation ("walking"):
- during sports, 103
- on the breath, 98 ff.
- visualization—
  of energy in yourself, 83
  of Jesus suffering, 126 ff.
  of people suffering, 126 ff.
  of your center, 85 ff.
  of your entire life, 59 ff.
  in crisis times, 185 ff.
- witnessing yourself, 102

use each of the senses, 96
use spaces/places:
- holy places, 166
- a special place, 164 ff.
- a tree, 211 ff.

Prayer:
during crises, 191
during sports, 104
for healing, 71 ff.
a mantra, or "seal," 174 ff.
offer each day, 162
offer up suffering, 128, 130

for others, 36 ff., 75, 185 ff.
practice of the presence of God, 171 ff.
prayers of other times and places, 179
the Psalms, 146
thanksgiving, 96, 113

Nature, tune in to:
animals, 64 ff.
plants, 68
sun, 216
trees, 211
weather, 216

Look at:
archetypal pictures, 224, 230
great art, 140
pictures of the Lord, 121 ff.
symbols:
- dream images, 236, 238
- from daily life, 207, 238
- traditional Christian, 203 ff.

Music:
in the background, 96
for a mantra, 174 ff.
to listen to, 121 ff., 124, 146
to sing (songs, hymns), 145

Other people:
do for them, 30 ff., 119
find God in them, 115 ff., 180 ff.
meet them through what they've left behind, 121 ff.
pray for them, 36 ff., 75, 185 ff.

GROUP 2: These need special time set apart for them.

Physical things:
gestured prayers (eurhythmics), 90
meditation ("sitting"):
- on the breath, 98 ff.
- on your center, 85 ff.
- accompanied by music, 193 ff
- witnessing, 102

Group sharing with other people:
finding yourself in the bible, 108 ff.
growth games, 148 ff.
"He touched me" moments, 54 ff.
shared prayer, 180 ff.

Write:
about your dreams, 232 ff.
about your "spiritual highs," 64 ff.
parables, 223
your life story, 62

Liturgy and worship:
celebrate feast days, 161

the Mass, 161
paraliturgical celebrations, 161, 162, 207
receive the sacraments, 74

Read:
the bible, 108 ff., 146, 223
fiction and poetry, 125
stories of others' souls, 58, 125

Art and music:
compose a tune, 142
domestic arts and crafts, 140
doodle, 139
draw a mandala, 48
draw your life, 59 ff., 156
draw yourself/your center, 136 ff.
Jesse tree, 206
make a calendar of celebrations, 158 ff.
make a song book, 145
"Me box," 206
music for meditation, 193 ff.
symbol drawings, 203 ff.

II. THINGS TO THINK ABOUT

Self-inventories:
on biblical and other checklists, 36 ff.
on difficult times in life, 191
on minivacations you enjoy, 162
on moments close to God, 54 ff.
on physical health, 80 ff.
on relationships (with others, with God), 30 ff.
on your gifts, 113
on your heroes, 115 ff.
on your highs, 64 ff.
on ways words can damage, 191

Symbols to research/soak in:
breath, spirit, 102
Christian symbols, 203 ff., 226 ff.
the cross, 131
the day, the week, the year, 162
dream symbols, 232 ff.
light, the candle, 96
the mandala, the circle, 48
musical instruments, 145
the sacred tree, 211 ff.
the spiral, 138
winged creatures (angels, birds), 151

Various topics to chew on:
death, 62
energy, biophysics, 83

getting high on God, 21, 64
guardian angels, 151
maps of growth, 119
mortification, voluntary penance, 130
nature and religion, 68, 217
pain, suffering, the cross, 71 ff., 126 ff., 185 ff.
the simple life, 131
space, spaces, 164 ff.
stewardship, 80 ff., 113
time, 153 ff., 158 ff.
unevolved people, 119, 185 ff.

Values clarification:
lifework planning, 156
of the "What's it all about?" questions, 47
of what's most important in your life, 44 ff.

Jesus:
in the Bible, 108 ff.
in Christ-bearers you know, 115 ff.
in sacred art, 121 ff.
in suffering and the cross, 126 ff.

Stories:
bible plots and characters, 223, 224
Christian myths and legends, 226 ff.
favorite plots and tales, 218 ff.

FINIS.